D1253959

DODGE CITY

Queen of Cowtowns

"The Wickedest Little City in America"
1872–1886

by
STANLEY VESTAL

Introduction to the Bison Books Edition
by Jim Hoy

UNIVERSITY OF NEBRASKA PRESS
LINCOLN / LONDON

⊗

First Bison Books printing: 1972
First Bison Books printing of this edition: 1998
Most recent printing of this edition indicated by the last digit below:
10   9   8   7   6   5   4   3   2   1

Library of Congress Cataloging-in-Publication Data
Vestal, Stanley, 1887–1957.
[Queen of cowtowns]
Dodge City: queen of cowtowns: "the wickedest little city in America."
1872–1886 / by Stanley Vestal.
p.   cm.
Originally published: Queen of cowtowns. New York: Harper & Row, 1952.
With new introd.
Includes bibliographical references.
ISBN 0-8032-9617-7 (pbk.: alk. paper)
1. Dodge City (Kan.)—History—19th century.   2. Frontier and pioneer
life—Kansas—Dodge City.   I. Title.
F689.D64V47   1998
978.1'76—dc21
98-8368   CIP

Originally published in 1952 by Harper & Row, New York.

To
The Memory
of
My Father
Walter Mallory Vestal
Kansas Pioneer

INTRODUCTION

Jim Hoy

Dodge City—the very sound of the name conjures images of the wild-est of the West: cowboys, Indians, gunfighters, buffalo hunters, caval-rymen, railroaders, gamblers, soiled doves. And of the final resting place for many of the real people behind these frontier archetypes: Boot Hill. "Get out of Dodge" has become part of the American lexicon, its mean-ing as well understood in the largest metropolis as in its place of ori-gin.

I recall several years ago when I was in Dodge City one July day and picked up a copy of the *Globe*. David Dinkins was serving his first term as mayor of New York City and, in response to some act of street vio-lence there, had made a comment that such an action would not be tolerated—that New York was no Dodge City. The mayor of Dodge, in a front-page open letter to his counterpart back East, was quick on the draw, letting Dinkins know that Dodge City was no New York City and that the locals were glad it wasn't. Safety in the streets, he correctly pointed out, was much more of a problem in the metropolis than in Dodge City. But while he was boosting the merits of life in Dodge City over those of Brooklyn and bemoaning the stereotype that had led to Mayor Dinkins's remark in the first place, I could detect a touch of local pride in that same image: Dodge City may have been "civilized" for a century, but it would always be known as the Beautiful Bibulous Babylon of the Frontier. Hell on the Plains. The Wildest Town in the West. The Wickedest Little City in America. The Roughest Place on the Face of the Earth.

Dodge City, even in its heyday, was never as deadly as many other towns on the frontier, but it was noisy and boisterous and full of vice. Like its most famous lawman, Wyatt Earp, who killed only one man in his tenure there, Dodge City had a reputation that carried far more weight than any amount of reality could. Back in the cattle-trailing era, so goes a story that has become legend, a drunken cowboy boarded a train in Wichita. As the conductor was collecting tickets, the cowboy said he didn't have one. No problem, the conductor replied, tell me where you're going and I'll sell you a ticket. "I'm agoin' to hell," was the response, followed immediately by the conductor's classic line: "Dodge City, two dollars." In the early 1970s when I first began to teach at Emporia State University, one of my colleagues went on sabbatical leave to a remote provincial village in France. No one there, he told me on his return, spoke English, and the villagers knew the names of only two towns in America: New York City and Dodge City. It seems *Gunsmoke*, in dubbed French, was a favorite on local television. From its origins in the early 1870s to today as we near the end of the twentieth century, Dodge City seems destined ever to epitomize the glamour of the cattle-drive era.

The number of killings in Dodge City may have been exaggerated by television and the movies, but the town was without question one of the liveliest on the frontier. Beginning as a soldier's town situated just west of the military reservation at Fort Dodge, with the usual camp followers in attendance, it was also a jumping-off point for buffalo hunters and a shipping point for the hides they acquired. Its legendary reputation, however, is a product of its glory days as the Queen of the Cowtowns—the title it won as the greatest of all the railroad shipping points in Kansas, where more cattle were shipped in the quarter century following the Civil War than in any other western state, the title it retained in Stanley Vestal's classic account of the life and times of "The Wickedest Little City in America."

Stanley Vestal was one of the most prolific recorders of the lore of the plains region to ever set pen to paper. His writing career, from his first publication (a 1904 article in *Holiday Magazine for Children*, written when he was seventeen years old) to his last (an article on the death of Custer published in *American Heritage* in 1957, the year of his death), spans over half a century and encompasses over two dozen books, over 125 magazine articles, sixteen biographical sketches for *World Book Encyclopedia*, four scripts for CBS Radio, and half a dozen other books that he edited or for which he wrote chapters or introductions. Included in his books are four novels, seven biographies, seven histories, four writing textbooks, one reference book, and a book of poetry.

Walter Stanley Vestal was born August 15, 1887, on a homestead near Severy, Kansas, the son of Walter Malory Vestal and Isabella Louise (Daisy) Wood. Vestal, a lawyer, died within six months of his son's birth.

Daisy moved back to her mother's boarding house in Fredonia, some thirty miles east, and returned to teaching school, leaving young Walter in the care of his grandmother, Sara Wood. On the Kansas prairies Walter learned to ride, hunt, and fish, and he was introduced to the fascinating world of the Plains Indians by a guest in the boarding house who displayed a collection of artifacts. When he was nine years old, his mother married James R. Campbell, superintendent of the Fredonia school system. Two years later, in 1898, Campbell accepted a similar post in the Oklahoma territorial capital of Guthrie, thus setting the course of Walter's life—and giving him a new name in the process.

In Oklahoma everyone knew Walter as Campbell, not Vestal. (He would return to his birth name a few years later when, as an academic in the English Department at the University of Oklahoma, he felt the need to separate his professional writing persona from that of the classroom teacher.) When the Campbells first moved to Guthrie, famous lawmen Chris Madsen, Heck Thomas, and Bill Tilghman were marshals of the town, and Indians would still occasionally camp along the banks of the Cimarron River north of town. Walter spent summer months at his uncle John Campbell's ranch near Watonga, close to the Arapaho and Cheyenne reservations. There, visiting friends among the Indian boys, he observed camp life first hand.

In 1903 his stepfather accepted the post of president of the newly formed normal school at Weatherford, in the middle of Cheyenne and Arapaho country, an ideal spot for Walter to learn even more about Indian ways. Walter became one of the first students, and first graduates, of the college, majoring in Latin and Greek and participating in most of the sports programs, thus meeting the athletic and academic qualifications to win a Rhodes Scholarship, one of his early ambitions. After four years at Oxford, Campbell was graduated with a B.A. (He acquired an M.A. in 1916, without any additional attendance.) After returning to the States in 1911, he took a job teaching high school at Louisville, Kentucky, which he did not like. His mind was on the plains, and his ambition was to become a writer.

In 1915 he accepted a position at the University of Oklahoma, where, except for occasional summer teaching stints in New Mexico, he would spend the rest of his professional career. Teaching literature, however, was merely a means of providing a living for himself and his new wife, Isabel Jones (who was also a writer), so that he could pursue his passion of writing. Using his birth name, Stanley Vestal, as his pen name,

Campbell had some early success in magazine sales but put his writing career on hold to join the army at the outbreak of World War I. He earned a commission as a captain of field artillery and was sent to France in 1918, arriving too late, however, to see active combat.

Two daughters, Malory and Margaret, were born to the Campbells, while their parents continued to write and while debts, many of them incurred by Walter's research trips, continued to mount. In 1927 both Vestal and Isabel had books accepted for publication. *Fandango: Ballads of the Old West*, a collection of poems based on historical figures and events, was Stanley's first book-length effort to see print, and Isabel's was a novel, *Jack Spratt*. From this point on, Stanley's career moved ahead steadily, while Isabel's was to falter, a circumstance that, in combination with the family's almost constant state of indebtedness, contributed to her demand for a divorce in 1938. For two years Campbell attempted a reconciliation, but after 1940 he resigned himself to bachelorhood.

Campbell prided himself on being the last homesteader in the country. Whether strictly accurate or not, he was certainly among the very last when he and Isabel took up a seventy-acre claim on a mountaintop near Santa Fe in August 1934, shortly before President Roosevelt removed public lands from settlement. The Campbells built a house on the claim in 1935, and it was proved up the following year, two years before the marriage dissolved.

One of Campbell's most influential actions was to establish, in 1938, the professional writing program at the University of Oklahoma. Although opposed by some members of the English Department, who felt that popular writing was not worthy of an academic department (and for that reason the program was later transferred to the journalism school), this program was one of the most popular and successful programs of its kind anywhere in the country, praised by such publishing luminaries as Bennett Cerf. Its purpose was to teach not technique so much as mind-set, to make prospective writers think like writers. Campbell wanted this program, staffed originally by Campbell and Foster Harris, to be judged by the accomplishments of its students, not by the qualifications of its professors. By the time of Campbell's death, the professional writing program certainly met his criteria for success: it had been experienced by twenty-five hundred students who had, in turn, produced among them some 250 books and over ten thousand magazine articles and stories. Along with his teaching of professional writing, Campbell published four textbooks on writing (under his professorial name, Walter Campbell).

Like most successful writers and teachers of writers, Campbell urged his students both to research potential markets and to write about what interested to them. The subject of greatest interest to Stanley Vestal was the American West, particularly the plainsmen, both European and Native, who had performed the heroic deeds that form much of the legendary appeal of our nation's history. Many of his books overlap in people and in places, but not in detail. Kit Carson and other famous mountain men (Jim Bridger, Joe Meek) are favorite topics, as are the Sioux leaders Sitting Bull and his nephew White Bull. Highways—the Santa Fe Trail and the Missouri River—are also dominant topics in Vestal's writing.

During his career Vestal had contact of one sort or another with many well-known American authors—Hamlin Garland, Robert Penn Warren, Mary Roberts Rinehart, Lynn Riggs, Sinclair Lewis, Erskine Caldwell—and knew such British authors as J. R. R. Tolkien and Christopher Morley through his association with Oxford University. He received a Guggenheim Fellowship to research and write his most successful book, *Sitting Bull: Champion of the Sioux*, and was the recipient of a Rockefeller Fellowship. Walter Stanley Campbell died on Christmas Day, 1957.

Because of his early association with Indians and his intimate acquaintance with their customs, Vestal was both eager to visit and able to glean information from many of the old warriors who had actively resisted white encroachment onto the plains. His method was to travel by car from Oklahoma up through Canada, interviewing as he went, then checking his findings against the written records held in various archives and libraries. In his youth he had learned many stories of Indians, the Santa Fe Trail, and Kit Carson, among other things, from those who had been there—John Seger, a Cheyenne agent, and George Bent, the half-Cheyenne son of William Bent.

Among professional historians Vestal's work is often seen as a source of good narrative that provides an authentic feel for the era, although not necessarily providing a firm source of fact or interpretation, an assessment that seems accurate for *Dodge City*. Vestal obviously did a thorough job of research in preparing to write this book, but rather than a straightforward, not to mention definitive, history, he produced instead an entertaining series of episodes, generally chronological, that give us a flavor of life in old Dodge City. Undoubtedly his method of composition favored this type of written product, for Vestal believed that once the research had been conducted and absorbed, the writer should put his notes away and write from his head.

For the general reader—the one for whom Vestal was writing—this kind of writing results in an accessible and readable text. However, the serious reader—one who would like to follow up on some of Vestal's assertions—is often frustrated by the casual documentation. Who, for instance, is the "bloody woman" described at the beginning of chapter 3? What are the "snuff mines" mentioned in chapter 9? Why did buffalo-hide buyer Lobenstein hire only Irishmen? Why doesn't Vestal give us more detail about "Dog" Kelley, the saloon keeper who once insisted that the town turn out for the funeral of one of his coyote hounds? And there is no mention at all of Tom Sherman, whose barroom was the original setting for the lamenting cowboy of folksong who was eventually transported to the "Streets of Laredo" by Texas cowboys.

Vestal protested often against the blood-and-thunder approach to the West taken by Hollywood, noting in his Dodge City book that the lawmen there deserve great credit for maintaining (relative) peace and quiet in raucous Dodge with a minimum of killing. Yet he, too, emphasizes the allure of a violent West, in chapter 1 celebrating a town in which even babies cut their teeth on the barrel of a Colt .45. Some twenty-five men out of a community of five hundred were killed in Dodge City's first year, he asserts, but without providing any evidence to back up this seemingly exorbitant claim.

Still, despite these lapses, Vestal provides the reader with a plethora of fascinating detail. The term "buffaloing," meaning to confound one's opponent, apparently originated in Dodge City, the result of Marshal Earp's nonlethal method of overpowering law breakers. So too, according to Vestal, did Dodge first give rise to the term "joint," referring to a saloon. And of the many boot hill cemeteries in the West, the one at Dodge was the first to bear the name. Early cowboys in the Dodge City area were called "buffalo whoopers," after their duties of scaring away bison to save the grass for cattle.

Vestal's strength as a writer is his ability to tell a good story based, as nearly as he could manage, on actual events. He can turn a good phrase and come up with a striking image: on the plains a man walking would get nowhere, "like a mud turtle on a world cruise." Perhaps no one could fully capture old Dodge City on paper, but *Dodge City* is one of a handful of books that provide a glimpse into its rollicking past.

So the legend that was Dodge City thrives today, even though the cattle that surround the town are grainfed feedlot steers, not trail-hardened longhorns. And although the mayor may occasionally rise to the defense of his town's progressiveness, still Dodge City belongs to the ages as Queen of Cowtowns.

Biographical Source: Ray Tassin, *Stanley Vestal: Champion of the Old West* (Glendale CA: Arthur H. Clark, 1973).

Table of Contents

Illustrations

DODGE CITY

Queen of Cowtowns

SURVEY

To ENJOY the story of Dodge City, you have to be reconciled to belonging to the human race. But if you read it aright, you will be proud to belong.

There have been many frontier towns on the Plains, each one part of the brave, hard story of the pioneers. But few of these rival Dodge City in rich human interest, adventure, and variety.

Though representative, Dodge was unique. For it was not just another cowtown—that community rooted in a military post became the booming camp of the buffalo hunters, where hundreds of thousands of shaggy hides were bought and sold. From the start it was the headquarters for the bullwhackers, whose groaning wagons carried freight to all the forts, ranches, and camps within two hundred miles. It was, moreover, for ten years the biggest cattle market in the world—the shipping point for Texas trail herds from which thousands of cattle cars every season carried rivers of beef to far-off cities.

Through two long depressions Dodge continued to boom. Abilene, Ellsworth, Hays, Newton, Wichita were only brief rehearsals for the drama that was Dodge. In fact, many of her citizens were graduates of those earlier cowtowns—seasoned frontiersman, Indian fighters, scouts, mule skinners, gamblers, railroaders, merchants, gun-fighters, and marshals.

Early in her career Dodge became notorious as "the wickedest little city in America," consisting largely of dance halls, brothels, and saloons infested with wild women and bad men. There, it was said, a man might break all the ten commandments in one night, die with his boots on, and be buried on Boot Hill in the morning. For nearly fifteen years Dodge City was the wildest town in the West. . . .

Fort Dodge stood on the north bank of the Arkansas River, astride the ruts of the Old Santa Fe Trail, roughly halfway between Missouri and Santa Fe. Five miles west of the post, at the edge of the military reservation—the hundredth meridian— a camp was started to sell whisky to the soldiers, and called Buffalo City. Soon after, in the summer of 1872, when the railroad came in, that camp became a town named Dodge City after the fort. But to the men of that day, it was simply known as Dodge.

At first there were only tents, shacks, and dugouts, and nearly everyone in town sold whisky or kept a restaurant. But its growth was rapid, and within a few weeks it began to look like a town.

On either side of the east-west railroad a row of one-story frame buildings sprang up, forming a wide street—Front Street or the Plaza—four blocks of wooden shacks and false-front stores. The chief engineer of the Santa Fe Railroad, A. A. Robinson, surveyed the street for the townsite company; some novice carried the chain. Or else some of the lots were measured with a lariat and never properly squared up; for half the proprietors on Front Street afterward found that their buildings encroached on some other man's ground, and so had to buy costly easements.

The town then had less than a thousand regular residents. There was no law nearer than Hays City, seventy-five miles away, beyond prairies infested with hostile Indians, horsethieves, and outlaws of every description. For after the Civil War all the guerrillas, bushwhackers, deserters and bounty-jumpers fled to this frontier.

From the beginning Dodge enjoyed a bad but enthusiastic press; many an ugly epithet was hurled at her, many a derisive phrase:

"The Deadwood of Kansas; the riproaring burg of the West;

Dodge City, as rough a community as ever flourished under any flag.

"Kansas has but one Dodge City, with a broad expanse of territory sufficiently vast for an empire; we have only room for one Dodge City; Dodge, a synonym for all that is wild, reckless, and violent; Hell on the Plains.

"The Beautiful Bibulous Babylon of the Frontier—with one saloon for every fifty residents; Dodge City dancehalls, where 'Hands up,' is oftener heard than 'Hands off.' There the only public buildings ever locked are the jail and the church.

"Dodge City, where was outfitted every expedition against Indians, horsethieves, bad men, where gunmen could be hired by the day. There, in the words of Jim Steele, the Kansas historian, they

> Called that day lost whose low descending sun
> Saw no man killed or other mischief done."

One summer day in 1876 a wagon train heading west reached Fort Dodge and made camp on the prairie.

After supper, Surgeon W. S. Tremaine, U.S.A., with one or two fellow officers strolled over to get the latest news. The travel-worn wagons stood deserted. Here and there they noticed bullet holes and iron arrow points wedged in the sideboards. Evidently they had been through hell and high water.

Passing the wagon corral, the officers were astonished to see the movers all assembled on the prairie, hats off, kneeling with bowed heads, while their minister, standing among them, led in prayer:

"Oh, Lord, we pray Thee, protect us with Thy mighty hand.

"On our long journey Thy Divine Providence has thus far kept us safe. We have survived cloudbursts, hailstorms, floods, strong gales, thirst and parching heat—as well as raids of horsethieves and attacks by hostile Indians.

"But now, oh, Lord, we face our gravest danger. Dodge City

lies just ahead, and we must pass through it. Help us and save us, we beseech Thee. Amen."

The service concluded, the wagon master approached Tremaine and requested a military escort through Dodge next day. This request, referred to the Commandant, Colonel Richard Irving Dodge, was turned down. But Surgeon Tremaine, having business in Dodge next day, considerately offered to guide the wagon train safely through Front Street next morning and on into the Western prairies. He later reported that the movers, shutting their women and children inside the white canvas of their covered wagons, drove straight through town, armed to the teeth, looking neither to the right nor left. They never halted, but kept going straight on until they were out of sight. Doubtless they offered up devout thanksgivings when they made camp that night.

The officers at the fort got a laugh out of this, for the troublesome characters in Dodge were nighthawks. Few of them appeared on the streets before noon.

Of course, the residents of Dodge City were not all Cyprians and gunmen. On the contrary. Most of the citizens had come west because they wished to better themselves. They were kept busy building homes, earning a living, freighting, hunting, fighting Indians, taming a harsh wilderness, making a city out of a camp.

For if Dodge were remembered only for wickedness and lawlessness, its memory might be willingly let die. But Dodge is remarkable chiefly for the heroic efforts made there to establish law and order. That required a hard fight, a long fight—a fight not only to tame trigger-happy transients, but a mighty exercise in self-mastery by her own citizens. The conditions that made Dodge a sink of iniquity were common to all cowtowns. But the outstanding heroism which finally got the better of those conditions flourished longer there than in any other camp on the Plains. Kansas can be proud of Dodge City.

Today it is the clean, orderly, up-and-coming metropolis of

southwest Kansas, a pretty, modern town, which now offers little enough to remind us of the old rough days. All that is left of frontier Dodge lies in state in the splendid museum there.

Still, if we exercise our imaginations, we can relive those vivid days, sense their strange quality, feel what those windy prairies, dusty trails, horned beasts, cruel savages—what those wooden shacks and dugouts, and all their gambling, fighting, and jesting meant to the men of Dodge.

Their rough way of life gave them a certain quality, a habit of mind and customs which differ from our own. Men who frequented Dodge were young, lusty, reckless—desperately human. To understand them and share their wild adventures will prove a rewarding experience, adding another room of sympathy to our house of life.

In this book our purpose is to recapture that experience, to understand what that fort, that camp, that wicked cowtown signified. Fortunately records are abundant, affording much that is fresh, accurate and new. From these materials we may glimpse striking characters, watch swift adventures, and see enacted brutal murders, daring deeds, rough practical jokes, touching sacrifices, and hilarious pranks. The lives of those pioneers were made, like our own, of hopes and fears, humors and despairs, petty schemes and difficult endeavors, and most of them had a fierce pride in the tough reputation of their town.

It stood at the edge of the flat Arkansas River bottoms, just under the bare hills to the north—"a hundred yards to water and a hundred miles to wood." But with all its discomforts, its garish pleasures, its rowdyism, gun-fighting, and sudden death, there was much hospitality, laughter, generosity and fun.

One day on a train rolling westward a surly cowboy told the conductor that he had no ticket.

"Where are you going?" Conductor Bender demanded pleasantly.

"To hell, I reckon," was the rough reply.

Bender grinned, "All right. Give me a dollar and get off at Dodge!"

But if old-time Dodge could be said to have horns and a tail, she came by them honestly. For all her prosperity rested squarely upon her bulls, her buffalo, her longhorns.

So let us see what all that shooting was about.

CHAPTER 1 :
PISTOL PRACTICE

F. C. ZIMMERMAN, the genial merchant, owned one of the largest and most important stores on the north side of Front Street. He sold a great variety of articles, but the sign painted in bold letters across the false front of his store well indicated the relative importance to the community of his various wares. The sign below his name read:

FIRE-ARMS, AMMUNITION

Below this were listed HARDWARE, TIN-WARE, and LUMBER, and on a plank nailed along the top of the wooden awning over the sidewalk in smaller letters was painted GROCERIES, PROVISIONS. Out in front, supported by an upright pole, a huge red wooden gun twelve feet long projected over the street, lest anyone should be stupid enough to miss the emphasis of the sign painted on the building.

Guns were just that important to the men of Dodge. They felt about guns much as Americans today feel about motor cars; they kill and maim far too many people, but we cannot get along without them. "But of course," the car owner will protest, "we do not intentionally kill people with our cars, but use them for many other purposes."

Yet if we could raise an old-time gun-toter from his grave on Boot Hill, he might answer, "I hear tell you kill more people with your cars without trying than we did with guns on purpose. But if you knew all I do, I reckon you'd admit we crowd you.

If all the killers in Dodge had been brought to trial, Ford County would still be paying off the debt. You say gasoline and alcohol don't mix. Take it from me, stranger, alcohol and gunpowder don't neither. But we didn't tote a gun just to kill people. Hell, *we* used our guns for many other purposes too."

Guns were used in doing business.

William Barclay "Bat" Masterson arrived in Dodge with the railroad.

He had contracted to grade the Santa Fe right-of-way on the mile extending west from the military reservation, the mile along which Front Street was being built. The subcontractor for whom he did the grading, however, was obliged to go east and neglected to pay Bat for his work.

Bat was little more than a boy then, barely nineteen years old, broke—and a long way from home. Tom Nixon hired him to drive team.

One day after the railroad had reached Colorado somebody tipped Bat off that his debtor was at Granada. Said he, "Bat, he's got two, three thousand dollars rolled up in his pocket, and he'll be through here on tomorrow's train."

Now Bat had not been working on the railroad just to pass the time away.

Bat asked Josiah Wright Mooar to go with him. They met the train. Mooar waited on the platform. Bat boarded the train, found the fellow, and brought him right out onto the platform at the muzzle of his six-shooter.

Then Bat said, "You owe me $300, and dammit, if you don't pay, you're never going back into that car."

The fellow protested, "You're robbing me."

Bat declared, "No sir, I'm not robbing you. I'm just collecting an honest debt. You owe it, and you're going to pay it right now."

So the fellow pulled out his roll tied with a buckskin thong, peeled off the right amount and paid Bat.

Bat thanked him, declared the debt settled, and the fellow was mighty glad to scramble back into that railroad car.

While they were having that argument a crowd had gathered to see the fun, and everybody hurrahed Bat about his method of collecting the debt. Bat set 'em up, and all the sporting men in Dodge rallied to him. Up until then he had not been much noticed there. . . .

Guns were used to see fair play.

One spring day in 1885 the two Mooar brothers were watering their teams at the well in the street just in front of Kelley's saloon. They had with them a dog, half buffalo wolf, which they had bought from an Arapaho Indian. Tous was a big black dog, weighing ninety-six pounds, a fierce fighter. A dozen of Mayor Kelley's wolfhounds (of which he was so proud) were on the sidewalk. Somebody sicked them on Tous.

But the wolf-dog did not scare easy. He never fought like a bulldog, grabbing and holding on, but always leapt in to snap, then sling his enemy aside. In that way he could cope with as many dogs as could get to him at one time. Soon the pack was getting the worst of it.

Just then Kelley came running out, six-shooter in hand, apparently to protect his hounds by killing Mooar's dog. Josiah Wright Mooar, holding a water bucket and unarmed, saw him coming. But before he could do or say anything he heard somebody behind him holler, "Drop that gun, damn you."

Mooar looked around and there was Big Jack Williams kneeling on one knee with his Big 50 buffalo gun at his shoulder, drawing a bead on Kelley.

Kelley put up his revolver, and old Tous "cleaned them dogs up to a finish." Mooar had not known that Williams was in town, but Big Jack was right behind him waiting his turn to water his team. . . .

Guns were used to prevent gunplay.

One afternoon a cowboy rode into town, tied his pony at the hitchrack in front of Wright and Beverley's store, and with his pistol in its holster, jingled his spurs down the rough boardwalk toward the nearest saloon.

Marshal Wyatt Earp stopped him. "Carrying firearms is not allowed in Dodge. You'll have to check your gun."

The Texan drawled, "Who's goin' to make me?" and reached for his weapon.

Wyatt did not reply. Swiftly he buffaloed the saucy stranger, laying the long barrel of his Buntline Special smartly against the man's temple, just under the hat brim. Down went the cowboy, as if he had been poleaxed, and later, in the words of the old song, woke up broken-hearted in the old Dodge City jail.

The term "to buffalo," used in this sense, seems to have originated in Dodge. . . .

Guns were also used to initiate tenderfeet and play pranks.

The Adams Express Company had an office in Dodge City. For some reason the old agent, Bob, was let go and a young tenderfoot named Billy sent to fill his place. Billy was quite a nice boy, a regular attendant at church and Sunday school and would blush bright red at the slightest impropriety or naughty word. In those days Dodge was a mighty tough place, and the rougher element pretty nearly ran the town. When Billy arrived, a committee presented themselves in his office and said:

"So you are the new agent? All right. We don't know you, and maybe we don't want to, but things are about like this: We're all friends of Bob's. We like Bob. The company hadn't ought to let him out. We ain't got anything against you, but if our freight ain't put through quick and delivered on time you'll hear of it. And when we want it, we want it right away, and no fuss about back charges, either. If things ain't run our way, then —well, you'll find out what'll happen then."

Billy did not have to wait long to find out what might happen.

His initiation began at once. No sooner had the delegation retired to the depot platform than the biggest man in the gang sat down with his back against the closed office door. The new agent did not like to disturb him, and so remained inside, a prisoner, for fully eight hours. Nearly every day on his way home from work he would be plastered with rotten eggs until he had no more clothes to spoil.

Then one of the roughs thought up something that made them slap their thighs and roar. They immediately hunted up the oldest and most bedraggled demirep in the camp. Next day when the train came in and the whole town as usual crowded the depot and platform, she rushed up to Billy, threw her arms around his neck, kissed him several times, and told him how glad she was to see him. "For now we can be married right away." She proposed that they hurry to the parson and get hitched without delay. "Come along, Billy," she urged.

Billy did not feel a bit like coming. But the old rep pulled a Colt's Navy out of her bustle and stuck it in his face, threatening immediate bombardment. Billy promptly caved in. He didn't like it, but he couldn't help it. The fellows who had planned this pretty scene offered to sign the marriage certificate as witnesses, but first insisted that Billy set 'em up, and led him from one saloon to another to provide the treat.

What might have happened if they had got liquored up and actually gone to the church will never be known. For while they were crowding round a bar Billy gave them the slip and ducked out the back door. His wedding was indefinitely postponed. . . .

Even babies in Dodge City found a use for guns.

One night a mother, alone in the house with her child, heard someone coming up the path. She looked out and saw a dirty, drunken tramp approaching.

Her husband's six-shooter hung on a nail by its trigger-guard. She snatched the gun down. It was not loaded. Still she meant to protect her baby with it, though her hand shook so that she could hardly hold the pistol level. She took her stand by the baby's crib.

Then she remembered her husband's warning, "Never pull a gun unless you aim to use it." If she tried to bluff that ugly tramp and failed, she dared not think of what might happen.

She decided to feed her unwelcome visitor and try to placate him.

Hastily she dropped the gun into her child's crib.

But then she seemed unable to say a word, and just stood there, shaking. The tramp took one look, insolently came through the open door into the house, and prepared to make himself at home. He staggered toward her. She stepped behind the crib. He looked down at the baby.

Then suddenly he turned pale, whirled around, and ran out the door. She wondered what on earth could have frightened him off. Then she saw what had happened. The little boy was teething.

The tramp was still running, heading for the lone prairie. He wanted nothing to do with a town where children cut their teeth on Colt's revolvers. . . .

Buffalo hunters made a living with their guns, and everyone in that hunter's paradise provided a part of his larder from the meat of wild game: buffalo, antelope, deer, prairie chickens, quail, waterfowl, and stray cattle. Guns were used to keep order in the courts of law. They were fired to start a horse race, and used to destroy pests such as rats, skunks, coyotes, rattlesnakes, and wolves. Horsemen might use a gun to crease a wild horse and so render him unconscious until he could be roped.

The celebrated Dr. Samuel J. Crumbine of Dodge City in his interesting book, *Frontier Doctor*, tells how a rancher with a broken leg, whom he had been treating, used a rifle to prevent him from returning to town and his other patients until the bone was safely knit.

For the first eight years or so people in and around Dodge City were never free from anxiety about Indian raids, and everyone with good sense when traveling in that Indian hunting ground took care to go heeled.

A bunch of horse wranglers from Texas nearing Dodge, who had run out of provisions and were almost starved, compelled a cow outfit to furnish hospitality at gun point. The cattleman was apologetic when he discovered that they were not horsethieves, as he had supposed from the large number of fine animals with them.[1]

Lone women left on the farm or ranch kept tramps and other visitors in order with guns when necessary.

Two such women were pestered by lightning-rod salesmen, who insisted on putting up the rods without permission, until the ladies brought out the family shotgun and ran off the "fiends."

Many a one on the frontier used his weapon in all manner of ways, yet never once shot at a man. But sometimes it had to be done—to defend a lady's honor. . . .

George M. Hoover, for years Dodge City's leading wholesale liquor dealer, pitched the first tent on the site of the town shortly before the railroad came in. But he was not long alone in the field. Tents, shacks, and dugouts appeared, and it is of record that nearly everybody in town sold liquor.

For months after the town started there was no law and order. Neither town nor county had been organized. The place had more than its share of wild women and bad men.

In those days before the railroad could bring in much lumber, a saloon contained only a barrel of whisky and a rude bar. Patrons stood at the bar, and wood being so scarce and costly, the bar was often made by stretching a raw buffalo hide over a framework of rough poles. Once dry, such a hide was stiff as a board and served its purpose well.

In general, men on the frontier treated women of all sorts with deference. And if one of them failed to do so, or even accidentally jostled a woman on the street, he was likely to find himself flat on his back with a bloody nose, while some avenger stood over him, pale and furious, reading him a brief but pungent lecture.

But in those earliest drunken days at Dodge such amenities were not always observed.

Among the characters who frequented the camp was a lady teamster who wore a man's clothes, led a man's rough life, and thought nothing of bedding down alone in a camp full of bull-whackers. This lady was left-handed, and like Calamity Jane in the picture[2] wore her holster on her right hip—but with the handle of *her* pistol to the front.

One wet night in one of those primitive dugout bars a drunken mule skinner made advances to her. Profanely she repulsed him. But he was too drunk to understand that she meant what she said. At the time he happened to have in his right hand a flat stick about a foot long with a hole bored out near one end through which depended a loop (made of small rope) three or four inches in diameter. This twitch was used to fasten on the nose or lip of a sick mule when it became necessary to drench it. It was also handy to control animals which would not otherwise submit to being bridled.

Suddenly the mule skinner applied the twitch to the reluctant lady, at the same time grabbing her right hand to keep it from her gun. As he pressed forward she was pushed back against the bar and so could not reach around behind him with her left hand to draw her weapon. All she could do was to pound his ribs with her left fist.

He paid no attention to her blows, but only tightened the twitch. Unable to escape, but determined to avoid his attentions, she kept shrinking away, moving along the rough bar toward her right. He kept after her, enjoying her struggles, intent on his caresses, and occasionally giving the twitch a tighter twist—apparently quite sure he would soon have her at his mercy.

Still she rubbed along the bar—until she had rubbed her belt halfway around her body, and so worked her holster clear across her back to her left hip. Then she stood still.

At that he shouted in triumph—just as she pulled her gun with her left hand and blew his guts out.

CHAPTER 2 :
: BOOT HILL

OF THE celebrated graveyards in America Dodge City's Boot Hill is the most famous, bar none.

That burial ground was short-lived and of small population, long since removed and interred elsewhere.

But Boot Hill, with a name so appropriate and a history so strange, remains a place of pilgrimage. Tourists flock up its slopes to see the memorials of early days and the grotesque fake graves with heads and boots of concrete sticking out of the ground, each with its lugubrious headstone proclaiming the manner of death.

During the first year of the camp no fewer than twenty-five killings occurred in a community of less than five hundred people—men knifed or shot in drunken brawls or as innocent bystanders, laid out in the back room of some saloon or thrown into the alley to await interment.

There were also early epidemics of smallpox and cholera which took their toll.

If the dead man or his friends had money enough or sufficient standing, the body would be taken five miles to Fort Dodge and buried in the post cemetery. Others, whether friendless, penniless, or unknown, were buried in the bottoms or the draws or on the hills around, wherever their friends or the marshal found it convenient to dig.

But this was obviously most unsanitary, and by the time Dodge City was organized in 1875 it was already becoming the custom to inter such persons on the hill just northwest of the range of shacks on Front Street. That hill was then a bold promontory protruding southward into the broad bottoms of the Arkansas River, made of gypsum, rock, clay, and sand, covered with buffalo grass, and decorated with clumps of soapweed and prickly pear, about half a mile north of the river. As the highest point near the town, it was a favorite lookout. From its top one could see the country for miles around—east, south, and west—spot the buffalo or antelope herds, detect the approach of Indian enemies, or—in the cowboy era—gaze out over the vast herds of cattle.

Various reasons besides convenience have been offered why the men of Dodge chose that hill for their graveyard. Some think it was to keep the water from the dead; others to keep the dead out of the water; one old-timer surmised that "they done it to give some of the folks buried there a boost nigher to heaven—which some of them sure needed."

This burial ground was not enclosed nor laid out in neat lots. Bodies were put away here and there, not only on the top, but on the slopes of the hill. In a town with such a large floating population and no undertaking establishment a man was promptly buried. A man killed in a gun-fight was buried just as they found him.

Other frontier towns frequented by gunmen had similar burial grounds, but Dodge City first used that name. Now Dodge City was nothing if not a sporting town, and it was considered the sporting thing to do for the man who killed a stranger to help defray his funeral expenses. A number of instances in which this was done are known.

On the Kansas plains there was no marble, and every stick of lumber had to be shipped in at heavy cost on the railroad. Coffins were expensive and on Boot Hill were often improvised from packing cases, if provided at all. One old-timer has been quoted: "If a man had a saddle blanket for a shroud in that day we thought him well provided for."

The interviewer asked, "But suppose he had none?"

"Well, then he was sure out of luck all round."

Few of the early graves were marked, and these only by a few words burned or scrawled on a board stuck in the ground.

The epitaph of a man shot down might well contain a euphemism. Whether the citizens preferred not to advertise the number of men so killed, or whether they acted in accordance with the old frontier custom of making a joke out of everything unpleasant, is uncertain. But one epitaph that has been handed down read as follows:

> BILL JONES
>
> BORN 1855   DIED 1876
>
> KILLED BY LIGHTNING

Some claim that the phrase, "Died of Lead Poisoning," was also used on a Boot Hill marker. One cattle rustler's cause of death was stated briefly: "Too Many Irons in the Fire."

The naming of the cemetery was explained by the county coroner, M. W. "Mike" Sutton, in a talk he made on February 4, 1880, at the dedication of the new schoolhouse on the hill. Sutton said that a man was shot in a gun-fight on the hill near where he stood while speaking. "The body lay nearly all day without anyone to care for it, when towards evening a grave was dug upon the identical spot where we have built the new school building. The grave thus made was followed by many others until this beautiful hill became dotted with little mounds to the number of twenty-five or thirty, and the hill itself was named Boot Hill because nearly all the tenants of its graves were buried in their boots."

Some have assumed that hundreds of bodies were laid away on Boot Hill, but even though Dodge did frequently, as they put it, have a "man for breakfast," the population of the camp was too small to afford so many killings.

No accurate record was kept of the names of those buried on Boot Hill. But among these in all probability was Enos Moseley, murdered near Dodge City in August, 1877,[1] and buried by Mike Sutton in proper style. It is unlikely that Sutton would have planted his young friend out on the lone prairie, and I can find no record that he was buried at Fort Dodge. By 1877 Boot Hill had become the recognized Dodge City burial ground.

On May 4, 1878, the *Dodge City Times* published this notice:

To Whom It May Concern

Dodge City, Kansas
  April 20, 1878
  All parties are forbidden to make interments on the property of the Dodge City Town Company, under penalty of the law.
                    W. S. Tremaine
                    Sec. & Treas. D. C. T. C.

Ten days after the date of this notice, the *Ford County Globe* remarks: "Hays has recorded the burial of the 64th victim of gunplay in her Boot Hill. Hays will soon be giving us a run." Shortly after, the paper mentions two more "gun-toters who were a little slow on the draw . . . buried on Boot Hill since the last issue."

On May 14, 1878, the *Globe* referred to the proposed five-acre Prairie Grove burial ground northeast of Boot Hill as follows: "Hurry up with that new cemetery."

Thomas Gallagher, a middle-aged cowboy employed by J. W. Driskill, was killed—along with his horse and a steer—by lightning, on Buckner Creek, eighteen miles northwest of town. Though he left no relatives and no property, the *Dodge City Times* (May 25, 1878) reports: "The body was buried in Prairie Grove Cemetery—the first burial there."

However, George Hoyt, a Texan mortally wounded by Wyatt Earp, was laid away on Boot Hill as late as August. One

Bill Lee was buried there in the autumn; there may have been others. Most of these would be men.

Yet Alice Chambers, who died May 5, 1878, was buried on Boot Hill, for on January 28, 1879, the *Ford County Globe* printed a notice that her body had been removed to Prairie Grove. From this it appears that the founding of Prairie Grove was not the end of Boot Hill.

There is a story that another woman, Lizzie Palmer, a dance hall girl, who died from an infected scalp wound received in a brawl with another woman, was laid away on Boot Hill. Her cowboy friends voted to give her a proper funeral. One preacher refused to conduct the service, it is said, but another minister, who was tubercular and was in Dodge temporarily for his health, readily agreed to act. The cowboys showed their appreciation by paying his railway fare home and providing an armed, mounted escort to the train. This may be legend, but certainly there was a Lizzie Palmer, as her name is mentioned as following the cattle boom from one cowtown to another.

At length, the city fathers voted to move the bodies from a designated area on Boot Hill to make way for the new schoolhouse. This was done. The *Ford County Globe* (February 4, 1879) commented as follows:

"The skeletons removed from the graves on Boot Hill were found to be in a fine state of preservation, and even the rude box coffins were sound as when placed in the ground. Colonel John W. Straughn, the coroner, who removed them, says they were as fine a collection of the extinct human race as he ever handled. Some were resting with their boots on, while others made more pretensions to style, having had their boots removed and placed under their heads for pillows. Only a few of them could be recognized, as all of their headboards, if there ever were any, had long since wasted away and nothing remained to denote where their bodies lay but little mounds of clay. They are now all resting side by side, like one happy family, at the lower end of Prairie Grove cemetery, northeast of the city. The enchanting click of the festive revolver they no longer hear. The sighs of the Kansas zephyrs are unheeded and the sportive grasshopper, perched on a headboard, chews his cud and chants his harvest song without the fear of God in his heart."

Thus the top of Boot Hill can have been tenanted for only about six years at most. Children attending the new school on the hill have recorded—in their later years—seeing the empty graves about the new building. Nearly ten feet of earth near the top of the hill was carried away to pave the race track. The bodies were reburied in a potter's field just outside Prairie Grove Cemetery.

But at least one other body was certainly buried on Boot Hill some distance down the slope where the road runs now. It was that of a buffalo hunter killed by the Indians in 1873 fifteen miles northwest of Dodge City. When the road was put through, Walter Straeter, the road builder, turned up a skeleton with his scraper. The skull had a round hole over the left eye where the Indian warrior's arrow had entered, while the iron arrow point, identified as Cheyenne, was still wedged halfway through the base of the skull which it had pierced. As a curiosity, this skull was given to a local physician who kept it in his office.

There a former acquaintance of the dead man used to amuse himself and his companions by holding one-sided conversations with the grinning skull: "Well, old-timer, so there you are! Not much to say, have you? They got you that time. You always were too careless about Indians. I hope this will be a lesson to you." And so he would continue making jokes at the expense of his silent partner.

There were those who felt that this sort of thing was a little indecent and waited for a chance to get back at the prankster. One day a traveling showman, a ventriloquist, turned up in Dodge. This seemed a golden opportunity to the boys and they induced him to lend his services.

They had no difficulty in persuading the prankster to visit the

Front Street, Dodge City, Looking East from Bridge Street

The Long Branch Saloon

The Scalped Hunter

Mysterious Dave Mather

William Barclay "Bat" Masterson

The Dodge City Peace Commission. Left to right: standing, W. H. Harris, Luke Short, William Barclay "Bat" Masterson; sitting, Charles E. "Senator" Bassett, Wyatt Earp, McLane, Neal "Skinny" Brown.

Colt's Manufacturing Co.

Frontier Model

The Peacemaker

Professor Foster Harris

Pavillion Model

doctor's office that night and put on his act with the skull for the stranger.

After hearing the prankster's remarks addressed to the cranium, the ventriloquist chipped in, throwing his hollow voice from the jaws of the skull. "Yes, damn you, they got me. You make fun of me because you think I can't get back at you no more. But I ain't all skull; I'm ghost too. If you ever come in here again to bother me, I'll h-a-a-u-n-t you. I'll never let you sleep a wink again."

Amazed, then frightened, then indignant, but still half credulous, the shaking prankster was led away to the Long Branch to set 'em up. He needed a drink. He tried to laugh it all off, but his laugh sounded hollow. And he entertained his friends no more in the doctor's office at the expense of the skull.

But Boot Hill was not only a resting place for the dead. On one occasion, at least, it proved to be a refuge for the living.

One day a man named—call him Sam Smith—turned up in Dodge with eight six-yoke teams of oxen and offered them for sale. He brazenly announced that he would give no title to the oxen. He would just give possession. This was as much as to admit that he had stolen them. But he found buyers and was paid in cash—$8,000 counted out and packed in a buckskin sack.

That was a lot of money to have on your person on a dark night in Dodge. Everybody in the camp knew that he had it. He wondered if he would ever see daylight. Then he had an idea equal to the occasion. Quickly he took his blankets and his buckskin sack up on Boot Hill and bedded down between two graves. Nobody would look for him there!

The city fathers, in their zeal for progress having removed the bodies from the most celebrated landmark of the community, scraped off its top and put up a schoolhouse, later replaced by a very handsome city hall. More recently men have gone to work and dug away the whole south end of the hill down to the level of the river bottoms in order to provide a site for a municipal auditorium—which so far has not been erected.

But no amount of destruction of the town's most notorious reminder of its lurid past can entirely kill men's interest in Boot Hill. . . .

Many a prose story has been woven around it. Here I will offer Josephine McIntire's poem:

> To any traveler who may pass this way,
> And climb this lonely Hill to pause and say
> A prayer for us who early found our rest
> Upon the prairie's wind-swept, ageless breast:
>
> Weep not for us who early made our beds
> Wrapped in our blankets, saddles for our heads,
> For we are happy here, secure and still,
> Locked in this rock-strewn, silent, sun-baked Hill.
> Ours was an age when strong men's blood was red,
> And hurtled through their veins like molten lead!
> Although our history's page was smudged with crime,
> We built an empire on the plains of time,
> And while we slumber in this snug retreat,
> It ebbs and flows around our booted feet.
>
> Weep not for us who early made our beds
> Wrapped in our blankets, saddles for our heads;
> We tamed the west when this, our land, was young,
> And sank into our graves unknown—unsung![2]

CHAPTER 3 :
: THE BLOODY WOMAN

ONE NIGHT a buffalo hunter left his camp near Dodge City, went into town and opened the door to enter one of the saloons. Here is his story:

"She was the hardest woman I ever saw and I have seen a good many. She was a beautiful woman with a fine physique and she dressed beautifully. I saw her sitting cross-legged on a corner of the billiard table next to the bar in a big white dress.

"Two men were standing at the bar; I saw one of them step behind it.

"At the far end of the saloon there was a wheel of fortune running and thirty or forty people around it, but there was nobody up in front but this woman. Just as I opened the door to go in there, the man behind the bar pointed and called the other man's attention to something down there and he turned his head to look. The man behind the bar had his gun in his right hand, put it to the other man's ear and blew his head off. He never knew what struck him.

"When he fell she jumped off the table, put the palms of her hands down into the blood that was running over the floor, jumped up and down and hollered, 'Cock-a-doodle-doo!'

"Then she held her hands up and clapped them in front of her, splattering the blood all over her white dress. He killed him just as I opened the door, and I closed the door and went back to camp and never told nobody I knew anything. I just closed the door and went back to bed. Oh, that was a wicked bitch!"

But one old-timer thought better of the scarlet women than of the men who patronized them.

Says he: "Some of the whores were the finest women you ever saw. I knew one in a dance hall there and because I knew of her good deeds and took her part, I come pretty near having a fight in the jury room over her. They had her up for vagrancy. I told them, 'All right then, punish her if *she* went to the other fellow's house. But if the man went to *her* house, get the man.' That was my argument. I said, 'Don't jump on the women and raise hell.' That hung the jury. It would not convict her."

In those early days, a number of soldiers from Fort Dodge were wounded, or killed, or got into serious trouble over Dodge City's Cyprians. The military did what they could to prevent such scrapes in Dodge City.

And so, when the soldiers failed to come to Dodge City, the girls invaded Fort Dodge—apparently by the *wagonload*. For in March, 1878, an order was published announcing that "no heavy wagons or wagons containing prostitutes are allowed to be driven through the Fort Dodge garrison."

Sometimes ladies of the evening had a difficulty in Dodge. One night about ten o'clock, two girls, Bertha and Sadie, were in a saloon. They had just returned from the dance hall and got into a quarrel, caused by jealousy. The two girls had words, so Sadie slapped Bertha's face. Then Bertha out with her knife and stabbed Sadie in three different places; one wound near the spinal column under the backbone, one a little forward, and one in the breast. A surgeon was immediately called and dressed the wounds, reporting them not dangerous. They were flesh wounds, quite deep but not necessarily mortal.

"The wounded girl was at once taken to her home in the house known as 'The Parlor,' and at latest accounts was doing well.

"The girl who committed the deed was promptly arrested, but is now out on bail."[1]

Rowdy Kate got her name from Rowdy Joe Lowe, her husband. She was a small, good-looking woman and always well dressed. Joe himself was something of a dandy, though he had a reputation for roughness which earned him his moniker. The Texans called his dance hall in Newton "the swiftest joint in Kansas." As was usual in dance halls, there was no price of admission, but patrons were expected to buy drinks for their girls at the end of every dance. In the fall of 1871 Joe killed a man named Sweet and was wounded in a free-for-all when a rival operator invaded his dance hall, firing into the crowd and bringing on a general engagement of those present. Though Rowdy Joe gave himself up and was bailed out, he never was brought to trial. Later Rowdy Kate had a dance hall at Dodge and many tales are current about her.

An old buffalo hunter in an interview recorded at the time declared: "I'll tell you a little story about her. With me it amounted to a good deal. I knew her at Hays and knew her at Dodge. I never had nothing to do with her. But I talked with her, and she was a pleasant and sociable person to talk to. I knew her when she came to Fort Griffin. The stage ran from Fort Griffin to Fort Worth and back. Rowdy Kate went down on the stage to Fort Worth. Coming back from Fort Worth she was the only passenger, and coming up Keechi Valley the stage passed a little girl afoot in the road, and the little girl stopped the stage and asked them if that was the right road to Fort Griffin, and the driver told her yes and whipped up and went on.

"Kate says, 'Why didn't you pick that little girl up?'"

"He says, 'I've got no right to pick her up. She didn't ask me for a ride, and I don't suppose she had any money to pay for it.' And the child didn't know how far it was.

"Rowdy Kate got a little warm. She says, 'You stop this hack and pick that girl up.' She pulled her purse out and paid the child's fare to Fort Griffin. Now Rowdy Kate was a smart, bright woman, and she went right to picking the girl what she was going up to Fort Griffin for—thought she had friends living there—and the thing proved that she was an orphan girl. She was living with an uncle down there, and there was a neighbor woman who had a spite against his family. She had put this child up to run away. This woman had told this little girl that she could go up to Fort Griffin and go in a dance hall, and that she wouldn't have to work but that she would always have plenty of fine clothes and money, and all that sort of thing.

"Rowdy Kate picked that all out of that little girl, and then she asked her if she had ever had anything to do with a man. She said no, but that this woman had examined her and said that she could.

"Kate had hours to pick this out of her, and when she got into Fort Griffin she asked the stage driver to stop just before they got into town. Rowdy Kate had a big dance hall herself at that time. She asked him to stop at the hotel, that was just at the edge of town. And Kate got out and run to the back door and called out the woman that I afterwards married. She wasn't my wife at that time. She was running this hotel at that time. And Kate told her she had a little girl out there that was running away and would she keep her two or three days and get word back to her uncle, who was her guardian, where she was, and keep everybody else away from her, and my future wife told her yes.

"They took the little girl in and my wife had a little adopted boy there that was going to school, and she sent her over the next day with the little boy to the schoolhouse, and the little girl got pretty well attached to the little boy and went right to school. She was a perfectly innocent girl, and they wrote down to her home and in about two and a half days up come her uncle.

"Well, my wife told him the story of what Rowdy Kate had told her, and he went over to Rowdy Kate's and had a long talk with her, and she explained the matter to him, and he come back. He saw then the dangers about this woman that was punching this girl up. It was just important to get her away from the influence of that woman, and he come back to the hotel and asked them if they'd keep her, and if they couldn't get work enough out of her to pay her board, why, he'd pay it. So my wife got kind of attached to her, and the little boy being attached to her it would give my wife more time to her business. They never charged this uncle anything, and the girl stayed right there and went to school for four years. . . .

"When Rowdy Kate died, it turned out she was a pretty well-off woman. She turned out to be a real church-worker."

Rowdy Kate is not to be confused with another Dodge City celebrity, Big Nose Kate Fisher.

Big Nose Kate was the friend to Doc Holliday, the gun-fighting dentist. Once when he was under arrest at Fort Griffin, Texas, she saddled two horses, set fire to the hotel to divert the attention of the town, marched into the room where Doc was held, covered and disarmed the guard, gave his weapon to Doc, and galloped out of town by Doc's side.

Some of the easy women in Dodge City were brought in, but a few girls came of their own accord, as moths to the flame. For Dodge, with its railroad, its fine hotels (then superior to anything west of Kansas City—short of California), its continual round of music and dancing, its crowded theaters, its throngs of free spenders, dandified sports and famous gun-fighters, and its general air of a summer carnival, proved irresistibly attractive to foolish young women from lonely farms, frontier hamlets or unhappy homes. To them the ramshackle camp was glamorous; Dodge City seemed the Hollywood of the Plains.

Dr. Samuel J. Crumbine of Dodge City in his autobiography, *Frontier Doctor*, may be quoted:

"The saddest case among those that came to my attention as coroner was that of a woman of unsavory reputation who chose suicide by poison.

"Here again testimony was illuminating.

"It revealed a tragedy that could have been prevented, it seems to me, one that apparently had its roots in an unhappy family life. Though this girl was the only child in a home where she was completely sheltered, she was dominated by parents who were continually quarreling over which one of them should control her. While she was 'possessed' by both parents, she felt that she 'belonged' to neither.

"Wearying of this, she listened to the 'sales talk' of a well-dressed woman whom she met by chance on a shopping tour downtown, a woman who drew her out, won her confidence, sympathized with her, told her she was 'a fool' to put up with that sort of thing, that she could make 'plenty on her own' and in a glamorous manner. Persuaded by this, the girl ran away the next time a quarrel began at the house. But whatever else home had done to her, it had not prepared her for her new life.

"The evidence of those close to her showed that she found the primrose path hedged with thorns that tore and bruised.

"Soon its 'roses' turned into poison ivy, its 'adventure and fun' into gall and bitterness. Sickening of all this and with no one to whom she could turn for help, the girl finally could think of nothing except to kill herself. But I have always thought the poor deluded child was only searching for what she had failed to find at home, that the greater sin was committed by parents who let themselves quarrel too much; worse still, let themselves quarrel over her instead of considering her feelings, for where could she turn for relief? At that time girls had too little relaxation.

"They had too few places to go when they needed a change.

"Unlike the men they could not turn to hunting and sports and in those days there were no movies, no inexpensive amusements."[2]

Sometimes a dance hall girl had better luck. On August 27, 1884, the *Kansas Cowboy*, published in Dodge, carried this story:

An Unfortunate Made Happy
Her Lover Takes Her Away

While a reporter of this paper was making his round last Friday evening skirmishing for news he stumbled on to a sensation. A well-dressed gentleman stepped into the dance hall and to his surprise found his long lost sweetheart, whom he had given up two years ago as dead. Such a meeting of the two lovers was a sight. After wiping the tears away, the lover commenced propounding questions to her as how come she was living at such a place.

The lovely unfortunate with dazzling eyes gazed up at him and said, "Charlie, I don't know; it has always been a mystery."

She made all kinds of apologies and told him of her trials and tribulations for the past two years in such language as brought tears into his eyes. She pleaded to be taken away from "this den of devils" as she expressed it. He agreed to, if she would make up her mind to be his "future happiness." She consented, and the happy couple left on the late train for Pueblo, where they will be joined in the happy bonds of holy wedlock.

This has been a love match for years back.

CHAPTER 4 :
: VIGILANTES

Dodge has usually been painted as a wild cowtown, but the camp was plenty wild before ever the big trail drives began to come there in 1875. The Texas cowboys were pretty tough and their talk was as big as their fighting quality. But bullwhackers and mule skinners had been rolling up the Santa Fe Trail for half a century. They had fought hostile Indians, Mexicans, horse-thieves, and each other all the way and were ready to crack down on any railroad man or soldier who stood in their path. Buffalo hunters for their part fancied themselves as the big bulls of that lick. They made their living with guns, often $100 a day, and could therefore afford more liquor and more ammunition than men on wages, whom they held in scorn.

Soldiers from Fort Dodge counted themselves professional fighters and were always ready to take a busman's holiday when on pass. So Dodge was full of men, all packing guns, with too much money and unlimited conceit, plenty of liquor—and not enough women to go around. There was no law nearer than Hays City. A man could get away with murder in Dodge.

The merchants with property and lives to protect and a business to conduct with these roughs and drunken gunmen were in a precarious position. They were constantly in danger of being robbed. The gamblers, though usually better shots, were in little better case. Their games were frequently held up and their lights shot out. The visitors aimed to run the camp.

Things went from bad to worse, until decent citizens could

no longer rely upon a single gunman to keep the peace and felt compelled to organize a vigilance committee. The Vigilantes at first were composed of the best men in the community. Their organization, secret as it was, for a time terrorized evil-doers, and hard characters warned to leave town promptly obeyed. But so tough were their customers that in self-defense the Vigilantes took in a number of roughs and killers to strengthen their hand. Then it was out of the frying pan into the fire.

The last straw was the murder of a polite, inoffensive, industrious Negro named Taylor. He had been a servant of the Commanding Officer at Fort Dodge, from which he daily drove a hack to Dodge City. On June 3, 1873, while Taylor was in a store making purchases, a lot of drunken fellows got into his wagon and drove it off. Taylor ran out and tried to stop them. This protest resulted in his death.

This unprovoked killing caused great indignation at Fort Dodge. There is a story that a body of Negro soldiers came from the fort, believed by the buffalo hunters in the camp to have "orders from Washington to burn the town off the face of the earth," but that Tom Nixon got together forty buffalo hunters and met the soldiers at the edge of the military reservation. Tom, so the story goes, pointed out the forty hunters, each with a "Big 50" Sharps rifle, and a hundred rounds of ammunition in his belt, and told the Commanding Officer those guns would all be trained on him and his three white officers. Tom said the hunters would "take the damn Negroes down to the Arkansas River and drown them."

The story goes that the officer returned to the fort and telegraphed to Washington for instructions. When he came back again he came with a warrant for arrest and a search warrant for the killers. This time, so the story goes, he was allowed to search for the killer of Taylor, but failed to find him and had to go back without him.

I have found no record in the National Archives indicating that the War Department ever authorized the Commandant at

Fort Dodge to burn Dodge City, but Scott and Hicks, the killers of Taylor, might well have circulated such a story in order to enlist the sympathies of the buffalo hunters. Certain it is that Major Richard I. Dodge sent the following dispatch to the Governor of Kansas:

> *To Governor Thomas Osborn,*
> *Leavenworth, Kansas.*
>
> A most foul and cold-blooded murder committed last night by ruffians in Dodge City. County organized but no election yet. Had nobody with power to act. Please authorize the arrest of murderers.
>
> RICHARD I. DODGE,
> *Major Third Inf. Comdg.*

Governor Osborn replied as follows:

> Leavenworth, Kans.,
> June 4, 1873.
>
> *To Richard I. Dodge,*
> *Major Comdg. Third Infantry,*
> *Fort Dodge, Kansas.*
>
> Until Ford County is fully organized you are authorized to hold, subject to orders of the civil authorities of the proper judicial districts, all persons notoriously guilty of a violation of the criminal laws of this state. I desire that you should exercise authority with great care and only in extreme cases.
>
> THOMAS A. OSBORN,
> *Governor of Kansas.*

With the Governor's authorization Major Dodge left the post at the head of his troops for Dodge City. The cavalry blocked the streets leading from town while search was made for the killers.

"After the murder, the corpse had been thrown upon the sidewalk and covered with a buffalo hide. Walking up to the body and coolly jerking aside its covering, Hicks pointed to a certain bullet hole, with the remark, 'I shot him there!' "[1]

"Scotty" (as Scott was known in Dodge), the other wanted

man, hid himself in the icebox in Peacock's Saloon and during the night was helped to escape. Hicks was taken into custody.

On June 5 the following order appointing a provost guard for Dodge City was issued at the fort:

HEADQUARTERS, FORT DODGE, KANSAS
June 5th, 1873

Special Orders
    No. 79
Sergt. Elsner and Six (6) privates Co. "A," 3rd Infantry will proceed to Dodge City as a guard. Sergt. Elsner will pitch a tent somewhere within the limits of the town. He will keep a sentinel always on duty. He will not permit any soldier of his party to enter any Bar room, Saloon or other disreputable place in the town except under orders. The guard will always be dressed in Uniform and will habitually wear side arms when away from their tents. Sergt. Elsner will not interfere in any way with the Citizens of Dodge City, but he will arrest any person whatever engaged in flagrantly violating the Criminal laws of the State of Kansas. Any person engaged in rows, fights, shootings, will be immediately arrested and the facts reported to these Hd. Qrs. at once. Sergt. Elsner will arrest every enlisted man found in Dodge City day or night without a written pass from the Commdg. Officer or unaccompanied by an officer, except teamsters in charge of teams of the Govt.

By Order of,
MAJOR R. I. DODGE
THOMAS B. NICHOLS,
2d. Lieut. 5th Cavalry
Post Adjutant

Meanwhile, the Governor appealed to the County Attorney at Dodge City. If he expected any action, he was disappointed. On July 5, Major Dodge appealed once more to the Governor.

FORT DODGE, KAN., July 5, 1873

Gov. T. A. Osborn,
    Topeka, Kan.
Governor:—Since Judge Brown held court here there have been two more attempts at murder in Dodge City, a negro being the suf-

ferer in each case. The man shot last night will probably die, being
wounded in head and lungs.

It is hardly necessary to invite your attention to the fact that I
am not the proper person to exercise civil authority. Sec. 18, Act
Appd. July 15, 1872, provides that any officer of the army on the
active list who shall exercise the functions of a civil office shall
thereby vacate his commission.

In making the arrest of the murderers in the Taylor case I exer-
cised no function of civil office, but simply, as a citizen, obeyed the
order of the chief magistrate of the state. Should I, however, continue to make arrests of "persons found violating the criminal laws
of Kansas" it might be argued that I was violating the spirit if not
the letter of the law quoted.

Besides this, there is, as you know, throughout the whole country
a very great jealousy on the part of civilians and civilian officers of
any interference of the military, and officers of the army are, and
must be, extremely careful of their actions in such cases.

In declining to act any further against the ruffians of Dodge City
I feel it my duty to make a statement of some facts and to point out
some difficulties under which you will labor in undertaking to bring
the town under the control of the law.

Every one who has had experience of life in railroad and mining
towns in unorganized counties or territories beyond the reach of
civil law is perfectly aware of the necessity of "vigilance commit-
tees," so-called organizations which take upon themselves the right
and duty of punishing crime when otherwise it would go on unpun-
ished and unpunishable. Were it not for such organizations life and
property would be at the mercy of villains ejected from law-abiding
communities and whose only hope of life outside of jails is the
absence of the authority of law.

So long as these organizations confine themselves to the legitimate
object of punishing crime they are not only laudable but absolutely
necessary. It is not often that the property-owning and valuable
class of citizens is strong enough to do this work alone. They are
obliged to receive into their organizations some of the roughs. These
in turn take in others worse than themselves, until, as I have often
seen it, a vigilance committee organized by good men in good faith

has become after a while simply an organized band of robbers and cutthroats.

Another difficulty: Having banded together and taken certain obligations as to secrecy, mutual protection of the good men sometimes finds them obliged to aid and abet what in their own hearts they know to be cold-blooded crime perpetrated by their associates. The town of Dodge City is under the control of such a band of vigilantes—some good men, some bad. The murder of Taylor was committed by these vigilantes, who were called together on the first alarm, then dispersed to search for Taylor, and while Scott and Hicks (vigilantes both) dragged him from the drug store and shot him to death at least a dozen other vigilantes stood by ready and obliged to take a hand in the shooting if necessary. Among them were good men who would be shocked at the thought of committing individual crime, and yet they aided, abetted and became "particeps criminis" in the most cowardly and cold-blooded murder I have ever known in an experience of frontier life dating back to 1848.

Of course the vigilantes are only a small portion of the population of Dodge City. It is probable they do not number over thirty or forty men; but, being organized and unscrupulous, they are able to exercise a complete tyranny of terror over the really good citizens who lack organization.

In selecting a man from Dodge City to execute the laws, you risk appointing a member of the vigilantes (all the members being known only to themselves), who would use his power for the benefit of the vigilantes; or you appoint a man well disposed to carry out your views but paralyzed by terror and utterly powerless to do anything.

The government is supposed to give protection. It protects these citizens from the Indians at great expense, yet leaves them to the tender mercies of a foe a thousand times more bloody and brutal than the Indians and infinitely more dangerous because he is in our very midst.

I sincerely hope that you may be able to devise some means of giving security to these people.

RICHARD I. DODGE,
Major Third Infantry

The same day the following order was issued at the fort with regard to the provost guard posted in Dodge City thirty days earlier:

HEADQUARTERS, FORT DODGE, KANSAS
July 5, 1873

Special Orders
    No. 94

It having been reported to the Comdg. Officer that the Provost guard stationed at Dodge City has been behaving in a disorderly manner, Sergt. Elsner "A" Co. 3rd Infantry and the provost guard are hereby relieved from duty at that place and will return to this post without delay.

The Quarter Master Dept. will furnish one mule wagon for transportation.

By Order of
MAJOR R. I. DODGE
THOMAS B. NICHOLS,
2nd. Lieut. 6th Cavalry
Post Adjutant

Wicked Dodge was too much for the soldiers.

The correspondence continued on into the spring of 1874. The Governor appealed to Senator John J. Ingalls of Kansas, and also to the Secretary of War:

April 29, 1874

Hon. Wm. W. Belknap
    Secretary of War.
        Washington, D. C.
                SIR:

I have the honor to herewith enclose for your information copies of dispatches between Col. Richard I. Dodge late Military Commandant at Fort Dodge and myself in relation to the arrest of certain parties at Dodge City Kansas on June last, who were believed to be implicated in the murder of an inoffensive colored man at that place together with a copy of a letter from Col. Dodge in relation to an action lately brought against him for damages for false imprisonment by one of the persons arrested, with a printed notice thereof.

The town of Dodge City was at the time on the extreme frontier, in an unorganized County where Civil process could not be effectively enforced. And life and property was endangered by the desperadoes temporarily in possession of the town. And in my judgment the Emergency justified the action taken by Col. Dodge and I earnestly recommend that the United States District Attorney for the District of Kansas be instructed to defend the action brought against him in this case.

Very respectfully Your Ob't Serv't
THOMAS A. OSBORN,
Governor of Kansas

The course recommended was successfully carried out. Colonel Dodge paid no damages, and the killer was punished. The Vigilantes disbanded.

CHAPTER 5 :
: THE BUFFALO

WHEN white men first saw the Great Plains, it was one vast buffalo pasture extending from the Colorado River in Texas up to the Saskatchewan in the British Possessions. How many million shaggy beasts ranged those grasslands can, of course, never be known. But those who saw the herds covering the earth as with one great robe, sometimes hundreds of miles across, could hardly imagine that the supply of bison could *ever* be exhausted.

In spring the buffalo ranged northward across western Kansas devouring the grass as they went. Cattlemen claimed that where buffalo had grazed, the pasturage was spoiled for two years after. Soldiers of the tiny garrisons strung along the frontier heartily approved the destruction of the herds as the only means likely to keep the Indian on his reservation. Railroads pushing west, stopped by that long depression of the seventies, lacked business and were glad to ship meat, hides, and buffalo bones to Eastern markets. The pioneer settler, though fortunate in being able to support himself by hunting in those first hard years, nevertheless grew tired of an unchanging diet of wild meat and constantly hankered for a mouthful of salt pork. The boarders in Dodge City, where buffalo meat sold for only five cents a pound, also complained bitterly of the monotony of the meat ration. Merchants and freighters welcomed the business that came from buffalo hunting. Everybody on the frontier except the Indian approved the destruction of the herds.

Only the simple-minded savage wondered why men would

kill off native animals that took care of themselves in order to breed less hardy creatures that had to be taken care of.

The Treaty of Medicine Lodge (1867) provided that Indians might hunt in Kansas, so long as buffalo ran there, but that no white man should hunt south of the Arkansas River—the "practical" southern boundary of Kansas.

A number of buffalo hunters who attended that treaty council were asked to promise—and did promise—not to hunt south of the river. That was the Deadline.

But as soon as the buffalo in Kansas had been exterminated, the bolder hunters moved south. As early as 1870, when J. Wright Mooar visited Fort Dodge to ask the Commandant, Richard I. Dodge, what he would do if they went hunting in Texas, the officer laughed and said, "Boys, if I were hunting buffalo I would go where buffalo are."

The Army never made any real effort to enforce that agreement. The Indians resented that, retaliated, and the troops were kept busy defending themselves instead of the Indian hunting grounds.

Several efforts were made to protect the bison. The Legislature of the State of Kansas in the last days of the session of 1872 passed an act to "prevent the wanton destruction of buffalo." But this measure met with an executive pocket veto. The same year a bill introduced in Congress to restrict the killing of buffalo on public lands met the same fate. In 1874 Congress passed an act to "prevent the useless slaughter of buffalo within the United States territories"; this, too, met with a pocket veto. Even if made law, it would not have protected buffalo in the State of Kansas. In 1877 Colonel Dodge wrote, "The buffalo is virtually exterminated. No legislation, however stringent or active, could now do anything either for or against the trade of the 'buffalo products.' "

Several Northern States did enact statutes to protect the bison,[1] but the animals were slaughtered.

To achieve this massacre it was first necessary to find a market for the hides. This was provided by an English firm who asked their American agents to send them five hundred rawhides as a sample. Before that only the robes were used, dressed with the hair on, and could therefore only be taken in winter; but with a market for rawhides the hunter could keep busy most of the year.

Of course buffalo hide is much too spongy and porous for sole leather, but made quite serviceable buff. And so in 1871 word reached Dodge of an unlimited market for hides. When Josiah Wright Mooar brought some hides to Charlie Rath's new store in Dodge, the trader paid $2.25 each.

Said Rath, "The only difference now between a buffalo hide and a greenback is the figure that you mark on it."

The butchery began. The hunters soon discovered that the rifles available were not adequate for the job. Most of them used old Army guns, a Sharps cavalry carbine weighing about seven pounds for use on horseback, breech-loading, .50 caliber. Some had old muzzle-loading Springfields converted into breech-loaders, weighing about eight and a half pounds, .50 caliber. But the hunters wrote to the factory demanding a weapon that would throw a slug as big as a horse-pistol ball.

The manufacturer claimed that was too big a caliber. They were loading the shells with seventy grains, but with the larger ball would have to have more powder, ninety to one hundred grains, a smooth leaden bullet, eleven to the pound.

Shells measured about three inches long. Some were bottle-necked. Good hunters preferred to load their own shells with black gunpowder. Says Mooar! "We wrapped a piece of paper around that bullet before we put in in the shell. When we loaded the shells—we used to get ammunition by the thousand—I would fill the shell with powder within half an inch of the top. When we got that powder in there, we set that shell down and put the rammer in and hit it a lick with the hammer, putting a wad on top and then a little powder on top of the wad and the bullet on top of the powder. As time went on we went a little stronger on powder until we never loaded them with less than one hundred or one hundred ten grains."

Sharps buffalo guns came in different sizes, all bigger and heavier than the early models, some as heavy as sixteen pounds unloaded. Mooar preferred a lighter model. Said he: "I killed 6,500 buffalo with my fourteen-pound gun and 14,000 with the eleven-pounder. The barrel was octagonal halfway up from the breech, then it was round."

The first shipment of rifles went to Hays City, calibers .44 and .45. The hunters were not satisfied, and finally prevailed on Sharps to build one to their specifications—the so-called "Big 50,"[2] for which they might pay from eighty to one hundred dollars or more. They never used a sling on the rifle, but supported the heavy barrel on cross sticks or a tripod. Some hunters preferred to fire from a sitting position, so that the boom of the gun would not resound so loudly.

Unlike range cattle, wild buffalo would sometimes attack a man on horseback but paid little heed to a man afoot. Their eyesight was none too good, but they had a keen sense of smell and when alarmed usually ran against the wind so that they would not head blindly into danger.

Seasoned hunters were in no hurry to leave camp in the morning. They waited until the herds had grazed, filled up, and were ready to lie down. Says J. Wright Mooar: "At nine o'clock by the watch I left camp to hunt. I didn't calculate to shoot the gun off before ten o'clock ne'er a time. I went out horseback ahead and my three wagons and my skinners followed me. I calculated to get out and find some buffalo sometime between nine and ten o'clock when it was getting warm. I wasn't in no hurry in the morning and I generally did all my shooting by noon. Then I'd sit up on a high hill somewhere while my men were scattering around doing the skinning. I kept watch to see that nobody bothered them."

When the hunter saw a herd standing, he would drop from the saddle and creep upwind toward the game. Hunters preferred a herd of about fifty to two hundred animals. Every such small herd, even when the country was covered with buffalo, had its own leader and grazed and traveled together. The ability to identify the leader of the herd was rare but very necessary if the hunter hoped to make a big killing at one stand.

As one old-timer said, "You just had to know somehow which one was the leader, and that's one thing you can't tell another fellow how you done. It's a kind of instinct, I reckon."

The hunter, wearing pads on his knees and a light-brown hat and clothes the color of autumn grass, would crawl on his hands and knees, trying to get closer. He crawled straight toward the herd, in that way being less conspicuous than if he had moved across the buffalo's line of sight. When he got within two hundred yards or so, he might begin to shoot, and keep edging forward as the killing went on. If the first shot were fired too near the herd they might take alarm and run. Says Wright: "You see, when you shot a buffalo in the lights, he threw blood out of his nose. He threwed it around, and he stepped backwards a step or two, and flopped over and died. If you shot him in the heart, he'd run about four hundred yards before he'd fall and take the herd with him."

At the sound of the first shot the herd would all crowd together. The sound startled them, all right, but it did not often stampede them. The roar of the Big 50 did not have the sharp, quick crack to it that a target rifle has. It made a deeper, heavier sound, but with a mellowness that wouldn't startle like the other. If the bunch the hunter was firing at was one of many in a great herd, hundreds and hundreds of the animals would drift away from the sound of the shooting. But the particular bunch whose leader had been shot down would stay and mill around him, while the hunter went on shooting until he had dropped as many as he wanted. Always he took care to shoot down any animal which headed away from the herd and so might start them all moving.

At an average stand he might get twenty-five or thirty or even fifty. There was no sense in killing more than the skinners could handle. Besides, the hunter, unless he had two rifles, would find his heavy barrel getting hot and have to let it cool. Some carried water and a wet cloth with which to swab out the heated gun.

As the hunter edged forward, he might sometimes approach to within fifty yards of the milling animals. Wyatt Earp, who killed ·buffalo with a shotgun, claimed to have done most of his killing at that range. Mooar says that men armed with rifles killed more buffalo at two hundred yards than at one hundred or less.

Fabulous tales are told of killing hundreds of buffalo at several stands all in one day, tales which a little mathematics will quickly discredit. Assuming that so large a number of animals would stand still to be slaughtered, the hunter would be obliged to load and fire his heavy breech-loading rifle every three minutes during a ten-hour day! But we do have reliable figures for some of the most successful hunters.

When the *Edwards County Leader* boasted that Mr. Warnock of Dickinson County had killed as high as 658 buffalo in one winter, the editor of the *Dodge City Times* snorted: "Oh dear, what a mighty hunter! Ford County has twenty men who each have killed five times that many in one winter. The best record, however, is that of Tom Nixon, who killed 120 at one stand in forty minutes, and who, from the 15th of September to the 20th of October, killed 2,173 buffaloes. Come on with some more big hunters if you have any."[3]

Mr. M. A. States, the nephew of Orlando A. "Brick" Bond, has given me definite figures showing Brick's bag of buffalo on his last hunt.

Someone had published some figures on Brick's bag and Mr. States questioned him about it. Brick went to the safe in his store and pulled out an old cowhide wallet. From this he took an ancient canceled check, on the back of which he had entered his score at the time, his bag every fifteen days for sixty days. The figures stand as follows:

November 1	1265
November 15	1354
December 1	1408
December 15	1828

One day Brick Bond killed 300 buffalo. This was just after a spell of bad weather when he feared his idle skinners had been stealing some of his skins. For this reason, he kept a daily record of his kill.

The grand total for Brick's bag amounts to 5,855 or about 97 a day. Brick summarized his kill as being usually about 120 to 125 a day. He employed five skinners. From the date on the check it is assumed that the figures were for 1876-77.

To kill buffalo, Bond used a Big 50 Sharps rifle, with octagonal barrel and a tripod.

During those years he hunted so constantly and shot so many buffalo that he was deafened by his gun.

The sound of a Sharps rifle was so different from that of other weapons that in Indian country several camps of the hunters would do their shooting within earshot of each other's weapons. So long as they heard only the mellow boom of the Big 50, all was serene. But when the sharp crack of a smaller gun was heard, all hurried to join forces and repel attack. Says Mooar, "I knew the sound of every one of my guns."[4]

CHAPTER 6 ·
: THE HIDE HUNTERS

HARDLY had the market for buffalo hides become widely known than the panic of 1873 began, which lasted for five long years. During those years most of the buffalo on the Southern Plains were destroyed. The American frontiersman had always depended in part upon wild meat for subsistence, and when people in Kansas realized that they could not only eat, but make good money killing buffalo, there was a rush to the Plains comparable to a gold rush.

All sorts of men rode, walked, or came on wheels to that great buffalo pasture between the Platte and the Arkansas Rivers. Family parties with a crate of chickens at the tail gate of the wagon and a milch cow tied behind, with children peering out from under the wagon sheet, moved onto the range along with every sort of killer, from the occasional English sportsman to the seasoned professional hunter.

They were armed with all sorts of guns, pistols, old Civil War muskets, squirrel rifles, shotguns, Colt's revolvers, carbines, and Sharps rifles. Every man wanted to shoot buffalo, but few were willing to do the dirty work of skinning and dressing hides. And in their greed for hides they seldom bothered to save the meat. Most of these green hunters were poor shots, knew nothing of the habits of the animals they hunted, and wounded far more than they killed. Most of them knew little or nothing about curing rawhides, and so spoiled four out of five of those they man-

45

aged to take. Thus, one hide brought to market might represent three to ten dead or mutilated animals.

This haphazard and cruelly wasteful slaughter soon gave way to a more systematic, but no less deadly, system of extermination. Businessmen in Dodge City and other towns along the railroad soon got the trade pretty well into their own hands by organizing and grubstaking parties led by crack shots—parties comprising skinners, cooks, hide handlers and a man who kept busy loading cartridge shells. They supplied ammunition, guns, wagons, horses, blankets, knives, and cooking utensils. A couple of ten-gallon water kegs, a coffee pot, Dutch oven, frying pan, tin plates and tin cups supplied the cook. His larder contained flour, some salt pork, a few pounds of coffee, sugar, salt, and beans; an A-tent or a lean-to made of hides gave shelter.

The pay of the men was in proportion to the number of hides they brought. Companies established central depots, such as Adobe Walls and Rath City, where they could supply hunters and receive hides.

In 1871 the buffalo were estimated by the millions, and many of the hunters entered the profession expecting it to prove a life-work, and despaired of killing off more than the annual increase of the herd.

Hunters encamped by water holes and along rivers where the animals had to come to drink, and at night built watch fires so that the slaughter could go on twenty-four hours a day.

Two years later where there had been myriads of buffalo there were only myriads of rotting carcasses. The air was filled with the sickening stench of death, and that great pasture, once teeming with animal life, was an empty, melancholy, putrid desert.

Josiah Wright Mooar hired outlaws for choice to skin and drive and cook for him on the buffalo range. They made good workers and were never tempted to quit, as they had no desire to return to the settlements—and prison. He was too alert to let his men steal his hides. And certainly on the buffalo range there were plenty of "hard cases" fit for his employment.

When the hunter had made his kill, he would signal his skinners waiting in the distance and then they would come along with the wagons. Mooar always had a gray lead horse in his team, so that he could recognize his outfit from afar.

The equipment of a skinner was a box of knives sharp enough to shave with. Every man carried knives of two kinds—the ripping knife and the skinning knife—with a steel at his belt to sharpen them with. The blade of the skinning knife was curved; the ripping knife had a straight blade. The skinners would walk up to the nearest carcass and get to work.

Skinning was hard, dirty, bloody work. The knife soon dulled. For in flytime buffalo rolled in muddy wallows and hooked at cut banks to sharpen their horns—their wool was full of grit and dirt.

When butchering a buffalo, the hide hunters slit the hide along the belly from neck to tail and down the inside of each leg. They skinned the neck all round, taking the ears, but leaving the skin of the head. They also skinned out the legs and a strip as broad as a man's hand along each side of the belly slit. Then noosing a short rope around the skin of the neck and bulky ears, they hitched a horse to that, headed the animal toward the buffalo's tail, and so pulled off the hide. Some thought it necessary to drive a stake to which the buffalo's head was anchored, in order to jerk the hide off quickly.

The skinners sometimes helped load the hides on the wagons. But ordinarily their time was too valuable to be taken up with that, and other men came along and loaded the hides—and meat, if that were being taken—following the skinners from one carcass to another. It took four good men to skin a hundred buffalo in half a day.

When the skinner ripped a hide from the carcass, it was rolled up and thrown into the wagon, and when all the hides had been gathered, they were taken back to camp, spread out flesh side up flat on the grass, or on a gentle slope if the weather was wet. Small holes were cut in the edge all round and the heavy hide was staked out on the ground with two dozen pegs a foot or more long and thicker than a man's thumb. The hides were "poisoned" against insects with arsenic. Otherwise, hide bugs ruined them.

Handling hides was heavy work. A good-sized green bullhide weighed about one hundred pounds.

In fine weather three days' sun would set the hides stiff as a board. Then the pins were pulled up and the hide turned over to dry the hair side. With both sides dry, the hides were piled in stacks about one hundred deep.

Then the hide had to be cured, and one of the men spent the morning taking the hides from the stacks and spreading them over acres of prairie flesh side up to cure until noon. Then he began where he started before, turned them all over to sun and stacked them all up again. They had to be stacked every night or dew would collect and the edges would curl up and the hide would be uneven and would not pack snugly on the wagon. Every day it was the same, until all could qualify as cured or "flint" hides. Such a hide had lost half its original weight. The hunters had only the actual weight to pay freight on. Cowhides averaged about twenty pounds, bullhides fifty. The hide of a spike—a young buffalo bull—was thin, light, and not so heavy. A good Studebaker wagon would carry five hundred flint hides weighing about five tons.

Not all outfits loaded hides alike. Some had wagons built like a hayrack and loaded the hides on spread flat, hair side up, lashing them down with chains or rope. Others, according to Billy Fox,[1] "broke" and folded the hides down the middle before they stacked them on the frames. Others, as photographs taken near Dodge plainly show, rolled each hide up like a carpet, hair side out, and stacked these lengthways in a wagon bed three or four sideboards high.

The market for hides varied, but generally brought two to four dollars on the Plains. Sometimes buyers would come out from one of the towns, forts, or trading posts to bargain for the hides. Sometimes these were sold by the hunters on the streets of Dodge City.

A single outfit with four nine-yoke ox teams and a big wagon with two others trailing to each team might bring in as many as four thousand hides, and buyers had to have plenty of cash on hand. There were no banks in Dodge during the heyday of the buffalo hunter. Eugene LeCompt was one of the Irish staff of Lobenstein, the great hide buyer, who would hire nobody but Irishmen.

One afternoon J. Wright Mooar's outfit rolled into Dodge laden with shaggy hides looking for LeCompt. LeCompt used to stand right out on the street in Dodge—both overcoat pockets stuffed full of greenbacks rolled up in rolls of different denominations—thousands of dollars, cash to buy hides. But that day some fellows had got him to cross the Deadline to the wrong side of the tracks to sit in on a game. Says Mooar: "I wouldn't sell my hides to anybody else when he was there. So I hunted around and finally found him in that saloon at a poker table.

"There was four of them in that game besides him with big stacks of chips in the pot. He had $100 in chips, I guess, besides a stack of greenbacks at his elbow."

Mooar didn't like the look of the other fellows at that poker table. He walked up to LeCompt like he was pretty mad, slapped him on the shoulder and said, "By Godfrey, if you want them hides of mine, get out there and count them. I want to get my money and go home."

LeCompt looked around at the "angry" buffalo hunter and said, "Can't you wait until I play this hand out?"

Mooar said, "Hell, no, I ain't going to wait for nothing. There's another buyer on Front Street who wants them hides."

LeCompt turned to the other players and said, "Gentlemen, will you please excuse me?"

They said yes. So he folded up his hand and left the cards there with all those chips and his greenbacks, and the two of them walked out to Mooar's wagon.

Then LeCompt said, "Drive around across the railroad tracks. I wouldn't go back in that house again for a million dollars. By God, you saved my life right there."

LeCompt never forgot Mooar's help. He had realized that he was framed, but had not dared try to leave the saloon or quit the game. So he just sat there until Mooar stepped in and got him out. . . .

Hides and meat were not the only products of the buffalo which brought money to Dodge City and its trading area. As the mighty slaughter continued, the Plains were covered with reeking carcasses, and the big buffalo wolves were everywhere. At first wolfers had done well, planting strychnine in the carcasses. But as the number of these increased, the wolves could get meat anywhere, and would seldom touch a carcass around which they smelled fresh human sign.

A greater source of profit were buffalo bones, which, shipped east on the new railroad, could be made into fertilizer or used to make bone china. Bone brought good prices. When a man drove to town to trade, he filled his wagon bed with bones and sold them on Front Street. The bones were piled up high as a man's head, extending for many rods along the track to await shipment. When the buffalo were all killed off and drought and depression again struck the Plains, many settlers who had lost their corn crop (before wheat came to be the main crop) managed to keep going by selling bones.

Freighters would buy bones from settlers at $2.00 or $2.50 a ton, haul them to the railroad and get up to $14 a ton. It took a lot of bones to weigh a ton in that dry air, so some dealers would throw water over the bones in their wagons before they drove in to sell them. Sometimes the same wet treatment was given to bones after they were loaded on railroad cars.

Apart from falling off a horse, being maimed by a bursting gun barrel, or trampled by stampeding buffalo, the actual shooting of the buffalo was not dangerous. In the summer mating season the bulls were fierce, but in the hunting season, fall and winter, the animals were fat and seldom vicious. Killing buffalo was hardly more hazardous than shooting cows in a barnyard. The principal risk was that they might take alarm and run away.

The greatest danger was weather. When a furious blizzard suddenly struck the level plains and filled the air with a white smother of icy particles, so that a man could hardly see his hand before his face, hardly breathe or dare to leave his cabin, wagon, or campfire, death from freezing was a terrible menace. Such storms blew away tents, blankets, smothered fires, filled a man's boots with snow, and set his animals adrift.

Colonel Richard I. Dodge repeats a report that more than one hundred frostbitten buffalo hunters perished along the Arkansas in two years' time (1872-73). He adds that seventy amputations were performed by his post surgeon on hunters or railroad men, and that over two hundred men lost hands or feet or parts of them near Dodge. John Riney of Dodge, who kept the toll bridge, was one of those crippled by frostbite.

Says Colonel Dodge, "One poor fellow had both hands and both feet taken off, and not only recovered but was a few months ago in good health and attending to his usual duties." He does not explain what those "duties" were.

And then there was always danger from hostile Indians. Of course, when they tackled buffalo hunters armed with the Big 50 Sharps rifle which could kill at seven hundred yards or more, they soon learned to be wary. But not every man could afford such a rifle.

In the spring of 1874 an incident occurred which aroused great indignation in Dodge City.

About the middle of June a company of four men with five horses and a wagon hit the trail from Dodge to the Cimarron to hunt buffalo. Jesse Fleming had a Sharps rifle. He was to do the killing. The others were to skin, drive, care for the hides, and keep camp. They made camp on Crooked Creek some sixteen miles from Dodge.

On the morning of Monday the fifteenth they discovered that during the night their horses had been stolen.

Two of the men remained with the wagon and their scanty supplies. Fleming, carrying his rifle, and Warren, unarmed, walked east to Mulberry Creek on the trail of the horsethieves.

There they found one of the lost horses which, having broken down, had been abandoned. . . .

Next day Jesse Fleming, carrying his rifle, came walking into Dodge City and reported that his companion Warren had been killed by a party of five Indians. Warren had refused to join Dirty Face Jones on a trip to Adobe Walls—because of danger from Indians!

A small company was organized at once to bring home the body, which they brought to Dodge City Tuesday night at ten o'clock.

Captain H. S. Bristol, Fifth Infantry, then commanding Fort Dodge, sent the Post Adjutant, Second Lieutenant Thomas B. Nichols, Sixth Cavalry, to Dodge City to investigate this alleged murder of a citizen by Indians.

Fleming told the officer that when he and Warren found the broken-down pony they despaired of catching up with the thieves on foot and decided to go to Dodge for help. Fleming went on to say that Warren, not having a gun, proposed that he should ride the horse into town while Fleming, being armed, should follow on foot by "a little different route." Shortly after Warren passed out of sight Fleming said he saw five mounted Indians swiftly circling around him, but—apparently because of the rifle—they kept at such a distance that he could not determine the tribe.

He showed his rifle and prepared to fight.

Then the Indians disappeared and he saw them no more. He was then about one and a half miles from the road to Camp Supply.

Fleming said he believed that the Indians discovered Warren and then went for him there.

Lieutenant Nichols reports: "The man Warren was shot in three places in the body; either shot should judge would have been mortal and his entire scalp taken off, leaving hardly a hair on his head, his body presented a ghastly sight this morning. There can be no doubt that it was Indian work. The case is a peculiarly hard one as all the man was worth was invested in his small lot of stock and he leaves a widow and six small children entirely destitute."

Lieutenant Nichols was not entirely satisfied with Fleming's story and brought him to Fort Dodge so that, as he reported to the Commanding Officer, "You can examine him yourself and judge of the correctness of his tale."

Two days later Lieutenant A. Hensly, Sixth Cavalry, reported a somewhat different story to the Post Adjutant.

He had been sent out with seventeen men of Company F, Sixth Cavalry, in compliance with orders issued June 17 to "a point on Crooked Creek where a party of Indians are reported to have been depredating, killing settlers, and running off stock." He rode to that point. The men left with the wagon reported that it had been agreed that Fleming and Warren should go to Dodge City for horses while the others stayed with the wagon until they came back.

Lieutenant Hensly's report continues: "Fleming (who accompanied me to the Camp and who related all he knew of the affair with as much reluctance, and who required as much questioning as an unwilling witness on the stand) states that himself and Warren had gotten as far as the head of Mulberry Creek about 10 miles from Dodge City when they saw a pony that had evidently been abandoned. Warren started to catch it and disappeared from Fleming's sight over a divide; shortly after, Fleming saw a party of five mounted men (He could not tell whether white men or Indians) who on seeing him appeared to have a consultation and then rode off. Fleming then walked into Dodge (It does not appear that he sought after his comrade who was unarmed). Fleming was armed with a Sharps, (sporting

Rifle) and as Warren did not come in that day, fears were entertained for his safety by his friends, and a party of citizens on
going out found his body a short distance from the place where
Fleming says he saw him last. He had been shot in the back with
pistols or a pistol and scalped. On arriving at the point which
Fleming pointed out to me as their camp, I found that the men
and wagon had disappeared. I found the trail of the wagon
which entered the road to Dodge about a mile from the camp
and as a party of citizens had gone from Dodge to bring them in,
about 5 hours before I started, I concluded they had found
them and started in that night, which fact was confirmed by a
party of wood choppers I found about six miles from the camp,
up the creek. These wood choppers state that they have not
been disturbed and have seen no signs of Indians. I could not
find any trail of horses or ponies near the Camp of the hunters;
the heavy rain of the 17th had obliterated any sign that might
have existed, so there was nothing that indicated the race of the
thieves, unless we consider that it was not done by Indians
(*sic*) usually do that kind of business. The order I received refers
to Indians killing settlers and running off stock. There are no
settlers on Crooked Creek, and the only stock is that possessed
by the wood choppers (a party of four men who are on the
creek temporarily) and any party of buffalo hunters who may
camp on the creek en route to Dodge from the Cimarron River.
I arrived at the Post this morning having been absent less than
48 hours. Marched about 70 miles, and saw no Indians or Indian
signs."

The well-known photograph taken "by Wm. S Soule" near
Dodge City, of a citizen lying scalped while a soldier in uniform
holding a horse and a man in citizen's clothes wearing white
gloves and a big black hat kneel beside the body, has usually
been identified as that of Warren, though sometimes merely
captioned "The Scalped Hunter."

There is no record to show what became of the broken-down
horse. The rain had obliterated all tracks, and it was impossible

to tell what had happened from the appearance of the ground.

The death of Warren resulted in his son going to work to support his mother and the other children. He was employed as bartender in the Long Branch Saloon and later presided over games for the house, becoming a skillful gambler. In after years he went east and was associated with Brady in similar enterprises. There, they say, someone asked him where he went to college. With a grin young Warren replied, "I am a graduate of the Long Branch Saloon, class of '78."

CHAPTER 7 ·

GAMBLERS AND GAMES

ONE DAY a stranger sat in on a gambling game in Dodge City and lost his little pile. Leaving the place, he walked down Front Street seeking Mayor Bob Wright. When he found him standing on the corner, he complained that the game was in violation of the city ordinance against gambling.

The Honorable Bob fixed the poor loser with a stern eye and barked, "So, you've been gambling, have you!" He turned to the Marshal near by. "Bill, this fellow has been gambling in violation of the city ordinance. Run him in. I'll make an example of these gamblers."

The Docket of the Police Judge of Dodge City shows that on June 2, 1886, two men were actually arrested and fined five dollars each because they "did gamble in the city of Dodge City contrary to law." This is the sole arrest for gambling recorded in the extant dockets prior to June, 1888, though these dockets cover periods totaling six years and three months. Yet an ordinance prohibiting games of chance in Dodge City with fines of ten to one hundred dollars for violation thereof was passed by the city fathers as early as 1878. The two men arrested paid their fines promptly. One of them, apparently, had come out ahead of the game, since he flippantly gave his name as "Vanderbilt."

It is clear that the city fathers neither hoped nor wished to abolish gambling in Dodge. The ordinance of 1878 was enacted

56

as a temporary and emergency measure to secure needed funds. It was a tax, not a fine.

The local paper made a joke of that: "Street interlocution: 'Have you paid your fine?' "

The paper (August 17, 1878) explains the situation:

"The ordinances in relation to gambling and prostitution are being vigorously enforced. Over $200 in fines have been collected. A sufficient amount will be collected to meet the expenses of retaining the police force, which was cut off one member.

"A number of hard wretches that infested this community have left for parts unknown. The community is well without them. The operation of the ordinances proved as we expected— the ridding of a class of dead beats, thieves and eye sores. The number of gamblers has been reduced, and of this class we feel charitable enough to say that their operations have been confined to what is known as legitimate and honorable gambling."

The very year the ordinance against gambling was passed by the city fathers the *Ford County Globe* expressed the following opinion:

"We believe that what is known as 'square games' are among the necessary belongings of any town that has the cattle trade. We don't believe there are a dozen people in Dodge who seriously object to this kind of gambling so long as this is a cattle town, but we appeal to our city officers 'to set down on' all showcase and other bare-faced robbing concerns. Keep them away from our town. They create more bad blood among both cattlemen and citizens than anything else. They are no good to any class of people in the community and they are even despised by gamblers themselves."

These "showcase" or confidence games, though frowned on, could not be entirely prevented. One anonymous contributor published in the *Dodge City Times* a request that the City Marshal inform the public if a City Marshal degrades his official position by standing in with so-called showcase games for ten per cent of the games. Marshal L. E. Deger indignantly replied:

"I consider that the city marshal who would take any per cent of any showcase game or other game of like character not only degrades his official position, but becomes a scoundrel. Sign your name next time."

When Dodge was young, the lottery swindler was free to fleece his victims on Front Street. His stock in trade consisted of a small showcase containing silver goblets, heavy hunting case watches, silver spoons, gold rings, diamond pins, and other jewelry. As the Plaza was part of the main highway to Santa Fe, plenty of passing suckers stopped there, and tinhorn gamblers and confidence men reaped a harvest. But after Kelley became Mayor such games were frowned on.

One June day in 1879 the City Treasurer, finding a showcase game attracting some unwary teamsters, offered them sound advice.

At this the proprietor of the game, one Curley, lost his temper and snarled, "Don't you interfere with my business again."

Hearing this, the City Marshal, speaking as a private citizen, said he would squelch the institution if the *vox populi* would back him. That assured, the Marshal gathered the showcase in his brawny arms and pitched the whole shebang into the street. Smash! Silver watches, jewelry, cutlery, diamonds, and other valuables rolled in the dust.

Somewhat later, the editor remarks: "The 'jeweler' has gone. . . . Before leaving, he secured an ornamental countenance which he will exhibit to his friends in the east as a specimen of the many novelties and wonders of the far west. In obtaining this curiosity he is said to have swallowed several teeth. Mr. Sutton says his mouth will compare favorably with that of a Chinese god."

Councilor H. E. Gryden afterward facetiously compared the Police Court with "the late showcase game." He said each comprised three outside men, one high cockalorum behind the case, and one inside capper!

The citizens of Dodge "no longer considered it necessary to

their success to encourage *every* species of vice." The swindlers were forced to decamp.

One morning, a week later, two monte men got off the westbound train. While they were standing near the water tank a passenger stepped to the platform and fired three pistol shots at the slippery Jacks. Both ran for their lives, stumbling over a rock as they went. The stumble may have saved them, as neither was hit. They explained that they had fleeced this passenger out of his pile. But as the editor put it, "There are gullible people who believe they can beat anybody at his own game; but they are invariably taken in and done for, and after all will be little wiser than before, being always the prey for the wiley card manipulator."

Games were maintained in nearly every saloon and dance hall in Dodge City, and nearly every game of chance that could be played with cards, dice, or a ball was played there. Faro, monte, hazard, and poker seem to have been most popular, and these games were generally presided over by a skilled professional gambler. Such men were generally of equable temper, with a cool head, steady nerves, and deft fingers.

Gambling, as Bat Masterson declared, "was not only the principal and best-paying industry of the town, but was also reckoned among its most respectable." Such a square-deal gentleman gambler as William H. Harris of the Long Branch enjoyed a prestige greater than that of a banker; and Bat Masterson, one of the most successful gamblers in the West, won a gold-headed cane worth twenty dollars on the Fourth of July, 1885, as the "most popular man in Dodge City," leaving Harry Scott, George Hoover, and others in the dust. It cost ten cents to vote in this contest, and of some 300 votes cast, Bat got 170.

A gambler's career usually fell into this pattern: first, a killing in self-defense; then a job as a gunman, and bouncer, in a gambling house; then a position as gambler playing on a percentage for the house; later, a partnership in or ownership of a dance hall, saloon, or other gambling place; and finally—on attaining years of discretion—a move to some safer place and job.

For though the gambler's reputation as a gun-fighter attracted trade to his table, there was always a chance that someone would try to run a bluff on him or pick a fight to see how handy he was with a gun.

However, it was sometimes possible in a gambling place of the better class to avoid quarrels. If a visitor presented his complaint to the proprietor instead of picking a fight with the dealer, an adjustment might be made. The proprietor would ask, "How much did you lose?" and return the fellow's money, adding this advice: "You're welcome to come in here any time to drink at the bar, but not to gamble. Bear that in mind."

Nearly everybody gambled in Dodge. Indeed the two deacons of Reverend Wright's church, Wyatt Earp and Bat Masterson, were professional gamblers.

My stepfather used to tell a story about a self-styled "preacher" who passed through Dodge. He hung his black coat on the back of his chair before he sat in, but always opened the game with prayer. He said he regarded chance as God's means of favoring the elect and punishing sinners. Once caught with an ace up his sleeve, he brazenly but blandly asserted that the Good Lord must have put it there.

Apparently he had donned the cloth to protect himself in case his tricks were discovered.

One character with a card up his sleeve found himself suspected of cheating. Hastily he ordered a sandwich, slipped the card between the two slices of bread and ate it. Thus he earned his moniker, "Eat 'Em Up" Jake.

The late James "Dog" Kelley, Dodge City's genial Irish sportsman and politician, used to delight in telling the story of a greenhorn who came to town.

Early one morning, the story goes, a tall, gangly, green-looking young man entered Kelley's restaurant and seated himself at a table in one corner of the room. As he gazed about him at the array of cowboys, freighters and gamblers, each with a brace of guns strapped on his hips, he seemed bewildered and afraid....

After finishing his meal, the greenhorn went over to where Kelley was seated. . . . Searching his pockets, he pulled forth a single silver dollar and paid the check. As he gathered up his change, he said in an undertone to Kelley, "Do they ever have any poker games around here?"

"Yes," replied Kelley, "but I advise you to let them alone. You are no match for these card sharks. And besides, in these games the sky is the limit."

Thanking Kelley, the stranger walked out of the door and started up Front Street.

The whole attitude of the stranger impressed Kelley, and he stepped to the door to watch where he went. The greenhorn walked slowly up the street, gaping at everything in sight. He crossed the railroad tracks . . . to the wagon yard, where he climbed into a freight wagon.

"Oh," thought Kelley, "a green country kid who wants to try his hand at being a Westerner."

That night, as the revelry was at its height, the "green country kid" sauntered into the Lady Gay Saloon and Dance Hall, and seated himself at a corner table to watch the big poker game going on. He was offered several free drinks, but declined with, "Thanks, I don't drink."

Thinking they had a sucker, one of the gamblers approached the young man, saying, "Want to try your hand in the game?"

"Yes," said the greenhorn, "but I guess I won't stay long, 'cause I ain't got much money."

With that, he took a buckskin sack out of his pocket, and after counting his money, he bought chips and sat down at the table to play. The spectators winked at each other, and the bartender said in an undertone, "A sucker and his money are soon parted. At that, I feel sorry for the kid."

It soon became evident to all concerned that the green kid knew the game and how to play it. He won pot after pot. The gamblers looked at each other in astonishment. One by one the players dropped out of the game, broke. Finally only two of the original six remained—the greenhorn and one of the city's smoothest gamesters. They battled until daylight, when the kid cashed his chips and slowly walked out of the door.

The bartender followed him out to the sidewalk and saw a well-dressed man join him. Together they mounted their horses and rode south out of town. As they shook the dust of the city off their boots, they turned to wave good-by to the bartender.

A bleary-eyed group of gamblers entered Kelley's restaurant for breakfast, and were greeted by a chorus of, "How about the green kid? How much did he trim you fellows out of?" And one gambler replied, "He broke up the game." He added, "We gave him everything in the deck, extra cards, marked cards, but he just kept on winning. He was the greenest-looking kid I ever saw. Even in shuffling and dealing the cards he was awkward and clumsy. But," he said with a sigh, "that face—he never moved a muscle. It was just like looking at a graven image."

The story of the greenhorn who broke the game in the Lady Gay spread all over town, and the boys were in for no end of joshing by the followers of the Great American Game.

Said Kelley, with a twinkle in his eye, "The kid taught those Knights of the Green-Covered Table a valuable lesson in that no matter how good you are at a game, there always is someone better. Mark Twain was right; you can't tell how far a frog can jump by looking at him."[1]

CHAPTER 8 :
: THE BULLS

THE SANTA FE RAILROAD did not stop at Dodge City, but immediately built on to the Colorado line, reaching it just in time to avoid the forfeit of public lands granted the company along the route. For years after, there were no towns of importance west of Dodge; she was for practical purposes the end of the line, and so remained the great distributing center for the Southwest. Trails radiated in all directions; and over these all supplies went by wagons serving the military forts in the region, the buffalo hunters' hide towns, the cattlemen's ranches, the Indian Agencies, missions, and inland settlements. These wagons were drawn either by oxen or mules.

More than forty years before the building of Dodge City, Major Bennett Riley, escorting a caravan of Santa Fe traders on the old Santa Fe Trail to the Cimarron Crossing (where the town of Cimarron now stands—about twenty miles west of Dodge), astonished everyone by using oxen to draw his wagons instead of mules or horses. At the time, the United States Army had no cavalry.

During the years that followed, the big Missouri mule was developed, and mule teams came into more common use. During Dodge City's heyday, both were used; bullwhackers and mule skinners played a great part in her life.

Their profane ejaculations and cracking whips were often heard on Front Street, and at any season their wagons and teams could be seen busily loading or unloading at the stores and warehouses.

With so many teams, wagons, and horsemen coming and going, Dodge City was necessarily well equipped with hitch-racks and corrals. H. B. "Ham" Bell in 1875 erected the first livery stable in Dodge City, where he also served as undertaker and peace officer. About ten years later he built a huge livery barn, the biggest building in western Kansas, to accommodate the trade. It stood south of the tracks on Bridge Street, and would stable more than one hundred head of horses or mules. The front of the building had painted across it a big elephant on the run, waving a banner; it was known throughout the West as the Elephant Barn. The corral extended for three blocks, clear to the edge of what is now Wright Park.

The Elephant Stable was a great rendezvous. Bell himself may be quoted here: "I have seen freighters meet in that barn by appointment made months previously. I have seen fifty men make their beds in the loft at night. The block across the street north was then vacant and freighters would come in with their eight-team wagons. They would leave an $80 gun, saddles, and all of their harness on those wagons and turn the horses and mules into the corral. Three or four days or a week later they would return, catch the horses, harness up, and away they would go. Not a strap would have been touched. People didn't steal then as they do now."

Bullwhackers prided themselves on being the toughest men on earth. Most of them were handy with a lariat, and all delighted in whip-throwing. A bull whip in those days cost $1.50. It had a stout hickory handle about two feet long. The lash itself measured twelve feet, with a buckskin popper a foot long on the end. Men armed with such whips boasted that they could kill a fly on the off ear of a leader of a six-yoke team and never bring blood. For the most part, the whips were used rather for cracking and inspiration than for actually lashing the teams, for such a whip cruelly used would flay where it fell.

Once a bout of lapjacket took place on Front Street, when two Negroes armed with such whips were egged on to lash each other in a duel which might have ended fatally, had not Marshal Joe Mason interfered.

In handling the whip, the bullwhacker grasped the handle in his left fist, coiling the lash with his right hand and the forefinger of his left. Whirling the whip around his head, he sent it flying straight out, then brought it back with a jerk. When snapped in the air, such a whip popped like a pistol shot. Some drivers, however, preferred to use a long oxgoad which they called a "*carajo* pole."

Government oxen were branded "U.S." on the horn. Many were shod.

There was no driver's seat in the lead wagon for the bullwhacker. The space aboard was too precious, and the wagons were packed chock-full of goods.

In the earliest days on the Santa Fe Trail before oxen came into use, the mule skinner generally rode a wheeler; and since white men mount from the left side, the saddle was placed on the near wheeler. In those days, the wagon brake was at the rear and had to be operated by someone other than the driver. Later, the brake was placed on the left side forward, with a handle six feet long to the top of which a rope was attached. This enabled the driver to manage the brake by pulling the rope, whether walking or riding.

Mule skinners carried whips of plaited leather, the handle therefore being a pliable tube of leather filled with shot to give it weight and afford a firm grip. The whip itself might be only seven feet long, with a whang leather loop at the end and a very long lash. The butt of such a whip when swung as a blackjack made a deadly weapon.

The mule skinner rode the near wheeler and managed his team with a jerk line three inches wide, extending to the lead pair of mules and attached to the near leader. Such a team could haul two or three tons in one wagon.

Both bullwhackers and mule skinners did a great deal of shouting and cracking of whips to keep their teams pulling together and at the right rate of speed. And so the Indians called cattle or beef "wohaw" and a wagon a "goddam."

Bull trains traveled during the early hours of the day and the late afternoon, resting during the heat of the day in summer. They averaged a dozen miles a day loaded, and half again as much empty.

A single wagon might be drawn by six yoke of oxen or a six-mule team, but as a rule, a team drew one large wagon with one or two smaller wagons trailing this. This arrangement proved economical. On good trails all three wagons could be handled easily by the team, and when the going was rough or boggy, or streams had to be forded or steep hills climbed, each wagon could be hauled forward separately and then all hooked together again when the obstacle lay behind them.

In that case, the animals were more numerous, and as many as twelve yoke of oxen might be used and six or eight pairs of mules, depending on the condition of the trail and the weight on the wagons. A wagon train ordinarily consisted of six teams, with two or three wagons to the team. The crew consisted of the wagon boss, the drivers, and the night herder. Commonly the boss had a saddle horse along.

Mules could travel faster and were less likely to stampede, but did not endure cold weather well and developed in their drivers an almost psychopathic irritability.

Charles Rath and Lee & Reynolds were the principal Army and Indian traders in Dodge City's earliest days and sent out many a wagon train to Camp Supply, Indian Territory, to Fort Elliott, and Mobeetie, its near-by settlement, in Texas. In 1876 Rath freighted to the Double Mountains in Texas, where he built a hide town of poles and buffalo skins to trade with the hunters. Two years later, when the buffalo in that region had been killed off, the Mooar brothers, with forty yoke of oxen, moved Rath City, lock, stock, and barrel, to Camp Supply in a single trip.

But while Rath City lasted, it was the metropolis of the buffalo hunters. In the hide-and-pole restaurant there, meat was the staple diet. The hunters knew that a man can keep fat and sassy on meat alone, provided that, like carnivorous animals, he eats the softer parts and internal organs as well as the steaks. So he obtains the minerals and vitamins he needs. The hunters ate buffalo tongue, tripe, kidneys—even testicles, which dainty souls referred to as "prairie oysters."

The hide-and-pole restaurant at Rath City was staffed with a cook and a waitress brought from Dodge.

One day a tenderfoot rode into Rath City to see the sights—or, as he put it, in a slang phrase then current, "to see the elephant." But first of all he wanted dinner, and went into the restaurant to get it.

The waitress was an innocent girl, but she naturally used the lingo of her regular customers. Said she, "Well, Mister, what'll you have—nuts, guts, or brains?"

The tenderfoot walked out. "I can go home now," he declared, "I've seen the elephant!"

From Dodge wagon trains went out to Indian Territory, Colorado, New Mexico, Texas, and western Kansas. One of the trails most used was the Tascosa Trail.

Storms, floods, raiding Indians, buffalo herds (which sometimes swept away the teamsters' animals) and stampedes were common hazards of the trail. Mules would stay with the bell mare if one were along, but oxen, more temperamental, were easily stampeded, and would take fright at any sudden noise or even the rattle of their own yoke-chains.

Oxen, better than mules, could cover long distances without grain. They were slower but surer; and on a long trip might even arrive before the mules, provided they had plenty of grass and water at short stages. On the other hand, mules, being faster, could go longer stages without water.

The bulls were better than mules in pulling through heavy mud because of the mules' small hoofs. Oxen, it was said, could pull a wagon through a bog that would mire a saddle blanket, but they were hard to shoe, apt to get sorefooted, and did not endure heat well.

Among other firms in the freighting business at Dodge City were the York-Parker-Draper outfit, Wright and Beverley, Culbertson and Nichols, supply houses and traders who had their own teams. There were also smaller outfits who hauled the goods of others. Generally, the rate was a dollar a hundred pounds on any long haul under, say, two hundred miles. We have some records of the quantities of goods freighted by these outfits. In February, 1879,[1] Lee & Reynolds moved nearly 500,000 pounds of stores for the Army. The following month they hauled 300,000 more. During 1883, the Santa Fe Railroad received goods (most of which went out of town by wagon) in monthly shipments of from nearly 2,000,000 to nearly 5,000,000 pounds; and a single rancher in 1884, according to Texas records, might order from 20,000 to 85,000 pounds of supplies. In 1883, 36 carloads of buffalo bones, weighing more than 8,000,000 pounds, were shipped from Dodge City, valued at $6.00 a ton.

Freighters usually loaded in the morning and drove out a few miles that afternoon to spend the night at one of the outlying camps around Dodge, and so get an early start next morning. Some of those camps, unpatrolled by Marshal or Sheriff, were wilder than Dodge herself.

There was much rivalry among the different outfits. The *Dodge City Times* (August 10, 1878) prints this story:

"A bull train race took place last week on the road south of Dodge. Russel made a trip to Fort Elliott and return in 19 days. Vance made it in 20 days. Culbertson made a trip to Supply and return, about half the distance to Elliott, in nine days. Culbertson claims the palm."

The bullwhackers had their stories and their songs. Once, they say, a storm cloud threatened in the west. The ground was already mud hub-deep. The bullwhackers well knew that a flash of lightning would stampede their cattle. Accordingly, they yoked their oxen, tied the tails of each pair together, and hitched each yoke with a log chain to one of the tree trunks of a small grove close by.

Crash! Lightning flashed. The bulls tried to run but could not get free. In the morning, when the boss woke up, he found his wagons two miles west of the grove.

Those bulls had pulled the grove through the mud two miles. "If you don't believe that," they said, "just compare the old map with the new one. Then you'll see!"

There were no traffic police in Dodge, no parking rules. Bullwhackers and mule skinners stopped their wagons wherever they pleased on the Plaza. Much of the year these jammed Front Street, and the hitchracks were lined with cow ponies.

By the beginning of 1874 the buffalo in Kansas had been virtually exterminated and the herds no longer migrated up and down the Plains, so that buffalo hunters in the Southwest, if they were to stay in business, had to head south.

The traders who bought their hides followed the hunters, freighting down supplies across the Neutral Strip to Hutchinson County in the Panhandle of Texas. There they established their stores near the ruins of the old Indian trading post known as Adobe Walls on the Canadian River.

General Kit Carson and his troops had attacked the hostile tribes there in November, 1864. Now, nearly ten years later, it was to be the scene of a fight between the tribesmen and the buffalo hunters.

Strictly speaking, the fight at Adobe Walls is no real part of the story of Dodge City; the battle has been described often.[2]

But Josiah Wright Mooar tells a story which throws a new and surprising light upon a most mysterious event which took place at the Walls before the fight occurred—the mysterious cracking of the ridgepole of Hanrahan's Saloon, which wakened nearly everybody so that they were dressed, armed, and ready when the Indians attacked. As the men in the fight outfitted at Dodge and some of them were citizens of the town then or later, this strange story may be included here.

Myers and Leonard arrived in March from Dodge City and erected a sod building with bastions at opposite corners and a picket corral with a log storehouse in the southwest corner. The corral stood on the banks of the creek, the store some distance south. Both faced the east. In April Charles Rath of Wright and Rath, also hide buyers, arrived and erected a small sod house just south of Myers' corral. It also faced the east. Tom O'Keefe set up his blacksmith shop, a small *jacal* or house of pickets, just south of Rath and Wright's building, and Jim Hanrahan, bringing a stock of whisky, erected a large saloon just north of Myers and Leonard's store to complete the line of buildings extending north and south; William Olds and his wife came along to run the restaurant.

Hanrahan's Saloon was built of sod, with a heavy ridgepole two and a half feet in diameter supporting the sod roof.

All this building provided work for a good many men. But before May Day everything was in order and business booming. The hunters were preparing to cross the river and assault a large herd of buffalo known to be there.

All this activity in the Panhandle gave the bull teams plenty to do. John Wesley Mooar was at Adobe Walls with his wagons while his brother, Josiah Wright Mooar, was out hunting. Late in June a military detail, a sergeant and four troopers, escorting Amos Chapman, a half-breed Indian and government scout, arrived at Adobe Walls from Camp Supply.

The buffalo hunters assembled there were curious as to their mission. The soldiers, who were not in on the real secret, replied that they had come looking for horsethieves. This statement roused resentment among the hunters.

That day the soldiers left Amos at Adobe Walls while they went scouting up the river.

Then it was whispered about that Amos was a spy for the

hostiles, and some of the boys in their cups told Hanrahan that they were going to hang Amos that night. This put Hanrahan in an awkward spot, for he, like Rath and Myers, had heard the news Amos had been sent to bring.

Lee and Reynolds, freighters and post traders at Camp Supply, were hand in glove with Robert M. Wright, post sutler at Fort Dodge and partner of Charles Rath. Lee and Reynolds traded a good deal with the Cheyennes and Arapahos in the Territory. Of course, you cannot keep a secret in an Indian camp, and they had ascertained the time when the hostiles were coming to attack Adobe Walls. This information they had sent confidentially by Amos to their fellow traders at the Walls, and had persuaded the Commanding Officer to send the soldiers along.

Hanrahan knew that if he divulged this information, the hunters would in all probability clear out and head for Dodge, leaving the traders and their precious goods to the mercy of the savages. So it was up to Hanrahan to save Amos.

Accordingly, that night Hanrahan advised Amos to slip out to John Mooar's wagon behind Rath's store and bed down there. Amos went in, had a drink, and declared in a loud voice that he was going down to Myers'. "Can I sleep here tonight?" he added.

"Sure," Hanrahan replied. "Come back."

Then Hanrahan set 'em up for all present while Amos slipped into the darkness outside. He hurried to John Mooar's wagon, explained the fix he was in, and crawled into John's bedroll. Grateful for this protection, Amos Chapman told John what his message was.

John drove down to Josiah Mooar's camp to warn him. They hurried to Adobe Walls and arrived there safely after a brush with Indians. There they learned that two camps of buffalo hunters had already been destroyed. It did not take the Mooar brothers long to load up and head for Dodge.

The brothers, because of Chapman's warning, had no part in the battle which followed on June 27.

Here is Josiah Wright Mooar's story of what really happened on the night before the fight:

Some time after midnight a loud crack was heard. Hanrahan shouted, "The ridgepole is breaking!"

Nearly everybody left his blankets and ran to support the mighty log. By a strange coincidence they found a prop already cut just the right length and hastily put it under the ridgepole. Mooar says the prop was only about eight inches in diameter and could never have supported the ridgepole if it had been really broken. And Billy Dixon, partner of Hanrahan, himself reports, "We never could find a single thing wrong with the log."

But now everybody was up. Hanrahan provided drinks, and most of the boys decided not to go back to their blankets. At daybreak, when the Indians came, directed by a bugler, all fought valorously, barricading the windows and doors of the buildings with sacks of grain and flour. The two Shadler brothers, sleeping in their wagon, were killed at the start. The other twenty-six men, in the buildings, were not caught napping. The Indians besieged the place for several hours.

Many of the Indians present took no part in the siege, but sat around on the hills, watching to see how their medicine man's "power" would work. Had the attackers succeeded in killing the whites, no doubt all the tribesmen would have joined in a campaign of extermination throughout the buffalo range. But as it was, the marksmanship of the hunters discouraged this.[3]

Only one man was killed in the fight that followed. Billy Tyler exposed himself; he was in a sitting position, facing the stockade gate, when an Indian only fifteen feet distant fired point-blank. The ball struck Billy in the left side of the neck, passed through his body, and came out under the right arm.[4]

William Olds, whose wife was the only woman present, afterward by accident shot himself with his own gun.

When it was over, several Indians and their Negro bugler were found lying dead. When the troops arrived weeks later, they found the heads of these dead enemies stuck up on the poles of the corral.

Rath and Myers did not remain to take part in the fight, but overtook the Mooar brothers' wagons, leaving the hunters to do the fighting for them.

Mooar believed that it was the crack of Billy Dixon's pistol, fired by agreement with Hanrahan, which simulated the cracking of the ridgepole. He says it was all a put-up job to keep the hunters from leaving the place undefended.

Naturally, those in the know dared not divulge this secret so long as any of the hunters survived. For the Indians had destroyed or swept away all their animals, endangered their lives, and killed three of their comrades. Had they known of this trick played upon them, it might have gone hard with those who had failed to warn them.

After this disaster no one dreamed of hunting buffalo in that region until the Indians had been brought to heel. Bat Masterson, Billy Dixon, and other hunters were very happy to join forces with Amos Chapman as government scouts (under Ben Clark) for General Nelson A. Miles in the campaign of 1874.

The weapons, war bonnets, and clothing of the slain Indians were carried back to Dodge as trophies and long adorned the walls of one of the saloons there. Frequently they were used in a prank played upon prominent visiting tenderfeet known to Dodge as the Indian Act.[5]

CHAPTER 9 ·
· PRANKS AND
· PRANKSTERS

DODGE CITY was no less famous for its pranksters than for its gunmen. For the men of Dodge were seldom willing to let bad enough alone.

On the American frontier it had long been the custom to make a joke of anything unpleasant—a practice which took much of the sting out of the isolation, the loneliness, the hardships and difficulties of frontier life. Laughter is man's best medicine, and on those empty plains infested with hostile Indians, rattlesnakes, hydrophobic skunks, mad wolves, horsethieves, and gunmen, where cholera and smallpox were epidemic and nearly every disease was incurable, a good dose of laughter was frequently needed.

Even in a booming town like Dodge there were no cheap amusements, little to fill a man's spare time. If he cared to read, he could pick up a weekly newspaper consisting of a couple of pages filled with stories and items of local news, which he had already heard by word of mouth before the paper came out, and four pages of boiler plate or patent insides. A man could exhaust such a paper in fifteen minutes.

The Dodgers, as some editors persisted in dubbing them, had to make their own fun. And since many of them, like their cowboy patrons, were or had been outdoor men—buffalo hunters, mule skinners, soldiers, railroad builders, ranchers or farmers—who roughed it in the open most of the year, they liked rough fun and practical jokes. Whatever the men of that town did, they did with all their might in a competitive spirit, determined to rise and shine brighter than citizens of rival towns.

Though stores and saloons were open twenty-four hours a day and those who tended them worked twelve-hour shifts, the sports of Dodge in the dull season had plenty of leisure. To do them justice, they tried hard to fill it with gaiety.

For they not only laughed at their own discomfitures, but heartily enjoyed their neighbor's plight—and if the plight did not produce itself, would go to great lengths to create it.

Often, too, their pranks served as a public protest, a lesson in behavior, a form of social discipline, which helped to build a decent community in a wild and lawless land.

And so they rejoiced in initiating tenderfeet or pulling the carpet from under anyone who put on airs or displayed a lack of that fraternity of spirit so necessary to life on the frontier. The braggart, the stuffed shirt, the high-hat, the critic and the sissy alike came in—not merely for ridicule and rawhiding—but sometimes for a rough time involving the risk of physical injury.

When Eddie Foy, who was to become one of the great comedians of the day, arrived in Dodge in 1878 he was dressed pretty loud, had "a kind of Fifth Avenue swagger and strut," and made some distasteful jokes about cowboys at his first performance. Foy later said, "Had I known the West better then, I might have been more careful."

The next day, when Foy appeared on Front Street, the cowboys soon had him roped, put him on a horse's back and led the pony under the big tree near the river.

There, as he sat with a rope around his neck, ready to be strung up, they had their fun. Sheriff Bat Masterson stood by ready to call "calf rope" if the play got too rough. But Eddie endured their hazing valiantly, determined to be nonchalant and not to let them think they were scaring him—even if they broke his neck. When they asked him what last words he had to say for himself, Eddie replied that he could say them better at the bar of the Long Branch Saloon. Says Eddie, "The whole affair ended in a laugh and a drink all around; that night I got more applause than ever and we stayed at Dodge all summer."[1]

As Robert M. Wright puts it, "They played pranks on him which Foy took with such good grace that he captured the cowboys completely. Every night his theatre was crowded with them. Nothing he could say or do offended them; but on the contrary, they made a little god of him. The good people of Dodge have watched his upward career with pride and pleasure, and have always taken a great interest in him and claimed him as one of their boys, because it was here that he first began to achieve greatness."

Eddie reports: "My bearing on that occasion must have given the town an exaggerated idea of my courage, for I was presently offered an opportunity to enlist as a hired gunman."

The expedition was to help the Santa Fe Railroad fight the Denver and Rio Grande for possession of the Royal Gorge in Colorado—the only possible right-of-way to booming Leadville. In April, 1879, the Santa Fe recruited a corps of gunfighters in Dodge City, wages three dollars a day and board. The *Times* reports that Sheriff W. B. Masterson and thirty men left Dodge City Saturday (April 5) for Cañon City. Doc Holliday, one of the group, urged Eddie Foy, the comedian, to go along. Eddie declined.

In May the Santa Fe recruited a second band of fighters in Dodge: As the *Times* put it: "Twenty of our boys; among whom might be named some of Dodge's most accomplished sluggers and bruisers headed by the gallant Capt. John J. Webb, put down their names, with a firm resolve to 'get to the joint' in creditable style in case of danger. . . . We will bet a ten cent note that they clear the track of every obstruction."

But it all turned out to be an almost bloodless junket.

The only Dodge City man shot was Henry Jenkins, of Sheriff Masterson's posse, who (the *Dodge City Times* alleged) "was shot in the back by a drunken guard of the Rio Grande force. . . .

The unfortunate man was climbing out of the depot window."

The *Times* later published an item from the *Pueblo Chieftain*: "Dr. Owen yesterday removed a rifle ball from the body of Harry Jenkins, who was shot in the railroad row at South Pueblo. The ball was found under the skin of the wounded man's breast, it having passed completely through him."

By all accounts the gunmen of both parties had a time loafing in the canyon and in the towns. The Dodge City boys returned disappointed that they had had no chance to show their mettle. For the Santa Fe staged the affair, not just to gain the Royal Gorge, but chiefly to distract her rivals from her line then building over the Raton Pass in New Mexico—the Pass she must possess to become a transcontinental railway. It had all been just another elaborate prank.

Occasionally a tenderfoot who was too self-assured, critical, or supercilious might have to endure rough horseplay at the hands of the Dodgers. But these were too tough and confident to be unduly severe on the stranger who was a mere innocent bystander.

J. Wright Mooar's brother arrived in Dodge looking for his brother in the fall of 1872—an obvious greenhorn wearing a stiff derby hat and city clothes, and wholly unarmed. Having spent an uncomfortable night at the Dodge House without enough bedding to keep him warm, he set out to find his brother.

It did not take him long to explore Front Street, and he then turned to the small scattered shacks on the slope of the hill. He came to one which had no window, and heard somebody talking inside. The door was half open. He looked in and said, "What are you doing in there?"

Two rough fellows looked round. They had paint brushes in their hands and a white horse between them half painted black. Neither one moved or spoke.

Caught at such work, some men would have killed the intruder at once; but one of these two had good sense. He saw that John was a perfect greenhorn. He said, "Come in, come in."

John stepped in and stared at them. His brazen host continued, "We stole this horse last night down on Rattlesnake Creek. Now we're going to paint him black, take him back, and sell him to the same man we stole him from."

It was the unalloyed effrontery, the sublime cheek of that horsethief that saved the boy's life. The horsethief was as good as his brag too, and no more afraid of the owner than of his dog. The owner bought the horse back; probably he recognized it but said nothing, since he could buy it cheap. The price amounted to a reward for bringing back the horse.

Bachelors abounded in Dodge City. The boys who boarded at the Dodge House were struck by the antics of a young fellow there who fancied himself as a lady-killer. His constant theme was his conquests as a "masher"—as a "wolf" was called in those days. To hear him tell it, he simply infatuated maidens and matrons, old and young. His fellow boarders were at first astonished at his brags, then amused, and finally everyone was tired of him.

Now nobody could annoy the men of Dodge with impunity. Social discipline seemed indicated.

The masher's fellow boarders concluded to check his mad career. They conspired to open up a correspondence with him under various fictitous names of imaginary females of unstable character. Day by day his mail grew heavier, and within a week he was kept busy answering not less than forty letters, which he first put on exhibit at the hotel! He also received several photographs of supposedly enamored girls, and was easily persuaded that he ought to buy an album to hold them, which cost him two dollars.

Seeing that he had swallowed their deception hook, line and sinker, his tormentors concocted a letter full of tender words, suggesting a meeting with one of the imaginary female correspondents.

They all wished to be in on the joke. Therefore the place they suggested for the tryst was the lumberyard east of the depot, the time ten o'clock at night.

Well before the appointed time some fifty men stowed themselves away among the stacks of lumber to wait in silent glee for the fun to begin.

They had hired the blackest, dirtiest, ugliest Negro wench in Dodge City to enact the role of the enamored maiden in search of a husband. The boys decked her out in spotless white with gloves to match, and her face was heavily veiled.

The masher arrived early and taking a cigar from his pocket and lighting it, he sat down on a railroad tie to meditate his approaching bliss; just then she turned the corner and hurried to his embrace. He arose, bowed politely, smiled and gave her, "Good evening."

They seated themselves in a quiet alley of the yard directly under the eyes of the audience and in a few minutes were on familiar terms. He hugged and squeezed her to his heart's content and called her many tender names.

This put a severe strain upon the self-control of the delighted spectators, who could hardly master the spasms of laughter which convulsed them.

Fortunately they did not have to hold in long, for when he eagerly tore away the veil from her face to kiss her, they all let go and the air was rent with deafening shouts and peals of mirth.

When he discovered his mistake and realized how he had been taken in, he tore off down the railroad track, like a speckled frog with a striped snake after him, his coat tail rolling in billowy undulations behind him, while his legs flapped together like the loose end of a lightning rod against the gable end of a barn. It was several days before he dared show his face on Front Street.

Sometimes pranksters would spend quite a bit of money to carry out their joke—much more than the unfortunate victim spent afterward in setting 'em up to the crowd.

One night in Dodge a bunch of cowboys were celebrating. They had just come off the long trail from southern Texas, shoved their cattle into the cars, and received their wages for the year just passed. Now they were on their spree.

They were all travel-worn and showed the wear of wind and weather. But one fellow, known only as "Hell-and-High-Water," his favorite oath, was positively ragged. His toes stuck out of his boots and there were holes in his hat.

They made it up to pick on him. They crowded round. As a precautionary measure one of the boys slyly relieved him of his pistol. Then the others ganged up. One jerked off his hat and tromped it in the dust. Two others had their knives out slashing at his boots, cutting the leather into kite strings, ripping off his shirt and trousers while he struggled and protested. Then they hoisted him, naked as a jaybird, upon their shoulders and paraded around the Plaza, finally carrying the naked man into a clothing store. There they all chipped in and bought him a complete outfit better than any he had ever known before. After that and a shave and a haircut, they repaired to the Green Front Saloon where the astonished victim of this stunt treated the crowd.

Strangers frequently came to Dodge looking for work, particularly during the two depressions. One of the stock jokes perpetrated upon an unsuspicious fellow of this sort was to send him on a fifty-mile hike to the Cimarron River to "find work in the snuff mines." The poker-faced pranksters, watching him set out, would say, "Oh, well, if he can't get it through his head, he can get it by shank's mare."

Another job frequently offered to men seeking work was that of herding antelope. The stranger, having come on the train, would object that he had no horse. "But you don't need any! Antelope herders never ride, because antelopes are scared of a man on a pony." And they would start the stranger off afoot on the ten-mile trail to a well-known ranch on the Saw Log north of town. . . .

Once, according to Noble L. Prentis, a prank was even played on a dead man. One winter morning, when it was twenty below zero, two men had the chill duty of burying a stranger, who, the night before, had got half shot, and then shot dead. The ground was frozen hard, and resisted their pick and shovel like so much iron. Near by, they spied a new grave where they knew an Indian's body had been buried, just a few days before.

One of the men stuck his shovel into the fresh mound. It would be easy to dig there. He looked at his companion and grinned. The other fellow caught on. Both went busily to work, sent the dirt flying, and dug up the Indian. They threw Poor Lo's body over the hill, and buried the white man in the red man's grave. "This was the first white man buried on Boot Hill."[2]

One day a cigar drummer from St. Joseph was in Dodge displaying his samples. A good many of the local men inspected his cigars, passing through the sample room.

Later the drummer discovered that several boxes of cigars had disappeared. He found a constable and with him went into every saloon and business house in Dodge City. Wherever they went they found smiling gentlemen happily smoking and praising his cigars, and every one of them told him that Luke McGlue had given him the smoke. But somehow nobody could find Luke McGlue.

This prank established the mythical Luke McGlue in Dodge City favor, and whenever an anonymous prank was played Luke McGlue got the credit.

The minister of the Union Church preached the gospel, but did not meddle with reforms. He accepted Dodge, if he did not approve of all its works. And Dodge accepted—and approved of—him.

One fine day Brother James Langton bought a Texas pony for the Reverend Mr. O. W. Wright, so that the minister could more readily visit the members of his flock. It was a gentle animal and bore the JA brand. The local paper records: "The man of God was wont to ride almost daily upon his earthly treasure out over the verdant prairie to breathe the pure fragrant air and it was very frequently the means of renewing his spiritual strength by imparting fresh vigor to his physical frame."

But to the pranksters of Dodge City nothing was sacred. Somebody stole the preacher's horse!

"The minister would not be comforted and for a time completely abandoned himself to paroxysms of grief." A little later the constable waited upon the minister to report the capture of the thief. The minister, he said, would have to decide whether the criminal should be shot or hanged.

Mr. Wright, gravely professing lack of acquaintance with their "advanced western customs," delegated his authority to Brother Langton, and the matter remained under advisement. The newspaper records: "Just before going to press we are informed that the thief proves to be the notorious Luke McGlue, who stole the cigars from the Saint Joe man last winter."

Luke McGlue rose rapidly in Dodge City society—from horsethief to Mayor—if the notice posted in his name may be admitted as evidence. The paper records in 1878 that "Luke McGlue, Mayor, gives official notice which is posted on the depot building, that he will enforce the vagrant law, thereby warning tramps who may infest those quarters. A timely action. Hope McGlue will extend his authority over the city."

But there was one prank peculiar to the town in which the men of Dodge delighted to engage, as it was not only clean fun, ending in a round of drinks, but reminded everyone as often as it was staged of the heroic part that Dodge City men had played in the hard-fought battle at Adobe Walls in 1874. The *Dodge City Times* for April 21, 1877, gives an account of one notable performance of this kind—a spectacle for the whole town:

ANOTHER INDIAN SCARE

A Kansas City Drummer Chased by
Fiendish Red Men

An incident occurred yesterday which agitated our city from center to circumference. It was a reproduction of the notorious Indian Act, as a benefit to and in honor of Mr. Elias Cahn, of the

House of Cahn & Co., clothiers of Kansas City, who was here trying to sell clothing.

All the morning the intrepid young Mr. Cahn had been relating to gaping crowds of our astonished denizens miraculous accounts of his own heroic exploits among the Indians, and expressing a bloodthirsty yearning for more Indians to conquer. Finally our boys resolved that he should be accommodated, and a hunting expedition was proposed, to which he eagerly assented. Mayor Kelley, Sam Sneider, of the firm of Somshine & Sneider, of Cincinnati; John Mueller, and our young Indian fighter made up the party. As soon as the hunters had started, Messrs. Ed. Garland, J. M. Manion, S. E. Isaacson, C. H. Schulz, Mr. Wolf, C. M. Beeson and Jas. Langton donned Indian costumes which were captured at the Doby Walls fight, and with faces hideously painted—superbly mounted, they started in a round-about way, to intercept Mr. Cahn and his party.

By the time the latter party had started the populace began to turn out. Roofs of houses, old freight wagons and telegraph poles were quickly covered with anxious spectators; mothers with young babies on their backs and older ones following behind might be seen frantically rushing up Boot Hill; the silvery locks of aged and decrepit men could soon be seen fluttering over the highest and most inaccessible pinnacles of the hills adjacent to our city.

When our party of Indian hunters had traveled about four miles they were suddenly startled by a fiendish Indian war whoop, and on looking up the hill on one side, they saw the bloodthirsty devils riding furiously toward them in regular Indian file. Mr. Cahn, although armed with a murderous revolver carefully loaded with blank cartridges by Mr. Samuels, decided very promptly that discretion was the better part of valor, and, turning his fiery steed toward Dodge City, applied whip and spur without restraint. When the first shot was fired by the pursuers, Mr. Cahn exhibited his skill at Indian fighting by dodging the bullet so dexterously that his elegant cap flew off his head and was seen no more. The firing was rapid, but Mr. Cahn's head dodged faster, and he arrived safely within a mile of the city, when firing ceased, and he began to think he was saved. However, it soon occurred to his mind that the city must be besieged, as the hill-tops were crowded with people, and an excited populace filled the streets. But his friend Sneider reassured him, and both hunters and Indians made a triumphal entry into the city together, warmly saluted by the gang with eggs, "Sitting Bull" having one burst against the side of his head, to his infinite disgust.

As usual, the drinks were on the tenderfoot, and Cahn took considerable banter—especially about the loss of his cap. Cahn maintained that it blew off. But one of them said, "No. Your hair stood on end and pushed it off!"

On another occasion in order to add to the fun of the Indian Act the victim of the joke was mounted purposely upon a slow horse so that his pals could outride him and leave him all alone to the tender mercy of the pursuing "redskins." When the charge was launched and they all turned to flee, the victim found himself falling farther and farther behind. A friend circled back and yelled, "Hurry up, hurry up! They'll get you."

The victim, who was spurring and quirting his nag for all he was worth, shouted back, "What do you think I'm doing—throwing the race?"

This Indian Act, as it was called, was frequently performed, but the laugh was not always at the expense of the tenderfoot.

A few months after Mr. Cahn's adventure the boys proceeded to initiate the new jeweler in Dodge, Mr. H. Harris. Beatty was the ringleader and proposed a ride out from town to view the herds of cattle and breathe the country air.

As was usual before starting, someone with a shake of the head gravely informed the intended victim that there were hostile Indians lurking around Dodge. The usual weapon loaded with blank cartridges not being offered him, Harris made his own preparations and unobtrusively slipped his pistol loaded with ball into his boot.

A few miles west of the city the "Indians" dashed out of hiding with war bonnets and feathered lances.

"Run for your life," Beatty shouted as he whirled his own horse around.

Harris would have stood his ground, but his horse became unmanageable and joined the stampede toward town while the Indians, yelling hideously, pressed close upon their rear. But when Harris lost his hat, he reined in his animal. To ride into town bareheaded chased by Indians was more humiliation than he could bear.

He turned to face the foe and recover his headgear.

As the Indians approached he pulled out his pistol, aiming at the head of the foremost chief and coolly waiting until he could see the whites of his eyes. Then he fired.

When the "braves" saw that gun, they scattered like quail under a hawk. The chief heard the ball whiz past his head, and rode for his life.

This time the drinks were on the "savages."

CHAPTER 10 ·
·
· THE LONGHORNS

From the first, the men of Dodge were cattle-minded. In the early seventies, those owning herds hired mounted men, called "Buffalo Whoopers," to frighten buffalo off the grass and so make room for their steers.

D. W. "Doc" Barton, then a youngster of nineteen years, with eight men drove two thousand cattle to Dodge City as early as 1872. Fearing Indians, he followed a very roundabout trail through New Mexico and Colorado to the Arkansas River, following the stream down to Pierceville and Dodge City. But as there were then no loading pens in Dodge, he moved on to Great Bend. It was not until 1875 that cattle came to be regularly shipped out of Dodge: then it became the Cowboy Capital.

Various other Kansas towns attracted Texas trail drives—Abilene, Ellsworth, Newton, Wichita, Caldwell, Hunnewell, and Ellis—each having its brief and prosperous season as a wild and wicked camp, until settlers blocked the trails, or decent citizens revolted, or the railroad, moving on, offered cattlemen some more convenient shipping point. As it pushed west across the prairie, the railroad also carried along the shacks and denizens of earlier cowtowns—the famous Hell on Wheels.

But Dodge differed somewhat from those other towns. She had been the booming camp of the buffalo hunters before ever the cattle came, and her newer citizens—many of them seasoned graduates of earlier cowtowns—were better prepared to cope with rowdy cowboys and tough killers. The gunmen and wild women who followed the cattle trade from camp to camp by this time were well-acquainted with each other, and had worked out a way of life that gave Dodge a certain stability: they knew how to raise hell and make it pay.

The men of Dodge had become accustomed to living high. Buffalo hunters readily made one hundred dollars a day; and when the trail drivers came in, money circulated just as freely.

During the sixties the wild longhorns of Texas had multiplied while the men were away at war. It is estimated that there were three to six million wild cattle then running loose in Texas—almost as many horned beasts as there had once been buffalo on the High Plains. And in fact, it was rather less expensive to drive a longhorn steer to the Kansas market than it was to kill a buffalo and bring in his hide. A steer could be driven from southern Texas to Dodge City at a cost of seventy-five cents—and all the way to Montana for one dollar. Nature provided the cattle as she had the buffalo; and the grass was free. Cattle cost only the trouble of branding and marking them, and they carried themselves to market.

The cowboy worked for thirty or forty dollars a month and "chuck," and for this was prepared to labor, fight and even risk his life for his employer with a fierce loyalty. He would put in eighteen hours a day in the saddle—or even twenty-four hours in an emergency—with never a thought of overtime, strikes, or unions; and out of his meager wages bought his clothes, his bedding, his expensive hat, boots and saddle, his bridle, leggings, rope, and spurs, his six-gun and ammunition. His diet, provided by his employer, was simple and monotonous—biscuits, beef or salt pork, beans and spuds, dried fruit and coffee.

The trail drives began just after the Civil War when Texas was impoverished, and money almost unknown there. Some early outfits had no wagons, but carried supplies on packsaddles. The diet of cowboys on the Northern Plains was much more varied and appetizing even after the Texans became prosperous; this was largely because Texas owners seldom traveled with their herds; whereas a Northern owner often rode with his cattle, and so his cowboys ate as well as he did, with flapjacks and sorghum, peppersass and pie. "Pie-biter" was a common nickname in the North. Usually there were about two hundred head of cattle in a trail herd for every cowboy along. Each rider had his string of two to six horses, usually belonging to the employer.

A trail herd might average twenty-five to thirty-five hundred cattle, which moved along ten to fifteen miles a day, flanked by riders at point and swing and drag; while far ahead the cook drove the messcart or chuck-wagon with its chuck-box over the tail gate, its wagon bed filled with bedrolls, and a cowhide "possum belly" swung underneath to hold wood or cow chips for the fire. He drove ahead to make camp and prepare supper at the bedground. Besides the cook and the cowboys, there was the horse wrangler and the trail boss. His aim was to arrive at Dodge with the same number of cattle he started with—or maybe a few more. It was the courtesy of the trail to pick up any strays lost by herds ahead.

The Texas longhorn little resembled a modern beef steer, which, in fact, could never travel a thousand miles at that rate and fatten on the way. The longhorn was wild, fierce, and sensitive, of mighty stamina, and muscled like a stag. There was nothing logy about him. He had narrow shoulders, a sharp backbone, tucked-up flanks, and a sway-back. There was more horn, hoof, and bone than beef about him, though he could get rolling fat. Most cattle get up slowly, hind end first, but the longhorn—like the buffalo—seemed to spring up all at once, like a jack-in-the-box. He had a long tail, long legs, and was built to travel.

He trod the buffalo grass with long strides and elastic step, always alert, uneasy, apt to stampede. He was tall and rangy, and his horns often had a spread of six feet or more.

Because of the indiscriminate coupling of these wild cattle, their coloration was as remarkable as their conformation. Colors varied, though generally dull—pale red, white, dun, speckled or spotted, bay or yellow, mouse-colored or blue of various shades, with many a brindle—calico cows.

They were used to walking long miles on their home range to find grass and water. On the mat of rich buffalo grass of Indian Territory and Kansas, they gained weight as they marched; and when at last they reached Dodge, their owner or buyer often held them there for weeks or months to fatten before shipping them to market. At Dodge, a mature longhorn, four years old or more, weighed from eight hundred pounds to twice that, and might sell for ten to twenty dollars and up.

The very horses the cowboys rode were sold at a considerable profit. Dodge remained a good horse market long after her Texas cattle trade came to an end.

Buyers and owners reached Dodge well in advance of the herds. Their proceedings while they waited were lively. When the brakeman yelled, "Dodge City," they hurried to the Dodge House, ornamented the register with their autographs, deposited their gripsacks with Deacon Cox, and went to breakfast. There J. L. "Uncle Mitch" Mitchener expounded the cattle gospel to Ike Johnson, Captain Littlefield, Jim Reed, "and about thirty other sinners, with all the authority of his forty-second year as buyer."

Everybody not at the Dodge House was at the Alamo, then presided over by a reformed Quaker from New York. It was hinted that the manner in which he concocted a toddy (every genuine cattleman drank toddy) increased the value of a Texas steer about $2.75.

Everything you heard was about beeves and steers and cows, or cutting or brands, and toddies and cocktails, and everywhere you went you met Phillips, the Santa Fe Agent. He loaded, branded, and shipped all the cattle, gave everybody a pass that wanted one—or talked him into not wanting one—knew everybody, was "personally acquainted with every bull, beef, steer, or cow between Kansas and the Rio Grande," could take a drink —and was never busy!

Someone arrived just then with three thousand head, and reported, "The grass is fine, the water plenty, drinks two for a quarter—and no grangers."

No wonder Dodge was the greatest cattle market in the world.

The herds started north as soon as the grass was high enough to feed the cattle, and after thirty to one hundred days on the trail, reached Dodge City.

There the buyers would drive out in a buggy or buckboard to tally the cattle and arrange for their disposition.

Dodge City was not only a shipping point but a great cattle market—for ten years the greatest in the world. For by no means all the longhorns brought to Dodge were put through the chutes into cattle cars. Many trail herds were driven on through Dodge to Montana, Wyoming, the Dakotas, or Nebraska, to fatten on the winter ranges, and later to supply forts and Indian Agencies, or be shipped eastward on the Union Pacific from Ogallala. Sometimes a buyer would employ the old Texas crew to drive the cattle through. So many a Texan went to the Northern Plains, where not a few remained.

The Tenth Census of the United States offers these figures for the number of cattle driven over the trails to Dodge and smaller markets:

To Dodge and Ellis

1876	322,000
1877	201,159
1878	265,646
1879	257,927

To Dodge, Caldwell, and Hunnewell

1880	384,147

Of 164 droves coming up in 1880, 33 were herds of breeder "through cattle"—heading for the Northern ranges. Of all these, 22,000 head belonged to Ellison and Son. Captain George W. Littlefield, then holding 14,000 head at Tascosa, reported in

February, 1880, that at least 350,000 head would come north that year. By the end of August, 287,000 had reached Dodge City. In 1881, 223,000 were expected. In 1882, of 153,000 expected, over 100,000 had arrived by June 12. In the second half of that year, 100 railroad trains, consisting of some 3,000 cattle cars, each with a capacity of 20 head, carried 60,000 cattle out of Dodge. The average number of cars leaving Dodge per month that year was 511, total shipment 76,650 head.

By the end of 1883, 3,243 cars, carrying 75,769 head of cattle worth $2,666,915, rolled out of Dodge, along with 51 carloads of horses and 3 of sheep. The total shipped in 1884 was equally great. By July of that year, 239,324 had passed through Dodge City. In 1885, the last big year of the Dodge City trade, the Santa Fe shipped out 3,051 carloads of cattle.

Between 1866 and 1890 it is estimated that ten million cattle were driven out of Texas to market.[1] The profit to the Texas cattleman might run from three to twenty dollars a head. But his losses were sometimes just as great. The market was highly speculative and unstable; prices sometimes tumbled, while drought or too much rain might ravage the grass, storms stampede his cattle, or predatory Indians, irate farmers, or rustlers decimate his herds. A blizzard or a prairie fire might cause a big die-up.

And there was always the threat that Kansas would enforce the quarantine against Texas cattle.

The longhorn carried ticks which in turn carried a virus. This virus, to which the Texas steer was immune, was carried by his ticks dropped along the trail to whatever other cattle might pass that way; and other breeds, more especially those imported from abroad, once infected, soon died. To make matters worse, nobody in those days knew how the disease was spread. It was known as Texas, Splenic, or Spanish Fever.

What Kansas stockmen especially feared were "through" Texas cattle—those driven straight through from southern Texas (that portion lying south of Red River) to Northern markets. Texas cattle held and wintered well north of that line in Indian

Territory or the Neutral Strip, they believed would not infect their shorthorns.

Cattle bound for Montana and points north crossed the river near Point of Rocks four miles west of town. To guide drivers to that point, the settlers plowed a furrow from Five Mile Hollow leading northwest through the ford. Before barbed wire came in and the Herd Law was adopted by Ford County, such furrows were the farmer's only protection for his crops.

As settlement steadily advanced westward and barbed wire enabled cattlemen to make large (illegal) enclosures, it became more and more difficult for trail drivers to bring their cattle through. They had to go farther and farther west, until finally (July 21, 1885) the Governor of Kansas issued a proclamation forbidding all "through" Texas cattle to enter Kansas.

What Texans prayed and hoped for was a National Cattle Trail to be laid out by the Federal Government, six miles wide and fenced, leading from Texas to the Northwest. A bill was introduced in Congress to establish such a trail, but did not pass. . . .

Each year Dodge City made great preparations for the cattle trade. Before winter ended, anxious forecasts were made about the size of the Texas drive for the coming season. Invitations were sent south, and the Cowboy Band popularized Dodge in a swing around the country. Merchants combined to reduce prices on items in demand by cowboys, and publicized these price cuts in Texas, while everybody fixed up and painted up his premises and laid in ample supplies for the season. Cattle would begin to arrive as early as April, and by the end of May, the trail drivers brought in a steady flood of longhorns. By the Fourth of July two-thirds of the drive would have been bought and sold, though cattle continued to arrive into September, and those cowboys who had driven herds to Montana and points north would be riding back to stop at Dodge as late as October.

With the cattle came in more than a thousand cowboys and sometimes nearly twice that number. Many of these, riding herd on cattle held near by for fattening, or employed in cutting out, branding, or marking cow brutes, or just waiting to be sent home, might hang around Dodge for weeks or even months.

Most of these herders received six months' or a year's pay as soon as the cattle were shipped out or sold, and after purchasing such equipment as they needed, spent the rest in riotous living. The money with which they and their employers flooded the camp attracted a hardy army of thugs, swindlers, scarlet women, and other parasites to prey on the unwary.

It is no secret that entertaining a veterans' convention for only a few days can leave a large American city exhausted. Dodge was only a village, but she entertained a convention of veterans five months out of every year; and the veterans—who outnumbered her citizens two to one—were Confederate veterans, who had no earthly use for Damyankees or Damyankee law and order. And they were not armed with water pistols! After the hardships and monotony of months on the trail, the cowboy arrived r'arin' to go, and, as one editor put it, "to drive us mad with the rattling of his spurs."

Texans are not noted for hiding their lights under a bushel, and the Texas cowboys flaunted their arrogance, swaggering along the boardwalk from dramshop to honky-tonk, gloating at the annoyance they caused, shooting out lights, breaking up meetings, sticking up gambling houses to get money for another spree, and taking their pick of the dance hall girls. They delighted in charging up and down the boardwalks on their ponies, riding into a saloon or dance hall, and shooting it out with anybody who might oppose their antics. It was their dream to hurrah the town, smashing windows and mirrors in the saloons, to kill the Marshal or run him out of town, to "tree" the camp, and then, with DODGE painted on the canvas cover of their chuckwagon, to ride home to Texas and declare, "We taken Dodge."

Something had to be done to cope with these troublesome gun-toters.

After the Civil War, violence in Texas steadily rose to an all-time high. Even small boys and ministers of the gospel went armed. Bloody feuds raged there long after Dodge City's cowtown days. In Texas the judge had not been able to replace the private avenger.

And if Texans put private vengeance before law at home, they could hardly be expected not to do so in Kansas.

In those days—before Buffalo Bill's show, Will Rogers' humor, and Hopalong Cassidy's television had glamourized the cowboy—he was not considered either heroic or romantic, but only as a rough hired man on horseback, with a chip on his shoulder and a dangerous gun on his hip. A Texan felt naked without his weapon, and who can blame him for wishing to wear it when he rode into "the meanest town in America"?

After the Vigilantes disbanded, the businessmen and gamblers of Dodge City saw no way to preserve order but to hire gunmen with the reputation of fearless killers to defend them and keep the peace.

In February, 1872, Newton had been organized as a third-class city, and the following April city officers were elected. These officers named William "Buffalo Bill" Brooks as City Marshal. He had been driving stage between Newton and Wichita. At that time Billy was a handsome thickset man, nearly forty years of age, with long hair reaching to his shoulders. He stood about five foot eight in his socks. On duty he often carried a Winchester rifle.

Newton was a tough cowtown while it lasted.

Men in Dodge heard that Billy was as tough as Newton. In June he encountered three drunken Texans on the street and drove them out of town. Once on the prairie they turned and threw down on him, making three hits. One ball pierced his right breast. He caught the others in his legs. But that didn't stop Billy. He chased those Texans for ten miles before he turned back for first aid. Shortly after, he resigned, and soon was patrolling the streets of Dodge City. The story goes that he killed or wounded fifteen men during his first month as Marshal. Four brothers ganged up on him to avenge the death of a fifth, yet Billy fired four shots and killed them all.

But finally he showed the white feather and Dodge City saw no more of him.

Josiah Wright Mooar witnessed the gunplay which ended the career of Billy Brooks as City Marshal of Dodge. The sidewalks along the street were eight or ten feet wide, with here and there a bench on the outer edge. At intervals barrels full of water studded the street, for rows of wooden shacks in that dry climate were nothing but firetraps.

Mooar and his friends Mark Holloway and Phillip Sisk were sitting on a bench and they saw Billy Brooks coming down the boardwalk afoot. Mooar says that Kirk Jordan rode up on their right, jumped off on the sidewalk and "throwed one of these Big 50 guns down on Brooks; Brooks jumped behind the water barrel and Jordan let drive. The bullet hit the top of the third hoop on the water barrel and went through the barrel, coming out of the bottom of the same hoop. It lodged in the hoop but cut a hole through it so that the water spouted out and run down Brooks' neck. Jordan jumped on his horse and rode off. He thought he'd killed Brooks. Brooks stood up, extracted the bullet from the barrel, carrying it with him as he went into the saloon."

Apparently Brooks needed a drink.

When he came out, says Mooar, "we was all still sitting there, and Brooks come down and showed us the bullet while *boogle, boogle, boogle, boogle* the water was still running out."

This incident destroyed the famous gunman's reputation for courage. Men of Dodge felt that their Marshal ought to stand up and fight his enemies instead of taking cover—more especially as Kirk Jordan's Sharps rifle could fire only one shot before reloading, while Billy Brooks carried a weapon containing several cartridges.

However, they did not care to have their Marshal killed. Bob Wright and others hid Brooks under the bed in a livery stable until after dark. Then they smuggled him to Fort Dodge where he caught the train and cleared out. Brooks had killed too many Texans—the town's best customers—but dared not face a Dodge City gun-fighter like Kirk Jordan. When Brooks left, Wright called it "Good riddance!"

Billy Rivers and several others followed Billy Brooks into and hastily out of Dodge. The presence of a famous killer in the camp was a challenge to every gunman in Texas—and all the greater challenge because he was Marshal. The Marshal's killings also inspired reprisals, and law and order were forgotten in the smoke of battle. It was more of a struggle for championship than an effort to police the town.

When the last of their discomfited gunmen departed, the citizens took action. On Christmas Eve, 1875, a temporary town council met and, after bitter debate, passed the first ordinances relating to meetings, salaries of officials, licensing of dramshops, crime and punishment. P. L. Beatty, James H. Kelley's partner in the Alhambra Saloon, was chosen Acting Mayor until they could hold an election.

Ordinances made punishable disturbing the peace, the discharging of firearms or setting off of firecrackers or building bonfires in the city except on Christmas, New Year's Day, the Fourth of July, and Lincoln's Birthday, or in any licensed shooting gallery or gunsmith shop. Cruelty to animals and public drunkenness were provided against, and resisting an officer, the use of profanity, indecent exposure, and the commission of nuisances upon any street, sidewalk or other public place. (This last item was interpreted by the officers as barring cow ponies from the saloons, sidewalks and dance halls.)

But Section 7 of Ordinance 4 was the principal concern of the council: "That no person shall in the city of Dodge City carry concealed about his or her person any pistol, Bowie knife, slingshot or other deadly weapon except United States, county, township or city officers." It was later provided that visitors to Dodge must check their firearms, immediately upon arriving, at check racks provided in hotels, corrals, stores, saloons, and gambling places; the proprietors of these places were not to return weapons so checked to a drunken man. A fellow with a load of whisky and a loaded gun was beyond control.

The Council of five members was closely divided on the advisability of attempting to enforce such ordinances. They passed by a majority of a single vote.

It was now up to Dodge to elect a Mayor who could find a Marshal able and willing to enforce these ordinances.

Dodge City paid little attention to party lines—though the town and county usually voted Republican. But in that small "cattle village," as some called it, with hardly more than a thousand residents, political campaigns commonly got down to personalities and the ever burning question of the wide-open town. Dodge was too free and easy a community to put up with reformers or long-hairs, but there was a group of substantial citizens who felt that the town could benefit by some measure of restriction on lawlessness, some controls.

The law-and-order faction was headed by such men as George M. Hoover, James H. Kelley, W. H. Harris, P. L. Beatty, and Deacon Cox. They declared that Dodge City now had "a sufficient number of families" to justify some segregation of the wilder members of the community. Gamblers and saloon keepers, who offered their customers only "a good time," most needed protection. For the "good time" was soon over, and often left the customers with empty pockets, hangovers, and rankling ill will.

Opposed to this faction were some of the wealthier merchants, such as Robert M. Wright, his Texas partner, Judge H. M. Beverley, A. B. Webster, and Charles Rath. The prosperity of these merchants derived chiefly from doing business with cattle buyers, cattle kings, and cowboys; they could see no point in annoying their best customers. Why shoot Santa Claus? These merchants' goods (including guns and ammunition) were not perishable, their customers were not resentful; seldom did anybody shoot up their stores. In his book Wright remarks, "A man might as well be dead as lose his property." For there was always a chance that the Texans might take their herds and business elsewhere.

The railroad men also favored a wide-open town, with no restrictions on the location of dives and deadfalls and no more law north of the tracks than south of them. It seemed to them that a customer whose business was worth thousands of dollars to Dodge ought to have special privileges.

George M. Hoover was elected Mayor. He ignored the pleas of those anxious not to disgruntle the Texans, and promptly brought in Jack Allen, a notorious gun-slinger, to serve as deputy under Marshal Larry Deger, Dodge City's man-mountain.

Shortly after, a gang of cowboys ran Jack out of town. The Mayor telegraphed, offering the job to Wyatt Earp.

CHAPTER 11 ·
· WYATT EARP TAKES A HAND

" 'THE MESSAGE that took me to Dodge had offered me the marshal's job,' Wyatt recalled, 'but Hoover told me that for political reasons he wanted Deger to complete his year in office. He would pay me more money as chief deputy than Deger was drawing. I would have power to hire and fire deputies, could follow my own ideas about my job and be marshal in all but name. The marshal's pay was $100 a month, but Mayor Hoover said they would pay me $250 a month, plus $2.50 for every arrest I made. Brown and Mason were discharged from the force and I was to appoint three new deputies at wages of $75 a month, each, and make my own arrangements with them about the bonus.

" 'Bat Masterson's brother Jim was in Dodge, a good, game man who could handle himself in a fracas, and I picked him as one deputy, took Joe Mason back, and was looking for the third when Bat himself came in from Sweetwater, Texas, still limping from the leg-wound he got when he killed Sergeant King. Bat's gun-hand was in working order, so I made him a deputy. He patrolled Front Street with a walking-stick for several weeks and used his cane to crack the heads of several wild men hunting trouble; even as a cripple he was a first-class peace officer.[1]

" 'I told my deputies that all bounties would be pooled and shared, but would be paid only when prisoners were taken alive.

99

Dead ones wouldn't count. Each officer carried two six-guns and I placed shotguns at convenient points, as I had in Wichita, but killing was to be our last resort.

" 'I figured that if the cowboys were manhandled and heaved into the calaboose every time they showed in town with guns on, or cut loose in forbidden territory, they'd come to time quicker than if we kept them primed for gunplay. Hoover had hired me to cut down the killings in Dodge, not to increase them. As far as that went, any one of the deputies could give the average cowboy the best of a break, then kill him in a gunfight; but even when gunplay was necessary, we disabled men, rather than killed them.

" 'With this policy, we organized for a fairly peaceful summer. There were some killings in personal quarrels, but none by peace officers. We winged a few tough customers who insisted on shooting, but none of the victims died. On the other hand, we split seven or eight hundred dollars in bounties each month. That meant some three hundred arrests every thirty days, and as practically every prisoner heaved into the calaboose was thoroughly buffaloed in the process, we made quite a dent in cowboy conceit. . . .

" 'We made no attempt to cut off the celebrations that the cowmen, teamsters, and hunters put on whenever they hit Dodge, but with a steady run of object lessons in the shape of buffaloed gun-toters, we certainly enforced a change in their ritual. And we held most of the hurrahing and fighting south of the Dead Line which we drew at the railroad. . . .'

"Below the Dead Line, as far as the marshal's force was concerned, almost anything went, and a man could get away with gunplay if he wasn't too careless with lead. North of the railroad, gun-toting was justification for shooting on sight, if an officer was so inclined, and meant certain arrest. Any attempt to hurrah stores, gambling-houses, or saloons along the Plaza was good for a night in the calaboose, and by proving that the Dead

Line meant something every time anyone broke over its restrictions, we kept trouble south of the tracks."[2]

This new policy, steadily enforced, was galling to the Texans. In their book, a gun-toter of any standing was entitled to a gun-fight in case of a "difficulty." He wanted a chance to draw his weapon and make his play. In the Old South, from which most of the Texans derived, only Negroes and poor whites engaged in fist-fights. A pistol or a bowie knife was the gentlemanly weapon. To be unceremoniously clubbed over the head, thrown into the calaboose, tried and fined, was not only painful, they felt, but scandalously unfair and degrading. That was an insult never to be lived down.

In fact, during the first season under Mayor Hoover's new policy, no prosperous cattleman gave any occasion to the police to buffalo him or run him in; only their hired hands, the cow-boys, came to grief, and these, apparently, soon learned their lesson—that if they liquored up, and went around shooting the doorknobs off the cathouses, taking pot shots at the wooden Indian in front of the cigar store, or disturbing the peace in some other way, a broken head and a fine were sure to follow.

But sooner or later, some wealthy cattleman was bound to defy an ordinance and so invite a test of the City Marshal's integrity and courage. For as J. Frank Dobie, a Texan born, has pointed out,[3] the Western code of violence derives from the South, where "difficulties" were plenty and there were actually more killings with knife and gun than in the Old West.

But it was not until the season of 1877 that a cattle king attempted to celebrate the sale of his herds by shooting on Front Street. Such a man, Wyatt Earp insisted, was "entitled to less consideration than a poor ignorant cowpuncher."

One evening, one of the Texans quarreled with a fiddler, inflicting a bloody scalp wound, and then pursued the terrified musician down Front Street, gun in hand.

Wyatt left his supper in the restaurant, pushed the fiddler through a door, and ordered the cattleman to drop his guns.

The Texan defied the Marshal, who promptly buffaloed him, and with the help of Neal Brown, lugged him across the tracks to the calaboose, ignoring pleas of the cowman's friends. Hurriedly, Bob Wright was sent for. He was the richest man in Ford County, member of the Kansas State Legislature, partner with the Texan, Judge Beverley, and an old-time Indian fighter, who had lived in and around Fort Dodge long before Dodge City was dreamed of.

Wright reached the calaboose as Wyatt unlocked the door. Wright protested angrily, "Here, you can't lock this man up!"

" 'What makes you think so?' Wyatt asked.

" 'Why, his business is worth half a million dollars a year to Dodge.' "

Wyatt readily admitted that fact. Meanwhile Neal Brown emptied a bucket of water over the prisoner's head to bring him to. Then the Marshal heaved him into jail. A crowd had gathered, and Wright, perhaps emboldened by their presence, made open threats.

"You'll let him go, if you know what's good for you," Wright warned.

The Marshal only locked the door. Furiously, Wright grabbed his arm. "If you don't let him out, Dodge will have a new marshal tomorrow," he shouted.

" 'Take your hand off my arm,' Wyatt said.

"Bob Wright erred. He snatched at the key in Wyatt's hand and grappled with him, mixing with muscular efforts a highly colored prophecy of the marshal's immediate future. Thereupon Wyatt swung open the door of the calaboose." Then he pitched the irate legislator into jail along with his friend the Texan.

" 'If I had done anything else,' Wyatt said, 'I'd have to leave town, because I'd have lost whatever edge I've got on these trouble-makers.' "[4]

Mayor Kelley, in spite of all persuasion, backed Wyatt's play; and the prisoner paid his fine.

Certain Texans were reported to have offered a bounty of $1,000 to the man who killed Wyatt Earp. After that, several persons fired at Earp. Wyatt was able to wound and capture one of these, a cowboy who, having gambled away everything he owned, had been given a shotgun and stationed where he might take a pot shot. The cowboy had no malice, merely needed the money, but would not identify those who had put him up to it.

The next thing Dodge heard, Clay Allison was coming from Colorado to cut Wyatt down.

Already Allison had killed the city marshals of Cimarron, New Mexico, and Las Animas, Colorado, and had been acquitted on pleas of self-defense.

He was a great dandy and show-off, but apparently one of those fellows who had to nerve himself with Dutch courage to face a skilled gun-fighter. One of his earlier victims lay buried on Boot Hill.

News of Clay's approach was brought to Dodge from Jim Tucker's ranch south of the river. Stuart Lake has penned Wyatt's account of what followed. His story clearly shows the dangerous situation in which a Dodge City Marshal found himself.

"Wyatt Earp, while marshal of Dodge, was on active duty in the streets until four o'clock each morning and, unless court business called him, slept until noon. Thus it happened that when Clay Allison hit Dodge City one morning, Wyatt was in bed. The marshal's first knowledge of Allison's arrival came with a message from the mayor that the gunman was in town, had been in several saloons buying drinks, and was boasting of the purpose of his visit. Clay was rapidly approaching the stage of intoxication at which he was most dangerous. Wherefor Mayor Kelley and his supporters were anxiously awaiting Wyatt's appearance.

" 'I'll be right along,' Wyatt said in response to the summons, then went about the routine of shaving and breakfast.

" 'With Clay in town the time for fussing was past,' Wyatt

commented. 'Now, it was up to me to leave Dodge by the back alley or go down Front Street and meet Allison.

" 'I did not intend to give Clay the satisfaction of thinking he had hurried me. He knew that I'd been sent for before I did, and I knew enough about the average braggart killer to be certain that a lot of Clay's fight would go into all the talk he'd be making while he waited. And the more I could irritate him by tardiness, the less sure of himself he'd be at the showdown.

" 'I wore my guns at breakfast on the chance that Clay might bring the fight into the dining-room. While I was eating, several men came to ask if they could help any, but beyond asking Bat Masterson and Charlie Bassett to make sure I was not ambushed by Allison's friends, I declined their offers. About ten o'clock I walked down Front Street toward Second Avenue.'

"Accounts of men who witnessed Wyatt Earp's meeting with Clay Allison do not differ in essential details, but few who have told their stories occupied positions as commanding as those of Chalk Beeson and Bill Harris, proprietors of the Long Branch in front of which the marshal met the gunman, and Luke Short who ran the Long Branch gambling concession.

"Between gun-fighter and gunman, one marked similarity was noted, in the colors of their clothing. Clay Allison had followed his predilection for black-and-white from the toes of his fancy boots to the tip of his huge sombrero, through the full array of white buck-skin and silver-trimmed accoutrements. Wyatt Earp was dressed as for any other midsummer morning. He wore no coat and his dark trousers were pulled down over the tops of his boots; a gun was belted to either hip; on his soft white shirt was his marshal's badge; for shade, he wore a sombrero as large and as black as Allison's.

"As Wyatt started toward Second Avenue, the north side of Front Street cleared instantly, a few spectators taking vantage-points in stores and saloons, a majority utilizing the ditch beside the railroad. As Wyatt neared the Long Branch, three doors from Second Avenue, Clay Allison came out of Wright and Beverley's door on the corner.

"Wyatt stopped and leaned against the wall of the Long Branch, just west of the doorway. Allison came along the walk, turned, as if to enter the saloon, and halted abruptly.

" 'Are you Wyatt Earp?' the killer demanded.

" 'I am Wyatt Earp,' the marshal replied.

" 'I've been looking for you.'

" 'You've found me.'

" 'You're the fellow who killed that soldier the other night, aren't you?' Allison continued.

" 'What business is it of yours if I am?' Wyatt countered, although the charge implied was without foundation.

" 'He was a friend of mine,' Allison retorted.

"As Allison talked, he had stepped close, and was actually leaning against Wyatt, thus shielding his right side and his right hand from the marshal's view.

" 'Clay was working for his gun all the time,' Wyatt said, 'trying to get into such a position that I couldn't see him start after it.'

" 'I'm making it my business right now,' Allison snarled.

"Wyatt felt the muscles of the body which pressed against him tauten.

"The watchers in the Long Branch said that Clay Allison had his thumb hooked around the hammer of his Colt's and the weapon half-out of the holster when stark amazement replaced the fighting scowl which had distorted his face, he dropped his gun as though the butt had turned red-hot, and jerked both hands, empty, above his waist. Then onlookers saw the reason for the transformation, although none had caught the action which brought it. The muzzle of Wyatt Earp's forty-five was jammed into Allison's left side, just underneath the ribs.

"With his gun against Allison's body, Wyatt waited for the other to move or speak.

"A few seconds of threatening suspense brought the strain to a pitch Clay could not endure. Hesitantly, Allison backed across the walk. With several feet between him and the muzzle of Wyatt's forty-five he found voice.

" 'I'm going around the corner,' Clay suggested.

" 'Go ahead,' Wyatt told him. 'Don't come back.'

"Allison backed out of sight beyond Wright and Beverley's. A moment later, when the marshal peered around the same corner, Second Avenue was empty. From across the road, Bat Masterson called. Armed with a shotgun, the deputy sheriff had taken his stand in a doorway to command three approaches to the Front Street intersection, thus precluding any attempt to gang-up on Wyatt from those quarters. Bat called that Allison had gone into Wright and Beverley's by the side entrance and that there were some twenty other men in the place who would bear watching. Then he pointed across the Plaza to Sheriff Charlie Bassett, guarding against a shot in the back from that direction. Wyatt returned to his post beside the Long Branch door. Allison's war-horse was hitched to the rail before Wright and Beverley's front doorway. Harris, Beeson, and Short could forestall any bush-whacking operations through the saloon. To reach his pony, Allison would have to come into Wyatt's line of vision, and from where he stood the marshal could keep cases until the killer made his next move.

"Allison probably was taking on liquid courage in Wright and Beverley's, and while Wyatt waited, the door of the Long Branch opened behind him and a double-barreled shotgun was thrust within reach of his hand.

" 'Take this and give him both barrels,' Chalk Beeson counseled.

"The proffered gun, incidentally, was the same fine English-made piece with which Bill Thompson killed Sheriff Whitney in Ellsworth. The gun belonged to Bill's brother Ben, and was his favorite weapon. Early in '77, Ben Thompson went broke in Dodge and posted the shotgun with Chalk Beeson for a loan of seventy-five dollars. Chalk kept the gun back of the bar while waiting for Ben Thompson to redeem it.

"Wyatt Earp, without taking his eye from the Wright and Beverley door, shook his head at Chalk's suggestion. Bill Harris joined his partner.

" 'Don't be a fool, Wyatt,' Harris counseled. 'Take the shot-gun and use it.'

" 'All Clay's got is a pair of six-guns,' Wyatt answered.

"Allison strode out of Wright and Beverley's door; Beeson and Harris ducked back through their own. The gunman, pistols in their holsters, walked straight to his war-horse, swung into the saddle, and sat staring savagely. He turned to the marshal.

" 'Come over here, Earp,' he suggested. 'I want to talk to you.'

" 'Make your talk,' Wyatt answered. 'I can hear you.' "

But Allison found he had nothing to say to Wyatt Earp. He saw himself alone and outnumbered. Profanely he complained that the gunmen he had expected to back his play had not showed up, and denounced the man who had promised to provide them.

Then, digging in his spurs, "Clay Allison wheeled his war-horse and started for the tollbridge on a run. As he reached the bridgehead, Clay pulled up and turned to face the Plaza. With a wild whoop, he jerked a gun, put spurs and quirt to his mount, and headed back toward Wright and Beverley's.

" 'Watch the store, boys,' Wyatt called to Masterson and Bassett, 'I'm going to get him.'

"The marshal walked to the middle of Second Avenue. Clay came at a gallop, gun in his right hand, quirt flailing in his left, yelling madly. When he was about fifty yards distant, Bat Masterson saw the Buntline Special move slowly from Wyatt's side to a level slightly above his waist. As Bat and the others waited for the roar of gunfire that would relieve the West of a killer or rob it of a peace officer, Clay yanked his war-horse to his haunches, in the sliding stop that only a highly trained cow-pony can achieve, wheeled, and rode breakneck again for the toll-bridge. This time he kept on, out of Dodge, toward Las Animas.

The showdown had come, and gone. Clay Allison had quit the fight."[5]

But Allison only rode away to fight again some other day. Next time he would bring plenty of friends of his own choosing to back his play. Next time he would not have to rely upon empty promises.

CHAPTER 12 ⋮ TRAIN ROBBERS

By the First Week of June, 1877, Dodge had livened up. The paper reported two hundred cattlemen in the city and money flooding the town. This state of affairs could not continue long in Dodge without an eruption, for the gang was in good shape for business.

Robert Gilmore was just a little fellow, known familiarly as Bobby Gill, and was often the butt of pranks and jokes. One day he was making oration on the street and passed some sharp remarks to which the gigantic Marshal Larry Deger took strong exceptions. Deger collared Bobby and started for the doghouse. Bobby, however, resented the interruption of his free speech and moved in a very leisurely and insolent manner, until Larry administered a few kicks in the rear.

At this, Bat Masterson interfered, winding his arm "affectionately" around the Marshal's neck, and so helped Bobby escape.

Larry then grappled with Bat, calling on the bystanders to take Bat's gun.

Joe Mason rushed up and took Bat's gun, but Bat would not give in, and almost succeeded in grabbing a pistol from among several of those handy.

At that time, Bat was one of the gamblers successfully engaged in relieving Texans of their hard-earned pay. Half a dozen of them came running to the Marshal's aid, pulling Bat loose and giving Deger a chance to draw his weapon and beat Bat over the head until blood flew, spattering Joe Mason.

But Bat fought with extraordinary strength, contesting every inch of the way. If he could have got hold of his gun, there might have been a killing; but at last they pushed him into the city dungeon.

The same afternoon, Ed Masterson, Assistant Marshal, performed his first official act by arresting Bobby Gill.

The editor remarks, "Next day Judge Frost administered the penalty of the law by assessing $25 and costs to Bat and $5 to Bobby.

"The boys are all at liberty now."

But the minutes of the City Council for July 3 reveal official sympathy with Bat in this affair: Mayor James H. Kelley, "with the consent of the Council, remitted the fine assessed against the defendant in the case of the city vs. W. B. Masterson." In November, at the Peoples' Mass Convention, P. L. Beatty, seconded by Messrs. Sutton and Manion, nominated W. B. Masterson for Sheriff. G. M. Hoover, seconded by Harry E. Gryden, D. M. Frost, and W. N. Morphy, nominated Lawrence E. Deger. Morphy and Sutton made speeches ("loud applause"), but Bat won the nomination on the first ballot. Deger nevertheless announced himself a candidate for Sheriff.

In November, 1877, Bat was elected Sheriff of Ford County by a majority of three.[1]

In January, 1878, Bat Masterson took the oath of office and became Sheriff of Ford County, replacing Charles "Senator" Bassett for a term of two years. Bat immediately appointed Bassett Undersheriff, for Deputy Sheriff chose Simeon Woodruff, and John W. Straughan for jailor. These appointments met with the approbation of the Dodge City people. They felt confident that Bat would do his duty. Before the month was out he had an opportunity to show his mettle.

Most of the excitement in and around Dodge City happened during the warmer months when Indian ponies were fat and warriors footloose and the cowboys from Texas were swarming up the trail to paint the town red—and furnish the paint. It was not easy to surprise Dodge City with a new kind of rascality, but on January 27, 1878, the town was electrified by a telegram announcing a raid by train robbers in near-by Kinsley. When the story broke, the newspapers of western Kansas gave it much space and followed it up religiously. These accounts and the court records give us fuller information about the raid and its aftermath than is usually available. For train robbing was something new out there in those days. Moreover, the business provided a test for the new Sheriff, Bat Masterson, and his colleagues.

It appears that six men planned the business at first and made rendezvous at the railroad water tank two miles east of Kinsley, intending to rob the eastbound train.

However, as it happened, the engineer had taken on water at Dodge City, needed none, and swiftly sped by the gang.

The robbers, having missed the train, rode to the station at Kinsley and dismounted. One of them remained on the platform as lookout. The other five walked into the office of the railroad depot and greeted Andrew Kinkade, the night operator, hardly more than a boy, with, "Good morning."

Their faces were blackened for disguise, which might have puzzled him but for their instant covering him with revolvers demanding the money in his charge.

Kinkade, looking into the barrels of their guns, exhibited remarkable presence of mind and declared, "I have no money here," at the same time jerking open an empty money drawer.

There was $2,000 in the safe in that office and of course Kinkade knew it.

The safe, moreover, was in plain view, and the man who seemed to be the leader of the gang barked, "Open the safe, damn quick too," at the same time shoving two cocked revolvers into Kinkade's face.

Kinkade explained that he did not have the key to the safe.

"Gardner has it. You can find him at the hotel; anyhow all the money in it went off on this morning's eastbound train."

While they argued they heard a train whistle somewhere east; the westbound Pueblo Express was approaching.

The time was short. The young fellow, surrounded by five armed highwaymen, never faltered.

They threatened to blow out his brains if he did not open the safe.

But Kinkade was a lad of courage. He had a small derringer in his hip pocket, put his hand in his pocket, cocked it, and attempted to draw. Perhaps they heard the weapon click or saw what he was up to. One of them shouted, "No you don't—hand that over." And Andrew laid it on the counter.

Kinkade knew that the hotel men would be there to meet the train within a few minutes.

But the bandits ordered him outside and marched him down the platform, their guns at his back. Even then Andrew Kinkade thought only of his duty, and his only fear was that he would not be able to inform the conductor of the danger to the train.

Seeing Blanchard of the Eureka Hotel coming toward the station, he shouted, "Go back, these men are armed." At that one of the bandits tried to strike him, but Andrew dodged the blow.

They seized Blanchard and another man, but while they watched the train Blanchard escaped, ran off and armed himself. The train was rolling in. Kinkade, followed by a shot, leaped across the track ahead of the engine, thus putting the train between him and the bandits. He hurried toward the rear to warn Conductor Mallory, shouting at the top of his voice, "Look out for yourselves. There are six armed men on the platform."

As it happened, James Anderson, the engineer, couldn't make the air brake work owing to a shortage of compressed air, so was unable to stop his train beside the platform and ran on by one hundred yards, leaving Kinkade exposed to the fire of the robbers.

They, however, had no interest in him now. They ran for the train. Two climbed into the engine, pistol in hand, commanding the engineer to start up the train. It was evidently their intention to run it out into the country where it could be robbed at their leisure.

But the steam was so low or the engineer's courage so high that the engine would not start immediately but stalled there near the station.

The train had rolled into the station on time. As it did so, Henry A. Brown, the express messenger, having a box weighing some fifty pounds to put out at Kinsley, opened the car doors (which were on hinges and swung inward). When the train whistled for the station, he placed the box in the doorway and stood beside it with his lamp and his book in hand. When the train stopped, he waited for it to back up to the station, and looking out, saw two men hurrying toward the engine and two others coming his way.

The latter suddenly rose up at the door of the car. One of them was six feet tall and Brown had a good look at his blackened face. He shoved a pistol at the messenger, exclaiming in a fierce tone, "God damn you, give up or I'll shoot."

Brown saw what was up, tossed his lamp into the coalbox, dropped his book, grabbed the six-shooter lying on a box near by, and without bothering to reply opened fire on his two enemies.

That did not faze the bandits. One of them tried to climb into the car. Brown fired full in his face and hoped that his target was, as he put it later, "a little damaged." At least six or seven shots were fired into the car at Brown, but missed the gritty messenger.

Two of the robbers had boarded the train to loot the passengers and the conductor, but the bandits on the engine, hearing the shooting at the express car, rallied to their comrades in the rear. When they jumped off the engine, the engineer started the train. The fellow in whose face Brown had fired fell off the train and those in the rear jumped down, running off, shooting as they ran.

Conductor Mallory stopped two miles out of town and went through the train to ascertain whether the messenger was safe and the engineer and passengers as they should be.

Nobody was hurt. Nothing had been stolen. The raid was a complete fiasco—owing to the courage and presence of mind of the Santa Fe Railroad men and the express messenger.

Immediately the Santa Fe Railroad printed posters offering $100 reward each for the capture of the robbers "dead or alive." The Adams Express Company took measures of its own to insure the capture of the bandits.

Though the crime had been committed in Edwards County, the reputation of the Dodge City gunmen was such that the Express Company called upon Sheriff Bat Masterson to go after them.

In their joy over their lucky escape, a number of the men on the train fired into the night. Perhaps, too, they thought a little shooting might further intimidate the bandits who were somewhere out there on the dark prairie.

Meanwhile, in Kinsley at that early hour the firing from the train caused misunderstanding. Instead of organizing a well-armed posse and crossing the river while the trail was hot, eight or ten citizens boarded a handcar and hurried to the rescue of the train. But the train pulled out before they reached it. In the darkness they saw the mounted robbers approaching and fired three or four shots at them. But the robbers rode on across the track, heading for the river.

Soon after, a telegram from Dodge City arrived announcing that the bandits had done no damage. About that time Sheriff Fuller organized a posse to take after them.

Those vast plains, broken here and there, laced with running streams and spotted with small patches of brush or timber, offered safe harbor for horsethieves, robbers, and assassins. The country, desolate and almost uninhabited, yet alive with game, allowed a fugitive from justice to ride off in any direction. He could demand food and shelter anywhere he found it, for the hospitality of the range was open to all comers and no questions were likely to be asked. Moreover, in No Man's Land, no great distance south and west, where by some error of Congress no law existed, or could exist, there was everywhere a horsethief ready to welcome his fellow criminals. Honest men, even if they knew, seldom cared to risk their lives by acting as informers. To find the train robbers in that wilderness required a man who knew it. Bat Masterson was that man. He had hunted buffalo all over that region.

They found that the robbers had crossed the Arkansas River twelve miles above Kinsley, riding south through the sand hills. Party after party went out, but all returned unsuccessful. It seemed probable that the robbers had split up and scattered and were far away. Part of the time they were protected by dense fogs.

Sheriff Bat Masterson took with him as his posse J. J. Webb, Prairie Dog Dave Morrow, and Kinch Riley. The first day they rode to Crooked Creek, twenty-seven miles. Heavy snow fell and they had to lay over one day. On the third day they rode to Harry Lovell's cattle camp at the mouth of Crooked Creek, more than fifty miles from Dodge, arriving there at sundown. There they remained next day until late afternoon. The storm grew steadily worse and by 5:00 P.M. was a regular blizzard. Masterson knew that the bandits would have to seek shelter in such a storm and he thought the trail might lead to Lovell's camp. While they huddled in their ambush their lookout about 5:00 P.M. saw four men approaching and recognized two of them as West and Rudebaugh, two of the train robbers. The other two were cowboys. The bandits came within a few hundred yards of the camp, where they discovered the Sheriff's buggy and horse. Alarmed, they halted and asked the cowboys what strange outfit that was. One of the cowboys recognized one of Bat's horses as belonging to Anderson's livery stable in Dodge and told the bandits so.

The robbers hesitated, but the horse herder yelled to them, "Come on," and they again rode forward.

Meanwhile Webb, who they could not know was a member of the posse, volunteered to go out and bring them in. It was certain that if Masterson himself had stepped out while they were yet at a distance gunplay must have followed.

Webb went out, met them and told them he was on his way to George Anderson's. The two robbers rode on in with Webb walking beside them, and were so decoyed to the dugout where Sheriff Masterson and his party lay in ambush.

When they had come within shooting distance, Bat, standing behind the doorpost, stepped quickly out from his concealment and with leveled rifle called, "Throw up your hands." West at once complied. Dave Rudebaugh's hand reached for his revolver, but Webb, standing behind him at close quarters, had his gun out. The click as Webb cocked his weapon and a warning word led Rudebaugh to change his mind. He raised his hands and both surrendered.

Then Kinch Riley searched them and took from one a Colt .45 Smith & Wesson improved and a pistol from the other man. Kinch supposed that was all the weapons they had, but Bat was more observant. He saw that Rudebaugh had another weapon. When he went to take it, the prisoner tried to hold onto it, but Bat wrenched it from him. On their saddles they also had guns, one a .40 Sharps sporting rifle, the other a .45 caliber government carbine.

Once disarmed, the prisoners wanted to know why they had been arrested. Bat replied, "On a charge of attempting to rob the train." They made no answer, no denial.

The two cowboys who rode in with the bandits had fallen in with them a short distance from the ranch while out looking for three good horses stolen shortly before from their employer, Harry Lovell.

Sheriff Masterson brought in his prisoners about six o'clock on February 1 after a four days' hunt. He and his gallant posse had succeeded brilliantly and were the heroes of Dodge City for accomplishing so adroitly so daring an adventure. Some who love blood and gunplay may be disappointed at this smoothly executed arrest. But from the professional point of view, Masterson's capture of these desperadoes without a shot being fired must seem an officer's dream, a real triumph.

Though Bat had brought in two of the robbers, four remained at large. On the night of March 15, Officer Nat Haywood, completing his round south of the tracks, happened to see Tom Gott *alias* Dugan in one of the dance halls. At that time, Haywood did not know that Dugan was charged with attempted train robbery.

Bat immediately summoned Undersheriff Charlie Bassett and City Marshal Ed Masterson and the three went looking for Dugan and Green. The natural place to make inquiries was a livery stable, and at Anderson's place they learned that two men had just passed the stable heading up the river bottom. The officers lost no time and soon came in sight of the robbers. These, watching their back trail, saw the officers and broke into a run, but the bright moonlight prevented their escape. They tried to put up a fight, but one of them caught his revolver in his clothing and the other was disarmed without firing a shot.

The officers felt pretty certain that Mike Rourke had been in the town. Next day the sheriff, with Charlie Bassett, J. J. Webb, and James Masterson, struck out on the trail of the two remaining robbers. Rourke, they knew, as recorded by the *Times*, was "no slouch." It was predicted that no light strategy and nerve would be required to bring him within the clutches of the law.

On February 12 Bat and his posse reached Lovell's camp again only to learn that Mike Rourke and two other men had left there just two hours before. Lovell's men told Bat that Rourke had openly declared that he well knew he was charged with the attempted train robbery and that officers were after him. But he swore, "I am ready for them any time, any place. They can send the whole city of Dodge after me. I will fight them anywhere."

The posse immediately pursued, trailing the robbers to Beaver Creek. The officers left their mess wagon far behind, and kept so close on the trail of the robbers that for thirty hours they rode without food.

Rourke and his companions had safely reached No Man's Land, where no law could follow.

So far nobody connected with the train robbery had been hurt. But on May 4, 1878, the *Dodge City Times* carried the following item:

"Last Friday night Andy Kinkade, night operator at the depot, heard a noise in the freight room. He picked up his revolver and started to see what was the matter, when the revolver accidentally went off, inflicting a severe fleshwound in his foot. (Kinsley *Leader*.)"

Soon after, Eddie Foy brought his troupe of entertainers to Dodge, and straightway Ben Springer introduced him to the Sheriff. Foy describes Bat as "a trim, good-looking young man with a pleasant face and carefully barbered mustache, well-tailored clothes, hat with a rakish tilt and two big silver-mounted, ivory-handled pistols in a heavy belt."[2]

In August the *Times* paid him this compliment: "Sheriff W. B. Masterson and Deputy William Duffy are indefatigable in their efforts to ferret out and arrest persons charged with crimes. Scarcely a day passes without reward for their vigilance and promptness. We do not record all these happenings, because evil doing is of such common occurrence. There is a pleasant contemplation in the fact that we have officers who are determined to rid the community of a horde that is a blight upon the well-being of this over-ridden section."

In October came news of Mike Rourke, alleged leader of the robbers. One of the gang gave his partners away. Mike was captured, made confession, was convicted and sentenced to ten years at hard labor.

Dodge was proud of the manner in which her officers had behaved in this business. Though the crime had been committed in another county, her Sheriff had captured four of the six robbers.

CHAPTER 13 •
• MARSHALS FOR BREAKFAST

THE EDITOR of the *Dodge City Times* stated the case for the gun-toting cowboy aptly:

"A gay and festive Texas boy, like all true sons of the Lone Star State, loves to fondle and practice with his revolver in the open air. It pleases his ear to hear the sound of this deadly weapon. Aside from the general pleasure he derives from shooting, the Texas boy makes shooting inside the corporate limits of any town or city a specialty. He loves to see the inhabitants rushing wildly around to 'see what all this shooting is about,' and it tickles his heart to the very core to see the City Marshal coming towards him at a distance while he is safe and securely mounted on his pony and ready to skip out of town and away from the officer.

"The program of the Texas boy, then, is to come to town and bum around until he gets disgusted with himself, then to mount his pony and ride out through the main street, shooting his revolver at every jump. Not shooting to hurt anyone, but shooting in the air, just to raise a little excitement and let people know he is in town."

Several times during the season of 1877, Dodge had been thrown into excitement by the firing of revolvers in the middle of the streets, and the officers had determined to put a stop to it. One September evening Bat Masterson and his brother Ed heard several shots fired in quick succession. Everybody around rushed toward the sound. Hatless men, and women with their back hair down, ran out to see if friends of theirs were involved. Bat was then Undersheriff of Ford County, campaigning for Sheriff.

Bat saw the Texan riding down Front Street, passing Beatty & Kelley's, and called out, "Halt!"

But the cowboy yelled, "I'm goin' to skin out for camp," and again, *Bang! Bang!* went his gun.

Bat jerked his pistol and fired at the cowboy's horse. A split second later Ed got in a shot. The horse seemed to wince, but the Texan laid spurs to its sides and dashed out of town over the bridge. Both of the officers fired again, but without effect.

Bat then mounted a horse and gave chase, swiftly gaining on the wounded animal.

But when he cocked his gun to shoot again, the gun only snapped. It had not a load in its chambers. There was nothing to do but return.

Mortally wounded though it was, the cowboy's noble animal carried its rider nearly two miles from the city on the run, before it fell.

The cowboy hoofed it the rest of the way to camp. The citizens hoped that this might prove a lesson to him and others of his kind not to practice shooting "just for fun" in town.

Somewhat later in the day, Charles F. Hoag, mail carrier, was driving toward Dodge. He was within seven miles of town when a man on foot stopped him, put a six-shooter to his head, and ordered Hoag to turn around. Hoag recognized the man, who made Hoag carry him five miles to a cattle camp on Spring Creek. There the cowboy got down, and obtained a horse from a man whom he seemed to know. But before he left, he swore Hoag to secrecy.

Said he, "The officers are after me, and have shot my horse from under me."

On Hoag's stage was a lady passenger. As soon as she arrived in Dodge she informed the officers. But Hoag stuck to his promise and refused to testify. Though there could be no doubt in anybody's mind as to the man's identity, there was no pursuit. He was not likely to trouble Dodge again.

On March 5, 1878, Mayor A. B. Webster published an editorial in the *Ford County Globe* in which he exhorted the peace officers of the town to rigid enforcement of the ordinance against carrying firearms within the city limits.

The editorial complains: "Some of the 'boys' in direct violation of the city ordinances carry firearms on our streets without being called to account for the same. They do so in such an open manner that it does not seem possible that our city officers are in ignorance of the fact."

Such caustic criticism appeared week after week in the *Globe*. City Marshal Edward J. Masterson had already suffered for his leniency in dealing with troublemakers. On November 10, 1877, the *Dodge City Times* had given an account of an adventure in which Ed Masterson came near losing his life for this reason. In Bob Wright's book the author declares that he remembers this shooting scrape well. He heard someone running by his store rattling the boardwalk, crying out, "Our marshal is being murdered in the dance hall!"

Wright with several others quickly ran toward the dance hall.

The newspaper gives the story in detail:

"Last Monday afternoon, one of those little episodes which serve to vary the monotony of frontier existence occurred at the Lone Star dance hall, during which four men came out some the worse for wear, but none, with one exception, being seriously hurt.

"Bob Shaw, the man who started the amusement, accused Texas Dick, alias Moore, of having robbed him of forty dollars, and, when the two met in the Lone Star, the ball opened. Somebody, foreseeing possible trouble and probable gore, started out in search of City Marshal Ed. Masterson, and, finding him, hurried him to the scene of the impending conflict.

"When Masterson opened the door, he descried Shaw near the

bar with a huge pistol in his hand and a hogshead of blood in his eye, ready to relieve Texas Dick of his existence in this world and send him to those shades where troubles come not and six-shooters are unknown. Not wishing to hurt Shaw, but anxious to quiet matters and quell the disturbance, Masterson ordered him to give up his gun. Shaw refused to deliver and told Masterson to keep away from him, and, after saying this, he proceeded to try to kill Texas Dick. Officer Masterson then gently tapped belligerent Shaw upon the head with his shooting iron, merely to convince him of the vanities of this frail world. The aforesaid reminder upon the head, however, failed to have the desired effect, and, instead of dropping, as any man of fine sensibilities would have done, Shaw turned his battery upon the officer and let him have it in the right breast. The ball, striking a rib and passing around, came out under the right shoulder blade, paralyzing his right arm so that it was useless, so far as handling a gun was concerned. Masterson fell, but grasping the pistol in his left hand he returned the fire, giving it to Shaw in the left arm and left leg, rendering him *hors de combat.*

"During the melee, Texas Dick was shot in the right groin, making a painful and dangerous, though not necessarily a fatal wound, while Frank Buskirk, who, impelled by a curiosity he could not control, was looking in at the door upon the matinee, received a reminiscence in the left arm, which had the effect of starting him out to hunt a surgeon. Nobody was killed, but, for a time, it looked as though the undertaker and the coroner would have something to do."

When Bob Wright and his companions reached the dance hall they burst in the door. Says he: "The house was so dense with smoke from the pistols a person could hardly see, but Ed Masterson had corralled a lot in one corner of the hall, with his six-shooter in his left hand, holding them there until assistance could reach him. I relate this to show the daring and cool bravery of our marshal, in times of greatest danger, and when he was so badly wounded."[1]

The fact is that, as Wright says, Ed Masterson, Bat's elder brother, was "a natural gentleman . . . cool, and considerate." But he was not, in the opinion of some more rough and ready officers, "a man of good judgment." Apparently he was a favorite of his mother, who had protested against his going west. Probably she had a premonition that the rough frontier was no place for a boy of his gentle, though courageous, character.

Bat, too, had misgivings. For in 1875, while Bat was an Army scout stationed at Fort Elliot, Texas, Sergeant King, a notorious gunman, had objected to Bat's dancing with a girl he called his own. King jerked his weapon, killed the girl, and shot Bat in the leg, bringing him down. From the floor, Bat fired and killed the Sergeant. This affair had taught Bat to shoot first and ask questions afterward—a lesson Ed never learned.

By April, City Marshal Ed Masterson had fully recovered from his wound received in the fracas in the Lone Star Dance Hall, the City Council paying $23 for his medical expenses. Ed may have been irked by the criticism of his work in the papers. But if so, he did not alter his methods sufficiently. Ed was twenty-six years old.

Bat Masterson, Sheriff of Ford County, seems to have felt some responsibility, as well as a natural loyalty to his elder brother, and tried to help him with his enforcement of the ordinance.

On April 9, 1878, Bat had just won golden opinions for his work in March in catching Green and Dugan, the train robbers.

The editor of the *Globe*, Frost, though Bat's political opponent, published this comment: "Hooray for our officers. They have done well."

Bat was now at the height of his popularity. Nearly everybody admired him. Those who did not feared him. One day a stranger in the town asked some man on Front Street how he could find Bat Masterson. A local lawyer within earshot spoke up: "Look for one of the most perfectly made men you ever saw, as well as a well-dressed, good-looking fellow, and when you see such a man, call him 'Bat' and you have hit the bull's eye."[2]

But if Bat was admired and feared, everybody in Dodge loved Ed.

About ten o'clock on the night of April 9, 1878, Ed heard pistol shots ring out below the Deadline. He and Assistant Marshal Nat Haywood hastened to cross the tracks. The commotion was in the Lady Gay Dance Hall. Half a dozen cowboys just off the trail from Texas were hell-bent for a good time, but some of them had absorbed too much hard liquor and were making a nuisance of themselves. "Jack" Wagner was noisier than the rest and particularly obnoxious.

Stepping into the hall, Ed could see that Wagner was packing a gun. Wagner made no objection to being disarmed, and Ed, finding the cowboy's boss, A. M. Walker, handed over the six-shooter to him, suggesting that he check it with the bartender in accordance with the law. Having no further business in the Lady Gay, the two marshals stepped outside.

Almost immediately they saw Walker and Wagner coming out through the same door. Wagner, staggering, caught his coat on the doorjamb. As it pulled back, Ed saw that Wagner's gun was back in his shoulder holster.

Ed stepped forward. Firmly he insisted, "I'll take that gun."

The drunken Wagner was tired of being bothered about his weapon. "Like hell you will," he replied. "Who the hell do you think you are, anyway?"

The two men scuffled, and those inside, hearing the fuss, came tumbling out to see the fun.

The Assistant Marshal warily came forward to back Ed's play. Then Walker and another cowboy covered Nat with their pistols. Walker warned Nat, "Keep your nose out of this, if you don't want your head shot off."

Seeing that Nat paid no heed and was reaching for his gun, Walker stuck his own in Nat's face and released the hammer.

Fortunately, Walker's gun missed fire. Nat turned and ran down the street for help.

Bat, heading for the Lady Gay through the dark when the first shots were fired, now heard the scuffling and yelling. He ran forward, and was within forty feet of the dance hall door when a shot was fired. There Ed stood alone, scuffling with Wagner, surrounded by his enemies. Someone had fired a pistol at such close range that Ed's clothing was on fire.

Bat cut loose.

The *Dodge City Times*, April 13, reports: "Masterson fired four shots, one of them striking Wagner in the bowels from the left side. Walker was struck three times, one shot in the lungs, and his right arm was horribly shattered with the other shots."

The crowd drifted down the boardwalk toward the Peacock Saloon.[3]

"Marshal Masterson walked across the street, and entering Hoover's Saloon in the agonies of death, said to George Hinkle, 'George, I am shot,' and sank on the floor. His clothes were still on fire from the discharge of the pistol which had been placed against the right side of his abdomen and 'turned loose.' Making a hole long enough for the introduction of the whole pistol, the ball passed completely through him, leaving no possible chance for life."[4]

Some of the flying shots grazed the face of one of the citizens and a cattleman. The shots were fired almost simultaneously, and the wonder is expressed that more death and destruction did not ensue, as a large crowd surrounded the scene of the shooting.

Wagner, mortally wounded, staggered into Peacock's Saloon, found Ham Bell, threw his arms around him and groaned, "Catch me. I'm dying."

Ham Bell shoved him away. "I can't help you now."

Wagner, dropping down, lay there on the floor until some Texans carried him away to Mr. Lane's rooms. There next day he died. As he lay dying, Wagner confessed that he had shot the Marshal. Wagner was buried on Boot Hill April 11, at 4:00 P.M.

Believing them mortally wounded, Bat did not pursue these men. Someone called to him from Hoover's Saloon that Ed was dying, and he rushed to the side of his brother. They carried Ed to Bat's room. There, in half an hour, he died.

Bat groaned, "This will kill poor Mother."

There was no fight left in Walker. His gun arm useless, he came tearing into the saloon, offering to surrender his gun to Ham Bell. Bell would not take it. "Throw it on the floor if you don't want it," he said.

Walker threw down his gun and staggered out through the back door of the Peacock Saloon. Discovered there by his friends, he was carried to a room above Wright, Beverley and Company's store. The *Dodge City Times* of May 11, 1878, states: "Mr. Walker, of Texas, father of the man who was wounded in the recent shooting scrape, arrived some days ago, and is attending his son. The wounded man is slowly recovering."

The four companions of the two wounded Texans were arrested as accessories to the murder of the Marshal,[5] but all were, after the fullest and most complete investigation, discharged by Judge R. G. Cook, as it was established that they were to blame only for being in bad company.[6]

Everyone in the city knew Ed Masterson. "They liked him as a boy, they liked him as a man, and they liked him as an officer." Every business house in the city closed its doors on the day of his funeral and almost every door in the city was draped in crepe. No one in Dodge, either living or dead, up to that time had ever had such honor shown him. Every vehicle in the city turned out for the funeral. The sermon was preached by Reverend O. W. Wright at the Firemen's Parlor. The funeral procession formed in this order: the City Council; the hearse; Sheriff Bat Masterson, the only relative who could be present; the Fire Company, sixty strong, in uniform and mourning; then buggies and wagons, followed by many horsemen. The *Ford County Globe* devoted the whole second page to the story. The Fire Company, of which Edward J. Masterson was a member, assumed the whole burden of the funeral expenses and would not permit Bat or his family to contribute. The Fire Company wore mourning for thirty days in honor of their departed brother.[7]

The cowboys, having killed a Marshal of Dodge, were more ready than ever to hurrah the town. A man might have supposed, from the way they behaved after Ed died, that Front Street was south of the Deadline. Wyatt Earp declared that if this had happened later, when the Texans were numerous in Dodge, their gunmen might have taken over the town completely.[8] On April 30, the *Globe* reported several new burials on Boot Hill.

On the other hand, the men of Dodge were all the more determined to enforce the law. They put up the money to recruit a strong force of peace officers.

Charlie Bassett succeeded to Ed Masterson's post of City Marshal. In May, 1878, Wyatt Earp returned from Fort Worth and took up his duties. Jim Masterson, Bat's younger brother, was to become Bassett's assistant in June. From the Docket of the Police Judge it appears that another man, John Brown, was added to the force about this time.

This force was not recruited without opposition. On May 18 an indignant taxpayer protested: "Look at our police force: one marshal at $100 a month; three assistants at $75 a month. Where is the necessity for such an army of policemen? . . . Three times more preparations are being made this year than last for the accommodation of the cattle drive."

Three days later the old veteran cattle king, Colonel J. F. Ellison, and his son were in town, also Captain Littlefield, J. W. Jeffries, W. F. Odom, John Saul, John T. Lytle, and J. C. Miller, all well-known cattle owners who had come to meet their herds. That day the *Globe* reported a number of cowboys "under the influence" in Dodge.

For as the waterfowl soared northward, cattle began to pour up the trails toward Dodge, some to be sold and shipped out of there, some to be driven north to Ogallala, Nebraska. Reports quoted in the Dodge City papers from the *San Antonio Express* show the following drives en route or about to start from Texas:

"James F. Ellison, 12,000; Lytle and McDonald, 10,000; Bishop and Halff, 8,000; D. R. Fant, 8,000; Smith and Savage, 8,000; Presnal and Mitchell, 8,000; Hood and Hughes, 4,000; E. B. Milett, 9,000; Mabry, 7,000; Quiniline and Montgomery, 6,000; John Frazier, 2,500; Waugh and Stephenson, 4,000; John Camp, 3,000; C. C. Lewis, 5,000; L. W. & Q. Johnson, 2,000; the Shiner brothers, 5,000; Littlefield and Houston, 15,000; Mr. Caruthers, 6,000; King and Kennedy, 15,000; Oge and Woodward, 4,000; Joe Matthews, 2,000; Hailer, 1,500; Reed and Rachal, 5,000; Chapman and Tuttle, 2,500; W. G. Butler, 6,000; Joe Croust, 2,000; Moore and Allen, 5,000; J. Birchfield, 2,000; W. B. Grimes, 500; J. L. Driskill, 3,000; A. S. Simpson, 2,000; Billet and West, 3,000; Mr. Pullan, 1,500; Snyder & Company, 25,000; Mr. D. Hawks, 1,500; Mr. Bates, 1,300; A. Adair, 500; Mr. Hineman, 1,200." Total: 207,000.

With these cattle came the cowboys, all set to whoop it up in Dodge. No wonder the editor of the *Globe* was relieved when Wyatt Earp returned. On June 18 he reported, "Wyatt Earp is doing his duty as Assistant Marshal in a very creditable manner, adding new laurels to his splendid record every day."

He was needed. Holdups in the town were numerous. Horsethieves continually operated in and around Dodge, while confidence men kept busy posing as land agents, selling worthless tickets to the Great Kentucky Lottery, and operating other crooked games for the unwary. The paper complains that the "showcase institution" in the west end of town was running "full blast all the time." Drunks were rolled. A man was found dead on the street. And it was complained that highway robberies were constantly committed in spite of "the expensive police force."

But meanwhile the building boom continued, there was more water in the Arkansas River than usual, the band got their "splendid new instruments" (paid for through a drive made by

Chalk Beeson and Judge Marshall), the Firemen's Ball was a grand affair, and the Glorious Fourth was celebrated for the first time in Ford County in fine style.

Dignitaries from Colorado, including the Pueblo Fire Department, were guests of honor in Dodge and were made welcome to "the biggest, wildest, happiest, wickedest little city on the continent."

Sergeant Holman, gunner, on the eve of the holiday fired fifty shots in rapid succession. The prolonged night life on the third caused the parade next day to start at 2:00 P.M.

Marshal P. L. Beatty presided. The band played "Hail Columbia." The Reverend Mr. Wright made "a long prayer." Mike Sutton made a brief oration on this the one hundred and second birthday of the nation. *Cheers.* In the pony racing Tobe Driskill's sorrel mare took first money ($8.00), William Matthew "Bill" Tilghman's horse second ($5.00). Joe Plummer's gray mare and Charles Reid's sorrel horse ran 400 yards for a purse of $50; the gray mare won. W. H. Loar won the 200-yard foot race, and Victor Collar was victor over P. L. Beatty in the wheelbarrow race (prize $2.00).

The most exciting and laughable event was catching—and holding—the greased pig. One Wright eventually captured it by falling on all fours on top of the squealing, wriggling porker.

The festivities concluded with the rendition by the band of "The Star Spangled Banner," a reading of the Declaration of Independence, loud applause, and "Yankee Doodle."

On July 16 the *Globe* reports: "Lively times in court last week. A dozen or more cases disposed of."[9]

But these were only preliminaries. On July 16 the Fire Company of Dodge City lost another brother; Ford County, a Deputy U.S. Marshal.

Harry T. "Mac" McCarty had just come up the street and stepped into the Long Branch Saloon. While he leaned on the bar talking to Mr. Jackson (the paper reports): "A half drunken desperado . . . snatched Mac's pistol, a .45 caliber Colt, from the scabbard, and as Mac turned to see who had so nimbly disarmed him, the assassin, giving the weapon a flourish or two, fired the fatal shot. The ball penetrated the right groin, severing the femoral artery, thence passing through the thigh lodged in the floor. The deceased staggered toward the door where he fell."

Another shot was almost instantaneously fired at McCarty's assailant by a bystander, the ball grazing his right side. Falling, he called out, "I am shot," and dropped to the floor, thus saving himself from the immediate penalty of his crime from the leveled revolvers about him.

McCarty died within a few minutes.

This killing, apparently so unprovoked, came near to bringing the men of Dodge to take the law into their own hands. The officers, however, managed to quiet the indignant citizens without a showdown. The prisoner, examined before Judge R. G. Cook, was charged with murder in the first degree. He waived examination and was recommitted to await trial at the next term of court. The dead Marshal was shown similar honors to those Ed Masterson had received.

Meanwhile, Nat Haywood had resigned his office and departed from Dodge City.

The January term of the Ford County District Court, S. J. Peters, Judge, was unusually busy in 1879. Sheriff Bat Masterson, Undersheriff Charlie "Senator" Bassett, and Deputies Duffy and James Masterson had done their part making it hot for law-breakers throughout Ford County. The criminal calendar listed one trial for murder, two for assault with intent to kill, two for stealing twenty-seven sacks of corn, one for stealing a horse and gun, and three for stealing horses; last of all was the celebrated name of Dutch Henry, horsethief extraordinary. After Thomas O'Hara was charged with the murder of Marshal Harry T. "Mac" McCarty, a petition for change of venue was filed (January 18, 1879). But shortly after, O'Hara pled guilty to manslaughter in the first degree and was sentenced to twelve years and three months in the penitentiary.[10]

Not long after, Sheriff Masterson wrote to the Colt's Fire Arms Manufacturing Company, ordering two .45 calibre revolvers for his "personal use"—nickel plated, with gutta percha handles. Bat wanted them "easy on the trigger," with front sights a little higher and thicker than usual, and barrels about as long as the ejecting rods.[11]

CHAPTER 14 :
: WYATT EARP
SHOOTS TO KILL

MEANWHILE, Mayor Kelley telegraphed Earp, who arrived in Dodge May 12. Two days later the *Globe* pointedly remarked:

"Wyatt Earp, the most efficient officer Dodge ever had, has just returned from Texas. He was immediately reappointed Marshal by our City Dads, much to their credit.

"Hurry up with that new cemetery. We know not the day, or the hour."

Some of the businessmen in Dodge, particularly those on the south side of the tracks, bitterly resented Wyatt's return. They catered to the Texans and had nothing but hatred for a Marshal who so effectively controlled their antics.

On June 18 the effectiveness of this "expensive" police force received this tribute from the *Globe* after a week of Wyatt Earp's activities:

"Three dancehalls in full blast on the South Side, stables jammed full, hundreds of cowboys perambulate daily, but two cases in police court. Who says we aren't a moral city!

"Wyatt Earp is doing his duty as a marshal, adding new laurels to his splendid record every day."

The bounty of $1,000 which irate Texans had offered to the man who would kill Wyatt Earp was still held out. On July 26, 1878, an attempt was made to collect it. We have four versions of this affair. Bat Masterson's, published in 1907,[1] Eddie Foy's,[2] Wyatt Earp's as given to Stuart Lake and published in his biography of the Marshal, and that in the *Dodge City Times*, July 27, 1878.

It was dark. Nearly everybody at large was in the Comique, where Eddie Foy and his troupe were performing to a crowded house. Marshal Earp was on duty in the street just outside. Through the thin walls he could hear the songs and patter of the comedians and still keep an eye on the Plaza. It was getting late when "Wyatt noticed a horseman pass in the road, turn, and jog by again. A block away he turned once more and came down the road at a gallop. As the pony sped by the point where Wyatt stood, the roar of a forty-five and a flash of flame sent a heavy slug through the plank at the marshal's side, across the stage, and into the opposite wall. A second, then a third bullet followed."[3]

Says Foy: "It had come to be one of my jobs to call the figures for the old-time square dances which were the favorites at Dodge—'All balance left! Swing the right hand lady! Alamon right!'—whatever that may mean; I don't know to this day—and at intervals of twenty minutes or so, 'Balance all to the bar!' —a broad suggestion to everybody to buy a drink. We were going merrily on with the dance when suddenly, 'Bang! Bang! Bang!' came a roar of eight or ten big pistols from the outer darkness, the crash of glass from our windows and shrieks from the women.

"Everybody dropped to the floor at once, according to custom. Bat Masterson was just in the act of dealing in a game of Spanish monte with Doc Holliday, and I was impressed by the instantaneous manner in which they flattened out like pancakes on the floor. I had thought I was pretty agile myself, but those fellows had me beaten by seconds at that trick. The firing kept up until it seemed to me that the assailants had put hundreds of shots through the building. They shot through the walls as well as windows, for a big .45 bullet would penetrate those plank walls as if they had been little more than paper."[4]

Lake writes: "Outside, Wyatt went into action toward the horseman, jerking his Colt's as he jumped.

"The rider had a mount of more spirit than steadiness. At the roar of gunfire the cayuse shied, plunged, and reared. Wyatt grabbed for the pony's tail with his left hand, to throw himself onto the animal's hindquarters and hold himself so closely against the pony's legs that he could not be hurt by flying hoofs while his weight would be more effective than hobbles against a speedy getaway. As he lunged, so did the pony, and Wyatt missed the hold. The rider shot at Wyatt again, and missed. The bucking spoiled his aim.

"Wyatt shot in reply, but also missed, as the pony jumped sideways, and was off toward the tollbridge on a dead run."[5]

At this Foy reports: "The firing had been going on for a minute or so when we heard a volley from another quarter—this time out on Main Street. Some of the city police and deputy sheriffs, hastily collected, were attacking the gunfighters in flank. At that the Texas men spattered a few pellets at the police and then galloped across the bridge in flight."

Outside Wyatt was having it out with the cowboy, who turned in his saddle and fired his final slug which flipped up the brim of the Marshal's big hat. To bring his target against the sky, Wyatt dropped to his haunches and fired again. He heard the pony's hoofs slow on the bridge, then halt. "The rider had fallen from the saddle, and at the south end of the bridge Wyatt found him, unconscious, with a bullet through the small of his back. At the calaboose Dr. McCarty pronounced him mortally wounded."[6]

It was not until the next morning that the wounded cowboy could be identified as George R. Hoyt, a Texan. It was later reported that he was a fugitive from justice. (In the year 1878—so the *Dodge City Times* reported—the State of Texas published a list of persons wanted by the law totaling more than four thousand names, "with forty counties still unheard from." Rewards offered for these men totaled $90,000.) According to

Stuart Lake, on his deathbed Hoyt confessed that some big cattlemen had promised to get the warrant against him quashed if he killed Wyatt Earp; Hoyt, loyal to his employers, did not reveal the names of those who offered him this bribe.

Neither Foy nor Bat nor the editor of the *Times* seems to have been aware of any bounty posted on Wyatt's head. Bat surmises that "the drunken cowboy . . . rode right by Wyatt, who was standing outside the main entrance . . . but evidently he did not notice him, else he would not in all probability have acted as he did. . . . Whether it was Foy's act that angered him, or whether he had been jilted by one of the chorus we never learned; at any rate he commenced bombarding the side of the building directly opposite the stage upon which Eddie Foy was at that very moment reciting that beautifully pathetic poem entitled 'Kalamazoo in Michigan.' The bullets tore through the side of the building, scattering pieces of the splintered pine-boards in all directions. Foy evidently thought the cowboy was after him, for he did not tarry long in the line of fire. The cow-boy succeeded in firing three shots before Wyatt got his pistol in action. Wyatt missed at the first shot, which was probably due to the fact that the horse the cow-boy was riding kept continually plunging around, which made it rather a hard matter to get a bead on him. His second shot, however, did the work, and the cowboy rolled off his horse and was dead by the time the crowd reached him."

It is amusing to compare the account of the experienced gunfighter, Bat Masterson, with those of the impressionable actor. Actually only five shots had been fired into the building by a single cowboy. But Foy, after mentioning the three first shots, "Bang, bang, bang!" imagines a "volley" and "the roar of eight or ten big pistols" and declares that the place was shot up "by a gang of rough lads from Texas." He concludes: "The marvelous part of the whole affair was that aside from a few harmless scratches and some perforated clothing, nobody in the dance hall was hurt."

It is quite clear from the account in the newspaper that Hoyt was at first the only assailant, that he fired at Earp, that he fired several shots, and was only wounded—not killed—at the bridge. The account in the *Times* (obviously *not* by an eyewitness) gives the hour as 3:00 A.M., reports that "one of the bullets whizzed into a dancehall nearby," described the wound as being "in the arm," states that Bat and others joined in firing after Hoyt and his companions as they galloped away, and described the Texan as "a rather intelligent looking young man."

The editor adds one comic detail: After the firing became general, "some rooster who did not exactly understand the situation, perched himself in a window of the dancehall and indulged in a promiscuous shoot all by himself!"

Hoyt's arm was "broken in two places."

The *Dodge City Times* (August 24) tells of Hoyt's ordeal: "He had been growing worse for several days, and the hot weather and the nature of his wound caused mortification to set in. On Wednesday morning the doctors decided that the arm must be taken off. The operation was performed by Assistant Surgeon Tremaine, U.S.A., in a very skillful manner." But Hoyt, "who was already very weak from long sickness never rallied or spoke after the operation. Just before he died he opened his eyes and seemed to recognize Mr. Day and one or two others, then with a smile on his countenance, he closed his eyes in death without a struggle. He . . . was like many other men who grow up on the Texas frontier, very bold and reckless, and we understand he was under bond before he came here; . . . however, he had many good traits, and seemed to have many friends among the Texas boys."

The cowboys did everything possible to brighten the last days of their fellow Texan and to honor him after his death. The *Ford County Globe* reports: "George Hoyt, the Texas cowboy, died on Wednesday, August 21st, and was buried on Boot Hill in grand style. . . ."

Bat Masterson, who at another time called Wyatt the softest-hearted gun-fighter he ever knew, describes this affair as being the only time he had ever known Wyatt while in Dodge City to shoot to kill. Hoyt was, in fact, the only man who died after being shot by Wyatt Earp during the four seasons he policed the camp.

Romancers, following the lead of the genial Alfred Henry Lewis, have spun too many yarns about the officers of Dodge City and exaggerated out of all reason the number of their killings. As a matter of fact, so far as can be learned from newspapers, available court records, and accounts of reliable eyewitnesses, the officers who followed Wyatt Earp's lead, arresting instead of shooting offenders, killed very few men while on duty in Dodge.

That is their glory—that they enforced the law with little bloodshed.

While he wore the star, Sheriff Bat Masterson killed Wagner and wounded Walker and Kennedy, as described elsewhere in this book. The other Masterson brothers, Ed, Jim, and Thomas, killed nobody in Dodge, though Ed wounded Shaw. Assistant Marshal Grant Wells once killed a cowboy in the camp. But Bill Tilghman never had to shoot a man there; apparently, neither did John Brown, Neal Brown, Larry Deger, or Charlie Bassett. Ham Bell assured Stuart N. Lake that he "never used his gun on a human being during his tenure as sheriff of Ford County." City Marshal Bob Vandenberg told Lake that during his term of office "he winged a couple, but killed none." Lake writes: "Wyatt always said that most of the cowboys were drunk when they started trouble, and that it was his job to fend off serious trouble rather than to kill drunks."

Apparently other officers felt about this matter much as he did. Certainly, the members of the Peace Commission of 1883 not already mentioned—Luke Short, William H. Harris, and Frank McLane (professional gamblers all)—also killed no one in the camp.

Several of the men named above, who later acted as officers

in other towns, did kill one or more men in line of duty; indeed it would be easy to prove that these same gun-fighters killed more men elsewhere than in Dodge. When one considers that two officers had been shot down in Dodge City, this shows remarkable skill and forbearance on the part of the others.

Joe Mason, it is true, killed Ed Ryan in self-defense, but not in Dodge. Ben Daniels shot Ed Julian, and David Mather, Tom Nixon in personal quarrels—not in their capacity as officers. Wyatt Earp accounted only for George Hoyt.

Apparently, George Hoyt's killing had its aftermath.

The *Ford County Globe* (August 6, 1878) carried this story:

"Clay Allison, one of the Allison brothers, from the Cimarron, south of Las Animal, (*sic*) Colorado, stopped off at Dodge last week on his way home from St. Louis. We are glad to say that Clay has about recovered from the effects of the East St. Louis scrimmage."

Allison must have arrived shortly after Wyatt shot George Hoyt, and would certainly have heard of the shooting during his stay, however brief. Later, he must have heard of Hoyt's death. At any rate, the story goes that it brought him back to Dodge.

In a letter to Floyd Benjamin Streeter, author of *Prairie Trails & Cow Towns*, Pink Simms describes Clay Allison as an honest man, a dangerous man when aroused, and one quick to take up the cause of the underdog. "Clay Allison hated gunmen as a whole, and the Kansas marshals in particular; he believed that they could accomplish their purpose to keep law and order without so much killing."

Pink adds that Clay "heard that a young cowboy had been killed by Marshal Wyatt Earp while he was harmlessly shooting his pistol in the street; the cowboy's name was Hoyt, and he was a friend or had worked for Allison. . . . It was my understanding that Allison wanted to register a protest at the needless killing, and that Bat Masterson, knowing that Allison was drinking, thought it best to avoid a meeting until he was sober. I also heard that he did meet Bat afterward and had a talk with him, and some say that he threatened to kill Earp. I do not think that he was looking for the Dodge City officers with the intention of starting a fight, though Siringo said he carried a pistol in his hand. Yes, '78 was about the time. Siringo told me the story himself, though he wasn't the only one that I heard mention it."

Charlie Siringo tells how in October, 1878, after the Dull Knife Raid, he rode into Dodge with a friend and saw "Clay Allison, the man killer come out of one of the saloons, holding a pistol in his hand."[7] Charlie describes Clay as "half drunk."

With him, says Charlie, was "Mr. McNulty, owner of the Turkey Track cattle outfit." With Clay were twenty-five mounted cowboys carrying rifles and following Clay down the street as he searched each saloon in turn, "hunting for some of the town policemen or the city marshal, so as to wipe them off the face of the earth. . . . Clay Allison had sworn to kill the first officer he found."

After all the saloons had been searched, McNulty succeeded in getting Clay to bed in the hotel. The cowboys dispersed. "Soon after," says Charlie, "the city officers began to crawl out of their hiding places, and appear on the streets."

Dane Coolidge makes much of this affair in his version of the matter,[8] making sport of Bat Masterson in particular as a cowardly "Town Marshal." Of course, this is all nonsense, as Bat Masterson never was City Marshal of Dodge. At the time Clay Allison is alleged to have frightened him into his hole, Bat was Sheriff of Ford County. At that time several unorganized counties were attached to Ford County for judicial purposes, and Bat had a large territory to police; but it was no part of his duty to arrest drunks and gun-toters on Front Street.[9] Though of course, Bat was usually willing to collaborate with city officers whenever trouble started.

Pink Simms remarks about this story, "I do not think that there was as much to it as some writers try to make us believe."[10]

Thomas Masterson has this to say: "Clay Allison has been written up by the whoop-em-up scribblers, and given the reputation of being a bad man and two-gun artist whose very presence on the streets of a city made the officers hunt their holes and stay therein until the terrible Clay tired of shooting up the town and took his departure. Nothing is farther from the truth. He might have had, in certain localities, a reputation as a bad man and probably did have, but in Dodge City he was just a member of a big gang . . . who came to town for the purpose of getting drunk with a six shooter on his hip. . . . On Allison's visit to Dodge City, that I recall my brother Jim was City Marshal, and Clay appeared on the streets with his gun on his hip. He was very promptly arrested, disarmed, and put in jail.[11] He later appeared in police court and paid his fine for carrying concealed weapons. His gun was returned to him when leaving town, but it didn't occur to Clay to shoot up officer Jim or even the town before bidding them goodbye.

"Clay might have been bad, somewhere, but he was wise to the extent of picking his points. Dodge City didn't quite suit him."[12]

Certainly, Clay himself was no great hero that day, if he had to take on Dutch courage and bring twenty-five rifles to back his play before he started gunning for the officers.

Some have argued that Bat was not in Dodge when Allison came to purge it. In October of 1878, he made several expeditions out of town, including his pursuit of James Kennedy. But there is no proof of this whatever.

Just why Bat Masterson should be singled out as the coward on this occasion is not at all clear. Wyatt, not Bat, was the man who shot down George Hoyt; and if, as Pink Simms declares, Clay "threatened to kill Wyatt Earp," Clay must have known that. Where was Assistant Marshal Wyatt Earp, that October day in 1878? According to Earp, Allison visited Dodge a few weeks after their difficulty in the season of 1877; and Lake quotes Wyatt as saying, "I never laid eyes on him afterward."[13]

This being so, Wyatt did not see Clay at the time Siringo says

Clay was looking for officers in Dodge; yet the Docket of the
Police Court for 1878 contains entries of Wyatt's name as making arrests or receiving fees on October 5, 14, 15, and 25. It also
enters his name for several arrests for September and November
of that year. Jim Masterson has quite as many entries in the
docket as Wyatt. They were both on duty in Dodge. It was their
job to police the town, and certainly Siringo—the only eyewitness who has left a record—makes no mention of the Sheriff,
but declares Clay was hunting for "town policemen or the City
Marshal." Some better evidence than this will have to be produced to make Bat out a coward. If anyone is to be criticized
in this affair, surely these city officers are as fair targets as
Sheriff Bat Masterson.

But if Bat did urge the city officers to let Clay alone until he
sobered up, perhaps they were smart to follow his advice. As it
was, Clay fired no shot, hurt nobody, destroyed no property.
Had he been challenged, somebody might have been killed—and
not necessarily the city officers.

The size of the mob of cowboys Clay brought with him
speaks eloquently of their respect for Dodge City officers.

The truth is that the average cowboy, spending his life in the
saddle, was hopelessly outmatched by gun-fighters of long experience, who practiced hours daily and knew how to handle
themselves in a fight. Says J. Wright Mooar, "A man was a
damned fool in those days who rubbed up against those fellows
and undertook to pit himself against them."

Bitter controversy rages still over the comparative courage,
proficiency with firearms and merits of the Marshals and other
famous gun-fighters of those days. To date, Opinion is all we
have had to go by.

What are the facts: How thoroughly did the Dodge City
Marshals tame troublemakers? What truth is there in the claim
that they enforced law and order in Dodge?

Fortunately, we may still consult the record—the Docket of
the Police Court of Dodge City.

Wyatt Earp served as peace officer in Dodge during three periods: May 17 to September 9, 1876; July 6 to late November, 1877; and May 12, 1878 to September 8, 1879.

During Wyatt's first tour of duty in Dodge, the cattle season of 1876, Stuart Lake reports that his salary was $250 per month. The bounty pool made up of fees received by all the officers at $2.50 per arrest, was divided share and share alike by Larry Deger, Marshal; Wyatt Earp, Assistant Marshal; James Masterson, Joe Mason, policemen, and Deputy Bat Masterson. The pool, Lake says, ran to about seven or eight hundred dollars a month—or about three hundred arrests and convictions.

During his second tour of duty, the cattle season of 1877, Wyatt Earp and his deputies—Neal Brown, James Masterson, Frank McLane, Ed Masterson, Bill Tilghman—and for awhile his brother, Virgil Earp—pooled the fees they earned by making arrests. Wyatt arrived to take up his duties July 5 and states that during that first month the bounty pool was nearly $1,000. As quoted by Lake, Wyatt reports, "The $2.50 bounty on a prisoner was still in force." That meant four hundred convictions.

On August 6, 1878, at the regular meeting of the City Council, among bills approved were the following:

Chas. E. Bassett, salary as Marshal	$100.00
Wyatt Earp, salary as Assis't Marshal	75.00
John Brown's salary as Policeman	75.00
James Masterson, salary as Policeman	75.00

Wyatt's salary is here reduced by $175 from what Mayor Hoover offered him in 1876, and the docket for 1878-79 shows the Marshal's fees for an arrest reduced to $2.00 from the $2.50 formerly paid.

All this would indicate a less pressing need for Wyatt's services.

It is interesting to see what fees Wyatt and his colleagues earned during this third tour, and to compare the record with the previous figures offered. Such a comparison will show whether or not, or to what degree, Dodge was able to tame the Texans, during Earp's service there.

Wyatt Earp's name appears as Marshal of Dodge City in the Docket of the Police Judge of that town only from the date of July 5, 1878, to August 5, 1879. The earlier docket seems to have disappeared.

During this period of exactly thirteen months Wyatt Earp arrested or filed complaints against thirty-five persons.

The total number of arrests by all officers recorded for 1878 is only sixty-four.

Some believe that the court record was not complete, inasmuch as the names of several well-known men (Tobe Driskill, Ed Morrison, Tom Owens) whom Wyatt Earp claimed to have arrested, jailed, and brought to trial during the season of 1878, do not appear in the Docket. Others point out that an inspection of the record shows that Judge Marshall was more meticulous than any later Dodge City judge in keeping his Docket, and suggest that some prisoners may have been haled before a justice of the peace. Yet, in that case, they argue, unless the Justice split his fees, the officer would receive nothing.

In every instance the fee paid the Marshal is recorded as $2.00 for a prisoner, which would bring the total pool during 1878 to hardly more than $100, inasmuch as certain prisoners were judged not guilty and discharged—barely one-tenth of the monthly pool of 1877.

Arrests made in 1879:

Officer Making Arrest	Number	Fees Paid
Bassett	7	$14
Earp	12	24
J. Masterson	10	20
J. Brown	0	0
	29	$58

Dividing this among the four officers, and fees collected by each in 1879 would approximate $15—a yearly pool of only $58.

Other records of the time support this finding.

In August, 1878, a local paper reports the sale of "$400 in bibles in Dodge City" which "would bear comparison to towns of lesser note."

Of that same year Eddie Foy wrote, "The majority of days passed rather peacefully in Dodge, with no killings and few fights."[14]

A year later the editor compliments the citizens on their admirable behavior at public meetings. Throwing rotten eggs, shooting out the lights, and cow-camp rowdyism had gone out of fashion in Dodge.

It is no wonder that Wyatt Earp turned to gambling, and before long headed for Tombstone. The law had come to Dodge City.

Meanwhile, Sheriff Bat Masterson was busy taming Ford County.

CHAPTER 15 ·
: INDIAN SCARE

SIX MONTHS had not passed since the Northern Cheyennes under military escort had passed through Fort Dodge, on their way to their new home on the reservation of the Southern Cheyennes, before people in Dodge City heard rumblings of dissatisfaction in the Indian Nations.

In those days there was always the chance that Indians might jump their reservation, and now that there were no buffalo left in Kansas, warriors on the loose, living on the country, were bound to kill cattle and steal horses—if they did no worse. The Northern Cheyennes under Dull Knife and Wild Hog had come from the Bighorn Mountains—a country with clear streams, cold winters, and abundant buffalo; now they found themselves in the hot, flat, malarial, gameless reservation of the Southern Cheyennes. The two divisions of the tribe had lived apart too long to have much liking for each other. Indeed the Northern Cheyennes had much Sioux blood or were married to Sioux women, spoke Sioux, and felt closer to that nation than to their own Southern relatives. On first arriving, they taunted their tame kinsmen, bragging of their own recent exploits at Custer's Last Stand and the battle with General MacKenzie on the headwaters of Powder River. The climate did not agree with them. Some died, many fell sick, and all were sick at heart.

The men of Dodge knew Indians. They had no illusions as to the character of the savages, and knew what to expect in the way of atrocities which those fierce warriors would perpetrate if once they hit the war trail. The traders, freighters, and soldiers who traversed the country to the south were well aware of the Indian's sorry plight, the ineptitude of the Indian Bureau, the corruption of the Indian Ring, and the Government's continual failure to fulfill the terms of Indian treaties. The Cheyennes found that the tools and training in farming promised them were not forthcoming, that the beef and other rations were always in short supply. Three days a week the Cheyennes went hungry. Few buffalo were to be found north of Red River, and more and more reports of depredations came from the south.

On the twenty-second of December, 1877 the *Dodge City Times* carried a typical account of what went on:

"Last Tuesday evening Mr. D. Sheedy arrived in this city from his cattle camp at the head of Salt Fork, 60 miles southeast of here, in Comanche county, and from him we learn the particulars of another sneaking, treacherous outrage perpetrated by the noble red man. On last Friday, five Indians from the Cheyenne agency came into Mr. Sheedy's cattle camp, and in their accustomed insolent manner, began each to select a horse from the herd. The men in charge of the camp, four in number, were unarmed, but supposing the Indians not to be dangerous, ordered them to leave. The Indians 'showed up' their guns and told white men to 'keep quiet or Indian would shoot.' The white man, after this injunction, held his peace, and the noble Indian proceeded to kill a fat beef, take what he could carry, and start off with four ponies. One of the ponies not being suitable, they let him go, and went on with the other three.

"The Indians claimed to be Arapahoes, but one of the men in camp who understood the dialect, said they spoke the Sioux language. These Indians evidently had reinforcements out some distance from camp, as seven or eight of the tribe had been observed lurking around that day. Mr. Sheedy has armed his men and instructed them to shoot the first red devil that attempts to lay a hand on anything about camp. He does not know whether the horses can be recovered or not, but intends to write to the agent about it. It is hardly probable he will ever get his property, as no one was ever known to get redress for depredations committed by these noble Government pirates.

"One of the Indians who helped to do the stealing was a noted chief, with but one eye, and he can be easily identified. We advise his Indianship not to wander in the vicinity of that camp again."

Indian scares were frequent in those days and the people of Kansas, who had suffered Indian outrages along the Santa Fe Trail and elsewhere for the generation past, with casualties in some years higher in proportion to the numbers engaged than the troops suffered during the Civil War, were quick to take precautions. Of them all, the men of Dodge City, because of their greater experience with the redskins, were most alert.

When news arrived that a large party of uncertain size of Northern Cheyennes had jumped the reservation and were heading back north to their beloved mountain country in defiance of the Government, rumors flew thick and fast. The Indian trail to the north passed only a few miles west of Dodge City and the citizens knew that, though the main body of women and children would follow the trail, the young warriors would be scouting, stealing, and killing for twenty miles or so on either side.

At first one of the newspapers declared the news of the outbreak a hoax, and when some persons reported killed turned up intact and some men said to have been robbed by the Indians denied the story, there was much uncertainty. There was, besides, the fear that the news of an Indian uprising would stop immigration, hurt business, and cut down traffic on the railroad. Some citizens, sparked by these fears, sent letters and telegrams East declaring that there was no truth in the rumors. On the one hand the Indian Agent announced the flight of the Cheyennes, while a brigadier general in the Army persisted in his opinion that there were no Indians within one hundred miles.

But the evidence was too strong.

On Wednesday, September 18, nine days after the Indians started north, the fire bell rang furiously. By two o'clock the citizens had assembled at the Engine House in a mass meeting. It was decided to distribute all pistols, all guns, and all the ammunition in Dodge.

The Texas stockmen who held herds on the surrounding prairie rallied to the call, bought weapons enough to arm all their cowboys, and prepared to fight shoulder to shoulder with the Kansans. On one point Texans and Kansans were in perfect agreement. Neither of them had any earthly use for redskins. They both believed heartily that the only good Indian was a dead one. And no wonder, considering what they both had suffered for fifty years past.

But more long-range guns were needed than Dodge City could provide, and the following telegram was immediately sent:

DODGE CITY, KAN., September 18, 1878

Geo. T. Anthony, Gov., Leavenworth, Kan.: Three hundred Indians are driving off stock and killing herders. They are now within six miles of our city. We are without arms, having equipped members who have gone south. Can you send us arms and ammunition? Situation alarming. We are powerless without arms and ammunition.

JAMES KELLEY, *Mayor*
C. W. WILLETT
H. E. GRYDEN
D. SHEEDY

The foregoing telegram from Dodge City was forwarded to General Pope, whose answer follows:

FORT LEAVENWORTH, KAN., September 18, 1878

Gov. Anthony: Gen. Pope in town. Telegram just received from commanding officer, Fort Dodge, who has for a week had his orders about these Indians, makes no mention of their being in the vicinity.

PLATT, A. A. G.

The facts stated in General Pope's telegram were repeated to Mayor Kelley and others of Dodge City, who responded as follows:

DODGE CITY, KAN., September 18, 1878

Gov. Anthony: No. U. S. troops here, and no arms at post. The country filled with Indians. Send arms immediately. Breech-loaders.

JAMES H. KELLEY, *Mayor*

DODGE CITY, KAN., September 18, 1878

Gov. Anthony: Indians are murdering, and burning houses within three miles of town. All the arms we had have been sent. Can you send us arms and ammunition immediately?

H. SHINN
R. W. EVANS
C. W. WILLETT
T. L. McCARTY
JAMES C. CONNOR

It is noteworthy that Bat Masterson's name does not appear, though he was Sheriff of Ford County. At the end of August, the *Times* reports that he had gone to Hot Springs, Arkansas, for rest and medical treatment, having suffered spells of vertigo since the beginning of warm weather. Bat did not return to Dodge until after the Dull Knife Raid was over, though on duty again early in October.

While the mass meeting was in session, smoke and flames were seen rising from the house of Harry Berry on an island four miles west of town. At once the rumor spread that Indians had fired the house. A locomotive loaded with armed citizens raced to the fire and arrived in time to save the stock and haystacks. P. L. Beatty, Chalk Beeson, Wyatt Earp, and S. E. Isaacson were principals in extinguishing the flames.

The families of H. P. Niess, George Horder, and Harrison Berry, who lived in that neighborhood, had seen Indians in the vicinity and had got out, heading for Dodge, only a few minutes before the fire started. Some supposed that Indians set that building on fire, others that the fire had caught from that left in the stove when the family skipped.

A second expedition rolled west to Cimarron, returning that evening without having seen any Indians along the railroad.

Meanwhile the stockmen had gathered their herds along the river. More stories of depredations were brought in as citizens were warned and abandoned their homes seeking safety in the town.

Indians had raided a number of camps or ranches south of Dodge, carrying off horses and killing several persons. The *Dodge City Times* brought out an extra. Meade City, consisting of three or four houses with perhaps twice as many inhabitants, who had just established themselves a few weeks before, lay on the trail to Dodge near Crooked Creek. The extra carried the story of what happened there when the Indians passed early Monday morning, September 16. S. M. Cook, who reported the event, saw thirteen Indians approaching. This advance party formed a circle about the hamlet, which narrowed as they approached to within a few hundred yards.

Suddenly the entire party of Indians came in sight and were soon in the village.

The settlers, having no means of escape, no horses, and being poorly armed, sensibly decided to face the music and trust to luck.

The chief of the band rode up, took off his hat and threw it on the ground in front of Captain A. J. French. The Captain, knowing something of Indians, tossed his hat down in like manner. The chief then motioned to the band indicating that everything was all right. They then asked for food.

The settlers gave them two quarters of beef, a sack of flour, coffee, and sundry other provisions. They shook hands with the Indians, who seemed very friendly, saying, "Me good Indian; me no hurt you." After eating, they raided a larder and carried off a gun with other articles. The chief gave a signal and the main party moved out. Fifteen remained for a time as a rear guard until the main party passed out of sight. As they left, the rear guard met Washington O'Connor, a mail carrier resident in the village, who was returning from Dodge in his wagon. While the settlers watched, one of the Indians fired at O'Connor and dropped him. After they were gone his body was found dead with its throat cut. He was buried near by.

The Dodge City editor identified O'Connor thus: "Some of our citizens will remember O'Connor as the sandy complexioned man who was victimized by the confidence man several weeks ago."

It was supposed by some that the Indians numbered a thousand. Certainly they outnumbered a company of eighty cavalrymen which had attacked them on the Red Hill of the Cimarron one hundred miles south. The cavalry was compelled to withdraw.

Meanwhile, there were only nineteen soldiers at Fort Dodge, and the Commandant had made no report of trouble to his superiors. Nevertheless the Governor agreed to "send arms by special in charge of Adjutant General, if U.S. troops are not protecting you."

LEAVENWORTH, KAN., September 19, 1878

P. S. Noble, Adj. Gen.: Go to Dodge City with two hundred stand of arms and ammunition, on to-day's train, unless otherwise directed from there. Do not issue arms except upon receipt of officers of county or city, joined by five responsible citizens.

GEO. T. ANTHONY

TOPEKA, September 19, 1878

James H. Kelley, Mayor, Dodge City, Kan.: Adjutant General will come with arms and ammunition by to-day's train, if you still deem it necessary. Gen. Pope says there are not seventy-five warriors among the Indians now at large. Answer at Topeka.

GEO. T. ANTHONY

On Friday, the twentieth, the Adjutant General of Kansas arrived with a stand of one hundred arms. He was met at the depot by a throng of citizens and the Silver Cornet Band.

DODGE CITY [Sept. 20, 1878]

Gov. Geo. T. Anthony: Have issued one hundred stand of arms and seven thousand rounds of ammunition to mayor of Dodge; forty stand and two thousand ammunition to citizens of Cimarron; sixty stand and ammunition to Capt. Friedly, upon urgent request. All quiet at Dodge now, and citizens feel confident that they can meet any emergency. Rumors that Indians are near Lakin, and United States troops concentrating at other points. Shall return, as nothing further can be accomplished by staying.

P. S. Noble, *Adjutant General*

Companies of cavalry and a hundred mounted infantry had already been sent from Fort Leavenworth to Fort Wallace to head off the redskins, and two companies of infantry sent from Hays to take posts on the crossing of the trail. An infantry company sent on from Dodge was posted at Pierceville and cavalry companies from Fort Reno were reported pursuing the Indians to be joined by the cavalry from Camp Supply with orders to follow. Colonel William H. Lewis, Commandant of Fort Dodge, was ordered to assume command of these troops as soon as they reached his neighborhood. Already Lewis had sent out scouts—Bill Tilghman, Joshua Webb, A. J. Anthony, and Bob Wright—to get the straight of things. The Colonel estimated the warriors in the party at about two hundred.

The troops south of the Arkansas whom Colonel Lewis was awaiting conducted their campaign in a manner that would have amazed Colonel Lewis. One cavalry officer sent out to contact the Indians, instead of sending in to Fort Dodge for ammunition and rations, repeatedly led his troop back to the fort, leaving the Indians to their own devices. Colonel Lewis was further hampered by an order requiring him to hold all troops arriving at Fort Dodge. And when several companies had united under Captain Rendlebrook and were joined by some fifty civilians and cowboys from Dodge armed with the weapons Mayor Kelley had issued, the troops went into camp on Sand Creek about the middle of the day, September 22, though they knew the Indians were encamped nearby, making no effort to contact the tribesmen.

The civilians, however, showed more energy, and within half an hour firing was heard in the direction they had gone looking for Indians. Three companies rode to the sound of the guns, found the civilians and Indians engaged, and skirmished with them. No attempt was made to surround the Indians. Two of the companies did not even leave camp to join the fight. They found the Indians in rifle pits, and skirmished with them until about 5:00 P.M., then moved three miles away and camped for the night.

Returning to the rifle pits next morning, they found the Indians gone. The Dodge City paper declares that Captain Rendlebrook had orders not to bring on a general engagement, but to follow the Indians and keep in contact with them. But with the whole night's start the Indians had, his troops could not overtake them.

On the twenty-fourth they camped on Crooked Creek and on the twenty-fifth followed the Indian trail north of the Arkansas River. At Cimarron station Colonel Lewis brought two companies of Fourth Cavalry from Fort Elliott, Texas, Captain Mauck, and one company of Nineteenth Infantry, Captain Bradford.

Colonel Lewis was infuriated by the incompetence of these officers in letting the Indians slip through their fingers, and promptly took command, pushing the pursuit to the north.

The scouts hastened back to report that the Indians were on the move again. Meanwhile Neal Brown, a partner with Bill Tilghman in a ranching venture, hurried his wife and Flora Tilghman with their children into his wagon. He drove on the run for Dodge City.

The Indians crossed the Santa Fe Railroad west of Dodge, leaving a trail seventy-five feet wide where they passed under a trestle near Pierceville. It appeared from the sign that one hundred and fifty horses were in the party. Near where the Indians crossed the railroad, they left the body of an old squaw wrapped in blankets and covered with a buffalo robe.

By this time authentic accounts of the depredations committed south of Dodge City came in. Here is what happened to one party:

Charles F. Colcord, one of the foremost builders of Oklahoma, began life as a buffalo hunter and ended as an industrialist and a financier. He was President of the State Historical Society at the time he made the address quoted (in part) here following; the address is incorporated in the twelfth volume (1934) of the *Chronicles of Oklahoma*. At the time of the Dull Knife Raid he was a range boss of the Jug Cattle Company.

"The morning of the Indian raid, Reuben Bristow and Fred Clark left our ranch headquarters on Red Fork Creek, driving a team of mules, with a wagon, en route to the Cimarron Salt Plain, for a load of rock salt, for use elsewhere on the range. They had evidently just reached the high divide between the Cimarron and Salt Fork watersheds near Jug Mott, when they met the band of Northern Cheyenne warriors, by which they were quickly surrounded. From the tracks and marks around where we found them, we could tell that the Indians had come up all around the wagon and had shot Reuben Bristow in the head from behind. The mules the boys were driving were very much afraid of a gun and the marks in the ground where they had been standing showed that they had been very restless. The tracks of the Indian ponies indicated that the Indians were all around the wagon and one could see plainly where, at the crack of the gun, the mules had plunged forward and jerked the wheels off the ground. Then the Indians had chased the wagon, filling the bodies of both boys full of arrows. The panic-stricken mules ran down the slope from the high divide into the valley of a small branch or ravine, where they were brought to a sudden stop by a thicket of willows which were of sufficient size and elasticity to lift its wheels from the ground when the mules could drag it no farther. The Indians had cut the traces and taken the mules, leaving the bodies of the two youths in the wagon-bed, where they had fallen.

"I pulled four arrows out of Bristow's heart, shot in from the right side under the arm, and drew three or four out of Fred's body. . . .

"A site for a grave for the burial of the remains of our slain friends and companions was selected, back up the slope, near the divide where they had met their tragic fate. The September weather was intensely hot and dry, there having been no rains for several weeks. It surely was a hard job to dig that gravel with shovel and spade in that dry joint clay.

"Always, two of us would dig while the third member of our party would remain on watch at the highest point on the nearby divide. When one of the two diggers would get tired, he would mount guard on the high point, while the one thus relieved would go down and take his turn at helping to excavate the grave.

"Finally, when the grave was large enough to hold the two bodies, our next effort was to extricate the wagon which was resting on those bent willow saplings. Some of the largest of these had to be cut. . . . Then, with riatas tied from saddlehorns to wagon-tongue, it was pulled up the slope, out of the ravine, and into position at the grave. The transfer of these remains from the wagon into the grave—swollen as they were by decomposition to twice their natural size—was a gruesome task as well as a sad duty.

"When we had finished covering the bodies in the grave someone said that a prayer should be offered. All three of us were uneducated cowboys who had had no chance to attend church services or Sunday school, so none of us knew what to say or do under the circumstances. Both of the other two declined to do what all of us thought should be done, so both said to me, 'Charley, you will have to say something.'

"Now we all believed, as all men who are reared out in the open must and always will believe, that there is a God, who rules and overrules in the affairs of men. We had watched the sun, moon, and stars in their courses; we had night-herded by the North Star, for years, using it as a time-piece; every spear of grass in the prairie verdure, every flower that spangled its face, every wind that swept the plain and every note sung by the birds bore witness to the existence of a great, unseen, Divine Power.

So, knowing in my own soul the existence of such a Supreme Being, I took off my hat and raised my face to the skies as I said, 'God, take care of these poor boys.'

"Such was the prayer that I offered."

Little Wolf, the war chief who led the Indians, afterward declared that—until armed civilians from Dodge joined forces with the troops on Sand Creek—he had warned his warriors not to molest the settlers.

If this be true, he was unable to control his young men. The engagement on Sand Creek took place on September 22 and, as will be seen from the list below, seven-tenths of the civilians killed by Indians south of the Arkansas and all the wounded hurt there were attacked by Indians before the men from Dodge joined forces with the troops.

CIVILIAN INJURIES AND LOSSES SUSTAINED SOUTH OF ARKANSAS RIVER

Killed 10

2 young men, nephews of Mr. Colcord, Sept. 12, 1878
Dow, cattle herder for Mr. Kinsley
John Evans, herder of Mr. Sheedy, Sept. 12, 1878
Warren Richardson, Sept. 13, 1878
George Simmonds, cook for Chapman and Tuttle, Sept. 18, 1878
Con-Red, herder for W. C. Quinlan, Sept. 19, 1878
Thomas Murray, from Quinlan's Camp, Sept. 21, 1878
Samuel Leforce, From Quinlan's Camp, Sept. 21, 1878
O'Connor, mail carrier, Sept. 24, 1878

Wounded 5

Walter Payne, leg broken and thumb shot off, Sept. 13, 1878
Charles Payne, 3 yrs. old, shot in body, Sept. 13, 1878
Nora Payne, 1 yr. old, shot through breast, breaking top of left shoulder
2 men, strangers, Sept. 13, 1878

Stock Stolen or Destroyed 640

400 sheep
126 horses
114 cattle

The Government later paid claims in the amount of $4,348.35.

So far as Dodge City was concerned, the Dull Knife Raid was just another Indian scare—bigger than usual, no doubt—but equally harmless to the townsmen. The ineptitude of the Army officers had largely foiled the efforts of the aggressive gun-fighters sent out, and the redskins had made their getaway almost without loss. The only effect of the civilians' share in the skirmish on Sand Creek was to make the Indians abandon their fighting and take to forced marches—and, of course, to make them bitter and revengeful towards *all* white settlers who stood in their path. One taste of Dodge City's fighting quality sent the fiercest Indians on the Plains skedaddling.

Comparatively few of the settlers and stockmen around Dodge suffered during the Dull Knife Raid. They understood Indians and the measures Dodge City took to warn them saved many.

But up near the Nebraska line on the Beaver things were very different. There the savages ravaged a settlement of Bohemians new to the Plains and quite unprepared to defend themselves. Other settlers in that part of the State suffered almost as much. In all forty-three persons were killed, about twice as many wounded, their property destroyed or carried off, two boys kidnaped, and five women and girls ravished. One girl who was in the hands of the savages all one night had nearly all her hair torn out.

A Dodge City paper under the headline HOW TO SETTLE INDIAN RAIDS quotes the *Kinsley Graphic*:

"The stockmen who have lost heavily by the depredations of the red devils, are justly indignant at the apparent studied effort of Pettibone to misrepresent the situation, and the milk and water policy of the government in pursuing and punishing the savage thieves and murderers. If left to the cattle men and citizens, those Cheyenne marauders would never repeat their little game in the Southwest."

In November the firearms sent by the Governor were called in. The Dull Knife Raid was over.

CHAPTER 16

: KILLING OF DORA HAND

THE PRINCIPAL places of amusement in Dodge City during its heyday were the dance halls. Admission was free, and the house derived its profit from the sale of liquor. Eddie Foy has given us our clearest picture of the dance hall and its women in those days:[1]

"Some of the proprieties were very carefully observed . . . for example, a woman, no matter whether she was a housewife, a dance hall girl or even a courtesan (and mind you, the last two were not necessarily the same), was treated with grave courtesy on the street. Any man who failed to observe this canon got into trouble.

"It was an eye-opener to me to discover that the women who entertained Dodge, no matter in what capacity, didn't as a rule dress in silks and satins, but in ginghams and cheap prints; and that goes for the dance hall girls when they were on duty, too. In some prosperous mining camps where there were lucky prospectors with their pockets stuffed with dust, some of the girls were togged out in all the flashy finery they could lay hands on. But really wealthy men were not very numerous in Dodge; certainly the cowboys who came there didn't have money to throw at the birds, though they sometimes spent six months' pay in twenty-four hours.

"There were other impressions of such towns which have

gotten slightly warped by time and distance also. Their profession may not appeal to the reader of today as having been a very moral one, but I want to say that many of those dance hall girls were personally as straight as a deaconess. I knew some who were widows, some married ones with worthless or missing husbands, and not a few of these had children. Of course their family affairs were not made public. These girls were merely hired entertainers; their job was to dance with the men, talk to them, perhaps flirt with them a bit and induce them to buy drinks—no more. They pretended to drink with the men, but if a girl drank with every chap who bought for her, she would have been thoroughly soused and out of commission before the evening was over. I knew a few of these girls who didn't drink at all; but for some such girl a bottle of wine might be sold a thousand times in a year.

"I wish I could present to an audience of today an adequate picture of one of those old western amusement halls. Writers and artists have tried to do it, the movies have tried it, but all in vain—the sounds are lacking—the songs and patter from the stage at one end, where the show began at eight o'clock and continued until long after midnight; the click and clatter of poker chips, balls, cards, dice, wheels and other devices at the other end, mingled with a medley of crisp phrases—'Thirty-five to one!' 'Get your money down, folks!' 'Eight to one on the colors.' 'Keno!' 'Are you all down, gentlemen? Then up she rises!' and a thousand other bits representing the numerous varieties of games that were being played, and which, though mostly spoken in a moderate tone, combined to make a babel of sound. All around the room, up above, a sort of mezzanine, ran a row of private boxes—and they were boxes, indeed! As plain as a packing case!—where one might sit and drink and watch the show. When the various stage performances were over, there was dancing which might last until four A.M. or daybreak."

During the summer of 1878 there was another performer in Dodge who enjoyed popular favor equal to that of Eddie Foy.

This was the beautiful woman known to history as Dora Hand, *alias* Fannie Keenan. A local paper on August 10 published the following notice: "Hattie Smith and Fannie Keenan take a benefit at Ham Bell's Varieties next Wednesday night. They are general favorites and will be sure to draw a crowded house."

Fannie Keenan was as handsome, generous, and talented as she was versatile. She was known as Queen of the Fairy Belles, the most popular of the dance hall women. It was believed she had once been a singer in grand opera, and certainly of nights she charmed her listeners singing sentimental ballads in Dodge City's theaters.

During the day she proved a kindly, resourceful, and energetic person, always ready to help anyone in trouble. If some raw boy from Texas who had never even seen a train before lost his pile at faro or drank too much redeye and was rolled south of the Deadline, she could be counted on to grubstake him or redeem his saddle so that he could ride home. She asked no security or even the names of the men she helped. When someone fell sick, she was willing to play the part of a practical nurse. Of course, in such a small community everybody knew all about everybody else, and few people in Dodge were more respected than Fannie Keenan. Stuart Lake quotes one old-timer: "The only thing anyone could hold against her was her after-dark profession, and by Godfrey, I allow she elevated that considerably."[2]

That summer of 1878 the Mayor of Dodge, James H. "Dog" Kelley, one of the proprietors of the Alhambra Saloon and Gambling House, one day thought it necessary to bounce a visiting Texan, James W. "Spike" Kennedy.

This altercation between Kennedy and Kelley may have taken place on July 29, 1878, since the Docket of the Police Judge of Dodge City for the following day records the arrest by Wyatt Earp of a man who gave his name as "James Kennedy" for carrying a pistol. The plea recorded was guilty and the fine and costs were collected immediately.

More probably, it happened on August 17, when Marshal

Charles "Senator" Bassett brought one "James Kennedy" into
court on a charge of being "disorderly."

Kennedy had proved no match for Kelley in a rough-and-
tumble, and not being allowed to carry arms in Dodge, for some
time found no way to have his revenge. At length he caught the
train to Kansas City, bought the fastest horse he could find there,
and brought it back to Dodge.

Bridge Street (now Second Avenue) ran north from the river,
bisecting the Plaza. East of Bridge Street and south of the railroad tracks, facing north, the principal buildings were the Comique Theater, the Green Front Saloon, and the Western Hotel.
Behind the Comique was a cottage. Behind the saloon and the
hotel a row of small two-room shacks had been built. In one of
these Mayor Kelley slept of nights when in Dodge.

Kennedy knew this, of course, and apparently planned to
ambush the Mayor there.

Meanwhile Mayor Kelley had fallen ill and had been taken to
the hospital at Fort Dodge for treatment. Kennedy, not wishing
to be seen in Dodge, arrived by night and so was unaware of
this.

Before leaving for the hospital Kelley had rented his shack to
Dora Hand and another singer. When the dance hall closed, the
two girls went there and went to bed. In those small rooms the
beds had to be in the same position at all times. Dora Hand slept
in the bed formerly used by Kelley, her friend in the other. On
that dull, misty October morning about half past four, a mounted
man rode up to Kelley's shack and blazed away, aiming at the
Mayor's bed.

Four pistol shots were heard. Pistol shots in Dodge, as the
paper notes, were of common occurrence then; but this firing
betokened something fatal. Assistant Marshal Wyatt Earp and
Officer Jim Masterson hurried to investigate. Before the firing
the barkeep had seen two men lounging in the dim shadows
outside the solitary saloon then open. Few night-walkers were

abroad at that unreasonable hour and he noticed that they drifted away.

Shortly after the firing Kennedy and his companion returned and entered the saloon. When the officers arrived, Kennedy mounted his horse, and as soon as he was out of pistol range galloped away down the road toward Fort Dodge. Earp and Masterson arrested his companion and threw him in the calaboose. The fellow declared he thought Kennedy had done the shooting, and the officers had good reason to believe him. Kennedy had headed east, though his ranch was southwest, near Tascosa.[3]

No doubt Kennedy was gloating over having killed the Mayor of Dodge; certainly he believed nobody in Texas would turn him in.

The story titled "Midnight Assassin" from the next issue of the *Dodge City Globe* (Tuesday, October 8) may be quoted:

"Dora Hand alias Fannie Keenan foully murdered while in bed and fast asleep. . . . On Friday morning about four o'clock two shots were fired into a small frame building situated back of the railroad track and back of the Western House occupied by Miss Fannie Garretson and Miss Fannie Keenan. The building was divided into two rooms by a plastered partition, Miss Keenan occupying the back room. The first shot after passing through the front door, struck the floor, passed through the carpet and facing of the partition, and lodged in the next room. The second shot also passed through the door, but apparently more elevated, striking the first bed, passing over Miss Garretson who occupied the bed, through two quilts, through the plastered partition, and after passing through the bed clothing of the second bed, struck Fannie Keenan in the right side under the arm, killing her instantly.

"The party who committed this cowardly act must have been on horseback and close to the door when the two shots were fired. From what we can learn those shots were intended for another party who has been absent for a week and who formerly occupied the first room. Thus the assassin misses his intended victim and kills another while fast asleep who never spoke a word after she was shot."

The paper also quotes the verdict of the coroner's inquest:

The State of Kansas, Ford County, S.S.

An inquisition holden at Dodge City in said county on the fourth day of October A. D. 1878 before me a Justice of the Peace for Dodge township, said county, acting as coroner on the body of Fannie Keenan, there lying dead, by the jurors whose names are hereunto subscribed. Said jurors on their oath do say that Fannie Keenan came to her death by gunshot wound and that in their opinion the said gunshot wound was produced by a bullet discharged from a gun in the hands of one James Kennedy, in testimony whereof the said jurors hereunto set their hands, the day and year aforesaid. P. L. Beatty, foreman; John B. Means, J. H. Cornell, W. Straiter, Thomas McIntire, John Lougheed, attest: R. G. Cook, Justice of the Peace, Acting Coroner for Dodge township, said county.

Wyatt Earp, City Marshal and Deputy U.S. Marshal, had demonstrated his ability to cope with Texas gunmen. Accordingly, Mayor Kelley sent him to lead the posse. The members of this posse are given with some variation by different authorities, but it certainly included Wyatt Earp, Bat Masterson, Charlie Bassett, and William Tilghman. Lake quotes Kelley as telling Wyatt to bring Kennedy in alive. Said he, "Dodge'll want to deal with him as a community."

Bat Masterson supposed Kennedy was heading for Cheyenne, Wyoming, but Wyatt and Tilghman had a hunch that the direction of Kennedy's flight was only a blind and that he would circle back and ford the Cimarron near Wagon Bed Springs. In this way he would avoid the direct route of the Jones and Plummer Trail and cut the Texas Trail miles away in the Indian Nations. Taking the short cut, the posse hoped to arrive ahead of the fugitive.

As they rode, the officers warned persons along their route to say nothing of their passing, and though Kennedy made diligent inquiries he never learned who the horsemen were.

They were delayed somewhat in the afternoon by a terrific hailstorm and rode all night through the rain, but at daybreak they had ridden seventy miles and reached the ford. Though the storm had badly washed the trail, they could find no sign showing that Kennedy had passed, and it seemed unlikely that he could have got so far before the storm broke.

A near-by settler whose sod house they visited said he had seen no rider pass before the storm. There they had breakfast, unsaddled their horses and turned them out to graze so as to avoid all sign of a sheriff's posse. About four o'clock that afternoon Tilghman saw Kennedy cautiously approaching. Wyatt got out his binoculars and identified the wanted man. Kennedy halted, afraid to come on. At that the posse took a position some distance from the house. When Kennedy saw the posse, Wyatt ordered him to halt.

Instead, though armed with a carbine, two .44 caliber revolvers, and a bowie knife, he put spurs to his horse, slashed it with his quirt, and wheeled away. Bat threw down on him with his rifle and Kennedy lurched, almost losing his seat, but the horse ran on. Wyatt, anxious to take Kennedy alive in accordance with his orders, fired at the horse. It fell, pinning Kennedy to the earth. The posse ran up and pulled Kennedy from under the horse. Bat took hold of the man's right arm, which his bullet had shattered; Bat could hear the bones craunch.

Since the posse had come for him, Kennedy naturally assumed that Kelley was dead. But to make sure he inquired and so learned that he had killed a woman. Furious, he turned on Bat and cursed the astonished officer for not making a better shot.

The posse took Kennedy back to Dodge where Dr. T. L. Mc-Carty, Dr. W. S. Tremaine of Fort Dodge, and Dr. E. B. Fryer of Kansas City attended him. They removed four inches of bone from his shattered right arm near the elbow, leaving it useless. During this difficult and painful operation, Kennedy lost a great deal of blood, but behaved with firmness and courage under the knife. (In those days, of course, transfusions and anesthetics were unknown.) Kennedy was ill a long time, but was finally brought to trial. His wealthy father came from Texas and at length Kennedy was acquitted on the ground that the evidence was not sufficient to convict. In those days ballistics had not been heard of and there was no eyewitness to the killing.

As for Kennedy, he is said to have used his left arm well enough to shoot a man or two after his acquittal. But before long he met another who was faster on the draw.

A Dodge City paper pays this tribute to Kennedy's lady victim: "The deceased came to Dodge City this summer and was engaged as vocalist in the Varieties and Comique shows. She was a prepossessing woman and her artful winning ways brought many admirers within her smiles and blandishments. If we mistake not, Dora Hand has an eventful history. She had applied for a divorce from Theodore Hand. After a varied life the unexpected death messenger cuts her down in the full bloom of gayety and womanhood. She was the innocent victim."

Dora Hand was buried in the new Prairie Grove Cemetery north of town.

CHAPTER 17 :
: CRIME AND
: PUNISHMENT

IN EARLY DODGE, as elsewhere on the frontier, men's conception of crime differed from that of our time. In those days, if a man shot dead was armed at the time, and had had fair warning and a chance to draw his gun, it was not called murder, but a killing. If his wounds were in front, it was usually assumed that he had been justifiably killed.

And though the ordinance against carrying a deadly weapon came to be enforced north of the Deadline, when a killing occurred south of it, the officers might ignore it, provided that there were no destruction of property or promiscuous shooting, dangerous to citizens of Dodge. In most cowtowns, it was hardly considered a crime for one transient to shoot another.

Much has been written of the code of the gun-fighter—the code which held that one must not shoot an unarmed man nor any man in the back. Many great gun-fighters and marshals lived up to this code, but such men were always in the minority. The notion that on the frontier killings were common and murders were rare is not borne out by the record. For every killing where the victim got an even break, several murders are known, and some of these were of the most shocking and cold-blooded kind; and even in a killing, it was always possible for the gunman to approach his victim from behind, call to him, and as he turned around, let him have it before he realized his danger.

In and around Dodge crimes of violence were more numerous

than those of any other sort. Not a few of these were crimes of passion, killings resulting from a fight over some woman, by two men, or by two women over one man. Yet, though assault and battery, mayhem, highway robbery, drunkenness, gambling, and fornication flourished, the record is singularly clear of the more bestial, cruel, and unnatural crimes. I have uncovered only one case of cruelty to animals, one of brutal flogging, and scarcely any of sexual perversion, abuse of children, wife-beating, dope-peddling, kidnaping, extortion, or rape. Dodge had no Jack the Ripper, no muggers—a woman was far safer in frontier Dodge than in any sizable city in the States today.

There is but one story of attempted poisoning, though every hide hunter had quantities of arsenic and every wolfer used strychnine. And though train robbers, horsethieves, and cattle thieves were numerous and busy, burglary was rare, and petty thievery almost unknown. Only one case of forgery turns up, and blackmailers, racketeers, and cracksmen were unknown. Tramps and dead beats, however, abounded; and sharpers, swindlers, pimps, and confidence men frequently infested Dodge. Still, outlawry and bold bawdry were more typical.

It is noteworthy too that most of the recorded crimes committed in and around Dodge were perpetrated by visitors and transients, *not* by citizens of the town.

This item from the local paper is fairly typical of the cattle shipping season in Dodge:

"The boys and girls across the Dead Line had a high old time last Friday. They sang and danced and fought and bit and cut and had a good time generally. Five knockdowns, three broken heads, two cuts, and several incidental bruises. Unfortunately none of the injuries will prove fatal."

Men were sometimes killed over what seem now very trivial matters.

Thus, in 1876, three buffalo hunters from Dodge were out on the prairie preparing to move camp, when two of the men then in the wagon fell out, because one of them kicked the other's pony in the ribs. The driver, to whom the pony belonged, had started the team off; but the pony, tied to the wagon alongside, balked and refused to move out. The other man in the wagon, without rising from his seat, kicked the pony. Apparently the animal was not abused, but its owner would not let the matter drop, and in the fight which followed was shot dead.

Again in 1885, a settler, having staked a claim near Dodge, came to town with his brother and three friends to file upon it. That evening he engaged in a game of seven-up with one of the local gamblers. The newspaper alleges that the dispute arose "about a matter of 50¢." Five shots were fired, one killing the settler instantly. Three bystanders and the gambler were wounded, but Sheriff Pat Sughrue courageously disarmed the brother of the dead man, thus preventing further bloodshed. Two men were arrested, but apparently nobody was ever brought to trial.

One day in 1878, a train master employed by Lee & Reynolds had a misunderstanding with his cook and fired him, telling him to report to the office for his time. The cook complied. But soon after the train master cooled down and relented. He followed the cook and asked him to go back to work.

The cook, still huffy, declined.

Then the train master, his dander rising again, said, "I'll see about that," and jerked his gun.

But the cook was just as quick on the draw as his boss. Both fired at the same moment. The train master's slug cut the cook's scalp, but he caught the cook's shot through the lungs and fell to the ground. The cook gave himself up and was confined in the guardhouse at Camp Supply. The train master slowly recovered in the post hospital. He exonerated the cook, saying, "Joe was not to blame, he only defended himself—as any man would do when threatened."

On another occasion, a man from Dodge turned up in Texas to hunt buffalo. It was then the custom never to ask a stranger's name, but to inquire, "What do you want to be called?" At this, the man from Dodge laughed and replied, "Oh, just call me Buffalo Bill the Second." The fellow's presumption so angered one of the Texans that one day soon after, as the fellow passed by, the Texan threw his Big 50 down on him. Then there was only Buffalo Bill the First.

Gunmen, in those days, usually fired at the body of their adversary, as it offered a larger target, and a wound in the vitals was generally fatal. Head wounds were rare, and usually were made by a club or gun barrel used as a club.

Nowadays, of course, abdominal wounds are more curable, and killers are more apt to aim at the head.

A frequent cause for killings in western Kansas in those days was the resentment of some discharged employee toward his former boss.

V. F. Wyman, a much-respected stockman, lived with his wife and their baby on Spring Creek in Comanche County, where he ran about five hundred cattle and a smaller number of horses. He had, as he thought, made settlement with a former herder of his who went by the name of Cherokee Dan. The two men could not agree, Dan claiming more than Wyman thought fair, and refusing to give a receipt for what was offered.

Some days later Wyman, with Thomas and Edward Harper and William Parker, set out for Dodge. Wyman and Thomas were on horseback, the other two rode in the wagon. They were overtaken by Dan, who without a word of warning fired twice, both shots hitting Wyman's back.

Then, passing Wyman, Dan turned and fired two more shots into Wyman, who fell from his horse. Dan looked at his writhing victim, said, "You are not dead yet, I'll give you another," and shot Wyman as he lay on the ground. They had a gun in the wagon and one or two pistols among them, but the shooting was done so quickly, and the party was so taken by surprise, that they made no effort to shoot Dan.

Having emptied his gun, the murderer, driving Wyman's horse before him, rode swiftly away.

Wyman lingered about half an hour.

The Governor of Kansas offered a reward of $500 for "Cherokee Dan."

When the Santa Fe was being built westward beyond Dodge City, Thomas A. Butler, the railroad contractor, had a construction camp twelve miles west of Fort Dodge. At every such camp there was a sod or shanty saloon.

One day Butler's bookkeeper had words with a workman who had been fired. That evening as the bookkeeper sat at table in the saloon, the other fellow came to the door with a shotgun and killed the bookkeeper. Butler and a close chum of the bookkeeper's were near by. Both carried six-shooters, and as the workman ran they fired and brought him down. Then the bookkeeper's chum in a frenzy of rage ran out, and standing over the wounded man, emptied another six-shooter into his body. Then in his fury he picked up the shotgun and smashed it over the man's head. In all, the man had twelve bullet holes in his body.

The coroner came out from Dodge City and returned with both bodies loaded in the back of his spring wagon. When he reached town he discovered that the murderer was still alive. The doctor treated him and he was held under guard. To everyone's surprise he began to recover, but evidently "played possum" on them. One night he skipped out and was never brought to trial.

Several times the mail stage was held up. In September, 1885, the Tascosa stage was rolling within a few miles of Dodge City, when three mounted men rode up. Their leader shouted at the driver, A. E. Davis, "Open the mail sack." Riding in the stage were Grant Wells and Lizzie Miller. Behind it Grant's young brother, Wilford, was riding a horse. The men went on back and assaulted Wilford. At that, Grant jumped from the stage and begged the men to stop abusing his brother, as Wilford was sick.

One of the ruffians said, "I am a wolf," and he and one of his partners fired a shot apiece at Grant. The latter returned the fire, making three shots, one of which took effect in the head of the one who appeared to be the leader. He fell from his horse and expired immediately. His companions deserted him and fled southward.

Grant Wells came on to Dodge in the stage and surrendered himself to the authorities. Soon after, the dead man's body was brought in and turned over to Ham Bell, undertaker. An inquest was held before Justice Lybrand, acting coroner. The verdict was that Robert E. Robbins had died from a shot at the hands of Grant Wells, and that the shooting was justifiable. Wells was thereupon released from custody.

The dead man and his two companions had arrived in Dodge City the week before with a cattle outfit. He was evidently hard up, from papers found in one of the pockets of his saddle bags. The following is quoted from a letter written to his mother in lead pencil: "I am going to rob someone tonight, and if I get out all right I will come home this winter. . . . I was raised by a good honest mother. My father was long before me gone and I will perhaps go tonight. . . ."

The National Police Gazette made this affair the subject of an illustration it published. The editor of the *Kansas Cowboy*[1] comments: "This picture doubtless resembles the original scene about as correctly as would a Dodge City street fight or the soldiers' encampment at Topeka!"

At the time Robbins was killed, a nickel was the only money found on his person. His body was buried in the Potter's field. His revolver, horse, and saddle bags, valued at $60, were sold to pay the expenses of his burial.

Ed Prather and Grant Wells were two notable gunmen who advertised by word of mouth day in and day out. . . . They seemed to be conscious of themselves all the time and looked for the slightest justification to admit that they were the "baddest of the bad."

Wells, while Assistant City Marshal, had a gun-fight with a cowboy in which both fired together. Wells killed his man, but the ball from his opponent's gun lodged in the shell ejector of Wells's gun. He never removed it. It became his proudest possession. He yearned for an excuse to spin the thrilling story in its minutest detail as he exhibited the gun with the leaden bullet in its mechanism.

One day in the late eighties, City Marshal McCoy tried to arrest Prather and some other members of the "gang" who were in the Green Front Saloon.

In this "Green Front Fight" many shots were fired in the darkness. McCoy was hit in the leg and Prather in the shoulder. Immediately, Assistant Marshal Wells, Prather's loyal friend, unceremoniously vacated his job and took Prather to a distant ranch to recover where the law could not find him.

Prather, after recovering from the Green Front Fight, went into the saloon business, and decided to put on a show which would attract customers.

The grand climax of the shoot-'em-up stunts came when Prather declared, "I am the great-grandson of William Tell."

He then placed a tin can on his head and told Wells to shoot it off—which he did.

Wells, not to be outdone, declared that he too had some of William Tell's blood coursing through his veins. He removed a silk hat from the head of a recent arrival from the effete East, set it on his head crosswise, folded his arms and called out, "Ed, shoot a hole through this hard boiled katy."

Prather took deliberate aim and shot a hole through the hat, giving the crowd a thrill. Prather then bragged to the crowd, "I'm going to put another ball through that same hole to prove to you that Dr. W. F. Carver" (the marksman with Buffalo Bill's show in its early days, then billed as "The Evil Spirit of the Plains") "has nothing on me in the shooting game."

Prather threw up his gun and fired. His shot hit Wells in the forehead, killing him instantly. This ended the street show. Prather shoved his .45 back into its holster, hastily left town, and rode off to join the county seat war at Leoti.[2]

Afterward, Bill Tilghman, then City Marshal of Leoti, had to kill Prather in self-defense.

There were few cases of lynch law in Dodge. But sometimes the officers were not successful, and citizens took the law into their own hands.

Enos Moseley, a Kansan, just eighteen, came to Dodge City in July, 1877, looking for work. Five years earlier the Kiowas had killed his father, and he and his brother John now had a ranch on the Medicine Lodge in Barber County.

John had commanded the Barber County Militia during the Indian outbreak of 1874; he and eleven others had attacked a large band of redskins—five of whom bit the dust. Now John was on the trail bringing cattle from New Mexico.

Enos found work, but when wages were reduced he quit. For a week he remained in town, looking for a better job.

Meanwhile a herd belonging to Murphy and Hines was moving up from Texas. One of the hands went by the name of William Samples; he was suspicious of every stranger who came his way. On the way, V. F. Oden, the boss herder, hired a stranger to help drive the herd.

Samples somehow got it into his head that the new hand was an officer come to arrest him, and one day when the two were out together, Samples put a revolver to his head and wanted to know if he had a warrant for him. The new hand talked fast, and convinced Samples that he was not an officer and had no warrant. Samples let him go.

The outfit went into camp on Saw Log Creek a few miles from Dodge City.

On August 1, Enos Moseley hired out to Oden and joined the camp on the Saw Log. He met the other fellows and had a brief casual conversation with Samples too—about tobacco. There was no disagreement between the men, nor any apparent cause for hard feelings or suspicion.

That night Moseley spread his blankets in the bed of the

wagon. But, finding it too warm there, he bedded down on the ground near the other men. Moseley's move may have roused Sample's suspicions. But Moseley never dreamed of danger and went fast asleep.

Oden and Bob Lauderdale had gone out to take a look at the herd; they came back to camp about 2:00 A.M. They had spread their rolls close to Samples' bed.

Samples always slept with a cocked revolver in his right hand.

Now, as they came to lie down, Samples called out, "Is that you, Volery and Bob?"

They answered, "Yes."

Samples said, "How's the herd?"

Oden answered, "All right."

Then Samples, pointing at Moseley, demanded, "Who is that laying at my feet?"

Oden replied, "That's a stranger." Then he noticed that Cartwright, another cowhand, who also lay close beside Samples, had his foot in Moseley's face; Oden told him to take it away.

Samples declared, "I believe that is the son-of-a-bitch I've been wanting to kill." He raised up and fired across Cartwright's body at Moseley's head.

Everybody jumped up, told him, "You have murdered this man."

Said Samples, "I don't care if I have. I heard him and Trimble say they were going to kill me tonight. This man got out of the wagon and was watching for me to go to sleep."

All the others were unarmed. Trimble—and no wonder—started for the wagon, where there was a loaded gun. But Samples asked Lauderdale who that was, threw down his pistol on Trimble and said, "I've got a notion to kill that son-of-a-bitch." Lauderdale bravely stepped between the men, saying, "Don't shoot!"

Samples, revolver in hand, kept the herders at bay, mounted a pony standing near, and galloped away in the darkness.

Moseley never awakened, but remained unconscious until death. The bullet had entered the top of his head about four inches above the left temple, and passed out through the back of the head.

The two men had never seen each other before Moseley joined the outfit—he had never been in Texas. He was moreover, a sober, hard-working young man, well-liked and of excellent reputation.

Dodge was shocked and furious. This was no ordinary killing. It was, said the *Dodge City Times* (August 4, 1877), "one of the most cowardly, sneaking, underhanded, villainous murders . . . that the annals of crime have ever been stained with."

The weather was hot, and since the burial could not be postponed until distant relatives might arrive, M. W. Sutton, who had known Enos well, undertook the funeral arrangements. The body was laid in a neat coffin and committed to the earth, Trustee P. L. Beatty officiating—presumably on Boot Hill.

Coroner Galland formed a jury and held an inquest.

Oden and Cartwright were first sworn and gave their testimony. Oden testified that Samples had worked for him about three months, and was not to his knowledge a drinking man. It was surmised that he was a fugitive from justice.

Here follows the coroner's report:

STATE OF KANSAS $\Big\}$ SS.
FORD COUNTY

An inquisition holden in the county and State aforesaid, on the 2d day of August, A. D. 1877, before me, S. Galland, Coroner of said county, on the body of Enos Moseley, there lying dead, by the jurors whose names are hereunto subscribed.

The said jurors upon their oaths do say that the said body is the body of Enos Moseley, who came to his death on the 2d day of August, A. D. 1877, and that said death was caused by a gun shot or pistol shot wound inflicted upon him on the 2d day of August, A. D., 1877, by William Samples, and that said wounding was done feloniously.

In testimony whereof, the said jurors have hereunto set their hands, on this 2d day of August, A. D. 1877.

Jurors, G. E. HADDER, *Foreman*.
JOHN MUELLER.
JAS. F. MANION.
G. M. HOOVER.
J. COLLAR.
P. SUGHRUE.
Attest: S. GALLAND, *Coroner*.

Sheriff Charles Bassett, Undersheriff Bat Masterson, Al Updegraff, and one of the herders were scouring the country for Samples. They were out two days, but found no trace of him.

Meanwhile, some of the cowboys took over.

The day after the murder, a man came to the cattle camp to tell Oden that he had seen Samples: "He came out of the brush to my house to get something to eat. I didn't let on I had heard about him, and fed him. After he ate he took to the brush again."

Three men saddled up and tracked Samples to the spot where he had gone into a clump of bushes on the creek.

As they approached, Samples jumped out. One called, "Give up your six-shooter, and you'll not be hurt!"

"I will not," he shouted. "You have to kill me first." With that he began to shoot.

Three times he fired, while they fired seven. Then he fell, but he was only wounded.

Again they demanded that he throw away his six-shooter, and again he refused.

One then threatened to shoot him again if he did not. Then Samples threw his revolver away.

The sun was going down as they carried him into the dugout. He was shot through the bowels and wounded in the neck.

News of the capture was brought to Dodge City late Thursday evening, shortly after the officers had come back from their fruitless search.

Soon after, Sheriff Bassett and M. W. Sutton went to the

dugout on Saw Log Creek. The wounded man lingered in terrible agony until the forenoon of the next day (Friday, August
4). Until the very last he kept begging for his revolver, and
boasted that he was as good as any six men on earth.

But before he died he confessed that he had killed Moseley
believing him to be the nephew of a man whom he had shot in
Arkansas. He also admitted that Samples was not his real name.

They rolled him in a blanket and buried him on the prairie.
It does not appear that an inquest was thought necessary.[3]

The Vigilantes and Marshals of Dodge City appear to have
got rid of their victims by warning them to leave town or, if
that failed, by shooting them. There were far more guns than
trees around Dodge, and the object of the law-abiding was not
so much punishment as good riddance.

According to Bob Wright,[4] there were only two such hang-
ings, both at the same time.

Wright says that one night long after sundown a small bunch
of men rode into Dodge, stopped at his store, bought a piece of
rope, then quietly mounted and rode away into the darkness,
heading northeast.

Next day news arrived that horsethieves were hanging in the
boughs of a huge cottonwood in the center of a nice little bottom
near the crossing of Saw Log Creek twelve miles from town.

Cole and Calahan were the men so punished and are mentioned by name in the Dodge City paper. Calahan was a well-
bred young man, the son of a Christian minister. The young
fellow had come to Dodge looking for work and was said to
have hired out to herd horses for Tom Owens, one of the leaders
of the notorious Owens–Dutch Henry gang. Bad company.

Sometimes the wrong man caught it.

One July afternoon in 1883 three cowboys rode into Dodge
to see the town. They took in a dance hall or two, and two of
them were soon somewhat under the influence of liquor. The
third, Johnny Ballard, who was perfectly sober, feared that his
friends would get into trouble and kept trying to get them out

of town. He quietly headed them for the bridge. It was the road past Bond and Nixon's Dance Hall. The others reined up their ponies, lighted down and went into the saloon. Ballard, still in the saddle, anxiously waited for his friends.

They came out again, but no sooner did they reach the street than one pulled his pistol and began shooting up the town.

At that Ballard, who was unarmed, kicked his horse into a run, heading for the bridge. The other two immediately forked their broncs and followed.

By that time, the *Ford County Globe* alleges, "The officers and a deputy sheriff or two were close at hand. All of them joined in the shooting." The three cowboys, Ballard in the lead, rode on the dead run, but just as Johnny Ballard reached the drawbridge, a bullet struck the back of his neck, passed through his head, and came out between his mouth and chin. Johnny dropped from his horse. His companions rushed on across the bridge and rode south hard as their horses could go.

With half a dozen or more men shooting at the cowboys at the same time it was impossible to know who fired the fatal shot.

D. M. Frost, editor of the *Globe*, was caustic in his indignation at this killing: "It was a very unfortunate affair that young Ballard should thus pay the penalty of others' crimes, if any have been committed. We do not countenance the promiscuous shooting off of firearms on our streets by individuals any more than we do by self-constituted officers as was the case in this instance."

Frost goes on to point out that if the ordinance against carrying firearms were properly enforced, such killings could not occur, and he puts his finger upon the great weakness of law enforcement in Dodge City—namely, that citizens of Dodge without official status nevertheless were allowed to carry arms. Says he, "Let officers of the law do this sort of work if it must be done, so that the responsibility may be placed where it properly belongs and not on individuals who are not officers yet who, it appears, are ever ready to lend a hand whether called upon or not."

Not everybody in Dodge liked Frost's criticism, and there was considerable indignation which found voice in the *Dodge City Times*. It was suggested that the two cowboys following Ballard had killed him. To this Frost replies, "If these boys did kill their comrade, why did not the officers pursue them and arrest them like they ought to have done and which it was their duty to do? By not doing so they really admit that they are guilty of no crime and were thus allowed to get away without any effort to arrest them and thoroughly investigate the matter."

The gunmen of Dodge City were always ready to back the play of friends who happened to be officers, and on the record there is little to suggest that the officers disapproved.

CHAPTER 18 :
: FAMOUS VISITORS

As Cowboy Capital, metropolis of the Southwest, and a division point on the Santa Fe Railroad, Dodge City was visited by many celebrities.

In the beginning there were the military officers, such as General William Tecumseh "Uncle Billy" Sherman, General Philip H. "Phil" Sheridan, General Nelson A. Miles, General George Armstrong Custer, and many a veteran of the Indian Wars who later rose to fame. Senator John J. Ingalls was known in Dodge, also a number of Cheyenne Indian chiefs—unwilling guests.

As previously noted, Eddie Foy spent several seasons in Dodge, and Ex-Governor Thomas Carney once visited the town in the guise of a hide buyer, to get into a poker game, and lost his shirt. His friends, however, recovered his watch and bought him a ticket home.

Even a visitor from the White House stopped in Dodge—President Rutherford B. Hayes. According to the papers, however, Hayes showed no interest whatever in Dodge City and remained in his special car during the time the train paused there.

Dodge was "profoundly indifferent concerning the presence of a live president in its midst. No curiosity was manifested to see him, no interest taken in his arrival."

The fact seems to be that General Sherman had to do the honors, and spent considerable time chatting with a crowd of men, many of them Confederate veterans. But soldiers respect each other, and the meeting passed off very pleasantly.

Many of the famous scouts and Indian fighters visited Dodge at one time or another, including Billy Dixon and other heroes of the fight at Adobe Walls, Frederick W. "Buffalo Bill" Cody, and on one occasion James Butler "Wild Bill" Hickok.[1]

Many a well-known cattle baron, whose names appear elsewhere in this book, visited Dodge season after season—such men as Charles Goodnight, Geo. W. Littlefield, "Shanghai" Pierce with his herds of "sea lions"—and many another famous cattleman whose name is enshrined in *The Trail Drivers of Texas*.

Last, but by no means least in the annals of the town, were the gun-fighters and gunmen who sojourned there, of which none was more celebrated in his time than the English-born Ben Thompson of Texas, and his brother Billy.

Among women celebrities of the old days Calamity Jane stands first among Dodge City visitors.

But not all the celebrities who frequented Dodge City were members of the human race. Indeed a few of the quadrupeds were as well or better known throughout the Southwest than most of the bipeds.

Mayor Kelley's pedigreed greyhounds and wolfhounds were reputed to be the best of that breed in the country, and many were the stories told of their exploits. So well known were they that their owner was named for them. In Hays, Kelley had been known as "Hound" Kelley. In Dodge he was familiarly called "Dog" Kelley, while some combined these titles and referred to him as "Hound Dog" Kelley.

General George Armstrong Custer, commanding the Seventh Cavalry, was very fond of coursing coyotes, wolves, antelope, and jack rabbits. Kelley—who while in the service had been Custer's orderly—had cared for the officer's hounds and acquired a passion for the sport. Some of his own kennel were whelped by Custer's hounds.

One October day a hunting party consisting of Mayor Kelley,

Chalk Beeson, Fred Singer, Neal Brown and others went out with hounds for an antelope chase. The crusty snow made the run difficult, but that day Kelley's greyhounds set a record. They headed west from Dodge, starting a herd of twelve fat antelope, and after a chase of four miles, four of the dogs pulled down six. The largest number previously killed by the hounds in a single chase was five. The party returned in high glee.

On another occasion Mayor Kelley and Lieutenant Gardner of Fort Dodge led a party, twelve in all, crossing the river east of the fort, and soon flushed two antelope from the hills. It was hot weather, but away they went, antelope, hounds, and huntsmen, a mile and a half at breakneck speed. As they topped the hill the hounds pulled down an antelope.

But the gallant dogs killed more than antelope that day.

Unable to stand, they were taken upon the hunters' saddles and hurried toward the river three miles away. Fly never reached the water. The others were taken to the river, bled, and rubbed, but to no purpose. Rowdy shortly followed Fly, also Kate, an elegant imported hound belonging to the Lieutenant.

These animals "for grace, beauty and speed" had no peers in western Kansas. Fly and Kate were "a very king and queen."

That was Thursday. But the end was not yet. On Sunday Lieutenant Gardner's hound Omar died from the effects of this hunt.

Mayor Kelley also owned some fine horses, Battery Grey and Old Calamity, described in the press as "the boss buggy team."

Fast horses were so important on the plains and Dodge City so prosperous, that many a fine animal was brought there. One of the most celebrated was Bill Tilghman's saddler, Chief. When Tilghman first saw this animal, it was in the possession of a Kiowa Indian named White Deer who laughed at all offers to buy it.

It was a "rich, blood bay, fifteen and a half hands high, with a small white star in his forehead, the off fore foot and opposite hind foot white. Every line of him—from his springing, slender pastern to sloping shoulder and long-muscled hips, his short back and deep chest, his thin, fine-haired mane and tail, his delicate ears, in which the veins stood out; his easy, powerful stride, and the pride of him—proclaimed him a chief, a king of horses indeed."[2]

But that king of horses fell into the hands of the king of horse-thieves, Dutch Henry, and one fine day Tilghman bought the animal for $85 and hit the trail.

When Dutch Henry realized that he had sold so fine an animal for so small a sum, he followed Bill and demanded the horse back, threatening that if Bill would not agree he would steal him. But when Bill gravely replied, "Henry, if you do, some-time I will kill you for it," the little Dutchman stood up and replied, "By Gott, Bill, if you think enough of that damned horse to kill me for him, just keep him."

Bill Tilghman later owned many fine horses, including Chant, winner of the Kentucky Derby (1894) and many another stake. But in Bill's opinion Chant lacked the "gameness, the stamina, good sense, and affection for his owner that Chief had."

But considering that the fame and fortunes of Dodge City rested squarely on the buffalo, the oxen, and the cattle, it was natural that her horned celebrities should outshine the rest.

For there were buffaloes to be found in Dodge. The most noteworthy of these, of course, was the mounted white buffalo killed by Prairie Dog Dave which was for so long an ornament of Wright and Beverley's store. The others were ordinary live animals, two tame two-year-old buffaloes belonging to P. G. Reynolds (of Lee & Reynolds). These wandered about the town so exceedingly tame and docile that they came right into the backyards and poked their noses into kitchen doors, begging for bread and other eatables. They could be handled and trusted not to do mischief as a rule. But once, when a large troupe of entertainers paid the town a visit, the two buffaloes—enraged by the drumming—horned in, charged the parade, and put the band to flight.

But neither of these animals rated with certain domestic cow brutes.

Most of the cattle which snailed up the long trails from Texas to Dodge had been branded in the open at a bull chip fire and might never have seen a fence, much less entered a corral. When one of these herds crossed the Arkansas River below Dodge City, pointed for the shipping pens and the loading chutes beside the railroad, it was something of a problem to get the steers through that gate.

Of course some outfits had lead steers which could be trusted to do this, but of them all Old Blue, Charles Goodnight's lead steer, deserved and enjoyed most renown. Old Blue was much too useful an animal to be turned into beef. Every year for eight years he led a thousand or more JA steers 250 miles to Dodge, sometimes twice a year. He pointed his first herd north in October, 1878, trampling out the Palo Duro–Dodge City Trail.

Old Blue was unique. Goodnight bought him from John Chisum. The animal was broken to the yoke. He was four years old when he made his first visit to Dodge City. On that drive Goodnight decided to bell his lead steer—something which had never been done before. Most lead steers were tough and wild and would have gone crazy with a clapper banging at their briskets. But not Old Blue.

"As that bell rang off the miles in tune to his stride, Blue was the proudest animal that ever switched his tail at flies. At night a cowboy pitched his rope around Blue's neck, for he was as gentle as could be, slipped a leather strap around the clapper or crammed the bell full of grass, and the herd bedded in peace. Soon the beeves learned to follow the bell, and if, perchance, the clapper came undone at night, the herd would be on its feet, ready to trail, in no time.

"Beyond the Beaver the outfit passed the only settler on the trail, and beside his sod house was a little field with pumpkins, squash, and melons. Cow-chips made good fuel, and the owner implored them to camp nearby, as he was twenty miles from wood. They trailed on to Seven Mile Hill, and at last looked down the slope to Dodge City. In the evening they camped on the south side of the river, while McAnulty and Cresswell had herds nearby. The JA boss turned his weather eye to the sky that night, and called to his boys: 'All saddle and tie up. We'll have hell before day.' About midnight it commenced sleeting and snowing, but all hands struck for the herd and managed to hold it, though the two neighboring ones were lost in the storm. At daylight the boss yelled: 'Loose the bell and take the river.' Old Blue broke the ice along the edge of the Arkansas, swam the stream in the middle, and headed straight for the railroad corrals as two thousand JA's crowded on his fetlocks. Soon he was at a run, and the frozen ground was shaking to the beat of four thousand hoofs. Inside the gate he prudently jumped aside and rested, while the herd swarmed and milled against the far side of the corral. The cowpunchers jammed the steers up the chute and into the cars, and as the train pulled out for Kansas City, they, and the saddle horses, and Old Blue, stretched their necks over the top rail of the corral and watched them go."[3]

"He stayed with the remuda and ate hay while the cowboys warmed their stomachs at a bar and their feet on the floor of a dance hall. After a day and a night of celebration, they had spent themselves empty and were ready to leave. So at Wright and Beverley's store next morning the wagon was loaded with chuck and sacks of shelled corn. The grains in those sacks were colored red, white and blue, and on the road home Blue learned to eat corn; in fact he loved it, and the colored grains seemed to add to his spirits.

"The weather was freezing cold, and as the outfit headed southward, men and horses alike felt like making time. Blue was ready to travel also. He had the stride of seven-league boots and could walk up with any horse. Sometimes the thirty-miles-a-day clip made him trot, but he never tired or lagged. Down on Wolf Creek one night a hungry band of Kiowas rode into camp and, pointing at the big steer, demanded 'wohaw' (beef), but Chief

Lone Wolf and all his warriors could not have taken Blue away from those Palo Duro cowpunchers."[4]

He was always a great pet, and often came to the chuck-wagon to eat whatever the cook or the boys offered him.

He lived to be twenty years old and when he died they chopped off his horns and put them over the door of the JA office. Old Blue's horns are now proudly displayed in the museum of the Panhandle Plains Historical Society at the West Texas State Teachers College in Canyon, Texas.

There are those who claim that Old Blue sired Paul Bunyan's mythical blue ox.

CHAPTER 19 :
: COCKEYED FRANK
: KILLS RICHARDSON

IN SPITE of the ordinances against gun-toting north of the Deadline and the success of the officers in enforcing the Law on transients, residents of Dodge could generally produce a pistol, when needed, in a hurry. On Saturday evening, April 5, 1879, a gun-fight occurred in the Long Branch Saloon. The Tuesday following the *Ford County Globe* devoted almost its entire second page to this notorious affair under the headlines:

ANOTHER TRAGEDY

Frank Loving and Levi Richardson
Fight With Pistols

Loving Comes Out With a Scratch and
Richardson Goes to His Grave

The editor writes: "There is seldom witnessed in any civilized town or country such a scene as transpired at the Long Branch Saloon, in this city, last Saturday evening, resulting in the killing of Levi Richardson, a well known freighter, of this city, by a gambler named Frank Loving."

After alleging that the hard feelings between the men arose from the fact that both had been interested in the same (unnamed) woman, the editor asserts that, "On one or two occasions previous to this which resulted so fatally, they have quarrelled and even come to blows. Richardson was a man who had lived for several years on the frontier, and though well liked in many respects, he had cultivated habits of bold and daring, which are always likely to get a man into trouble. Such a disposition as he possessed might be termed bravery by many, and indeed we believe he was the reverse of a coward. He was a hard working, industrious man, but young and strong and reckless.

"Loving is a man of whom we know but very little. He is a gambler by profession; not much of a rowdy, but more of the cool and desperate order. . . . He is about 25 years old. Both, or either of these men, we believe, might have avoided this shooting if either had possessed a desire to do so. But both being willing to risk their lives, each with confidence in himself, they fought because they wanted to fight. As stated in the evidence below, they met; one said 'I don't believe you will fight.' The other answered 'try me and see,' and immediately both drew murderous revolvers and at it they went, in a room filled with people, the leaden missives flying in all directions. Neither exhibited any sign of a desire to escape the other, and there is no telling how long the fight might have lasted had not Richardson been pierced with bullets and Loving's pistol left without a cartridge. Richardson was shot in the breast, through the side and through the right arm. It seems strange that Loving was not hit, except a slight scratch on the hand, as the two men were so close together that their pistols almost touched each other. Eleven shots were fired, six by Loving and five by Richardson. Richardson only lived a few moments after the shooting. Loving was placed in jail to await the verdict of the coroner's jury, which was 'self defense,' and he was released. Richardson has no relatives in this vicinity. He was from Wisconsin. About twenty-eight years old.

"Together with all the better class of our community we greatly regret this terrible affair. We do not believe it is a proper way to settle difficulties, and we are positive it is not according to any law, human or divine. But if men must continue to persist in settling their disputes with fire arms we would be in favor of the duelling system, which would not necessarily endanger the lives of those who might be passing up or down the street attending to their own business.

"We do not know that there is cause to censure the police, unless it be to urge upon them the necessity of strictly enforcing the ordinance preventing the carrying of concealed weapons. Neither of these men had a right to carry such weapons. Gamblers, as a class, are desperate men. They consider it necessary in their business that they keep up their fighting reputation, and never take a bluff. On no account should they be allowed to carry deadly weapons.

"Richardson was buried on Sunday afternoon in the cemetery north of town, and his death, be it said to our discredit, adds another grave to the already long list filled by those who have met death in a violent manner."

The editor then gives the evidence of those who witnessed the fight, and the verdict of the jury:

Adam Jackson, bar-tender at the Long Branch, testified as follows:

"I was in the Long Branch saloon about 8 or 9 o'clock Saturday evening. I know Levi Richardson. He was in the saloon just before the fuss, standing by the stove. He started to go out and went as far as the door when Loving came in at the door. Richardson turned and followed back into the house. Loving sat down on the hazard table. Richardson came and sat near him on the same table. Then Loving immediately got up, making some remark to Richardson, could not understand what it was. Richardson was sitting on the table at the time, and Loving standing up. Loving says to Richardson: If you have anything to say about me why don't you come and say it to my face like a gentleman, and not to my back, you dam son of a bitch. Richardson then stood up and said: You wouldn't fight anything, you dam—could not hear the rest. Loving said you try me and see. Richardson pulled his pistol first, and Loving also drew a pistol. Three or four shots were fired when Richardson fell by the billiard table. Richardson did not fire after he fell. He fell on his hands and knees. No shots were fired after Richardson fell. No persons were shooting except the two mentioned. Loving's pistol snapped twice and I think Richardson shot twice before Loving's pistol was discharged."

A. A. JACKSON

Wm McKeever testified: "About 8 or 9 oclock I was at the Long Branch, standing by the stove. Heard Richardson say something, did not understand what it was. Loving said to Richardson you dam son of a bitch, if you have anything to say about me say it to my face. The next thing I saw was Loving with his revolver out. Could not see Richardson as he was behind me. The first shot that I can remember of being fired was fired by Loving at Richardson, and I saw the fire on Richardson's coat. When I first saw Loving have his pistol out I saw Richardson, but did not notice that he had any pistol. As near as I could tell there were six or eight shots fired. Did not see Richardson have a pistol at the time he fell. Saw Richardson fire once."

W. McKEEVER

Wm. Fickensher, sworn, says: "I was at the Long Branch when the shooting occurred. Saw Loving coming in at the front door. Richardson was just going out at the same door. When Loving came in Richardson followed him back. It was then a few minutes before anything was said, when Loving said something to Richardson about saying things to his face. I was still behind the piano. Richardson was sitting on the table near the stove and Loving standing before him near the end of the bar. Richardson said I don't believe you will fight. Loving said just try me and see. They both then drew pistols. Richardson had his pistol out and had fired a shot just as Loving got his out. Loving's pistol snapped the first time. Loving then ran around the stove, Richardson after him. Richardson fired two shots, one of them passing over Loving's head. Loving then fired and hit Richardson in the left brest. Loving fired twice more, one of the shots hitting Richardson. Richardson fell back but kept on shooting at Loving."

W. F. FICKENSHER

Chas. E. Bassett testified: "When I first heard the firing I was at Beatty and Kelley's saloon. Ran up to the Long Branch as fast as I could. Saw Frank Loving, Levi Richardson and Duffey. Richardson was dodging and running around the billiard table. I got as far as the stove when the shooting had about ended. I caught Loving's pistol. Think there was two shots fired after I got into the room, am positive there was one. Loving fired that shot, to the best of my knowledge. Did not see Richardson fire any shot, and did not see him have a pistol. I examined the pistol which was shown me as the one Richardson had. It contained five empty shells. Richardson fell while I was there. Whether he was shot before or after I came in am unable to say. I think the shots fired after I came in were fired by Loving at Richardson. Richardson fell immediately after the shot I heard. Did not see any other person shoot at Richardson. Did not see Duffey take Richardson's pistol. Do not know whether Loving knew that Richardson's pistol had been taken away from him. There was considerable smoke in the room. Loving's pistol was a Remington, No. 44 and was empty after the shooting."

CHAS. E. BASSETT

Wm. Duffey testified: "I was at the Long Branch saloon. I know Levi Richardson, who is now dead. I know cock-eyed Frank (Loving). Both were there at the time. I heard no words pass between them. They had fired several shots when Frank fell by the table by the stove. I supposed that he was shot. I then had a scuffle with Richardson, to get his pistol, and threw him back on some chairs. Succeeded in getting his pistol. There might have been a shot fired by one or the other while we were scuffling. Cannot say whether Richardson had been shot previous to that time, but think he had, as he was weak and I handled him easily. Richardson then got up and went toward the billiard table and fell. I can't swear whether any shots were fired at Richardson by Loving after Richardson was disarmed. Don't think Loving knew I had taken the pistol from Richardson. It was but a few seconds after I took Richardson's pistol that he fell."

WILLIAM DUFFEY

Edward Davies testified: "The first I saw was the scrambling of the crowd to get out of the way. The next I saw was Levi Richardson with a pistol in his hand. He was chasing Loving around the stove. Am not certain whether any shots had been fired. Loving was on the opposite side of the stove from Richardson. Saw Richardson reach around the stove and shoot at Loving. Did not see Loving shoot. Loving ran around the stove and out of my sight. I then went into the club room and saw no more. Am a plasterer by trade."

EDWARD J. DAVIES

P. L. Beatty testified: "About a month ago Richardson stated that he had had words with Frank and that he had struck at Frank; said that he would shoot the guts out of the cock-eyed son of a bitch any way."

P. L. BEATTY

Lloyd Shinn testified: "I came into the Long Branch on the evening of the 5th between 8 and 9 o'clock, and was standing at the corner of the piano in the back part of the room. Saw Loving, who was in the front part of the room, with a pistol in his hand pointing toward some one behind the stove. Then the shooting commenced. The crowd rushed back and I saw nothing more of the fight until after the last shot was fired when I saw Duffey and Richardson scuffling. In the scuffle Richardson fell over on some chairs. Loving came up, and reaching over Duffey snapped his pistol once or twice at Richardson, but it did not go off. The two men were then disarmed."

LLOYD SHINN

W. H. Harris testified: "I was sitting at the table to the north of the stove. Richardson was sitting on the table south of the stove. Heard Richardson say in a sneering tone you won't fight. Loving replied you try me and see. Richardson raised up, pulled out his pistol and commenced shooting, and then both commenced dodging around the stove. Loving did not shoot after Duffey commenced to scuffle with Richardson."

W. H. HARRIS

Verdict

State of Kansas, County of Ford.

An inquisition holden in the county of Ford, state of Kansas, on the 6th and 7th days of April, A. D. 1879, before me, John W.

Straughn, Coroner of Ford County, Kansas, upon the body of Levi Richardson, there lying dead, by the persons whose names are hereto subscribed. The said jururs upon their oaths, from the evidence do say that the said Levi Richardson came to his death by a bullet wound from a pistol fired by Frank Loving in self defense, on the 5th day of April, 1879, in the county of Ford, state of Kansas.

G. E. HADDER
G. M. HOOVER
A. H. POLLEY
T. GOODMAN
JOHN RINEY
SAM'L GALLAGHER, JR.

Bat Masterson declares that, to be successful, a gun-fighter had to have three qualities: first, the courage to fight; second, skill in handling his pistol; third, the cold nerve to draw and shoot deliberately so as not to miss.[1]

Both Loving and Richardson were amply endowed with courage. Richardson, before tackling Loving, had killed several men by straight shooting. Loving, on the other hand, so far as the record shows, had never shot to kill.

In skill with weapons Richardson appears to have had the edge on Loving, since Wyatt Earp declared, "There were few men around Dodge who could beat Levi at the targets."

Loving won the fight because Richardson on this occasion lacked the necessary cold deliberation. If, as some of the testimony indicates, Richardson fired first and Loving's pistol only snapped, every advantage at the start was with Richardson.

But he had taken up fanning and so sacrificed accuracy for speed. Fanning, like every other method of rapid fire, where a man faces only one adversary, is unsound in principle, being based necessarily upon the unnerving conviction that you will miss your first shot. In those days, when clouds of white powder smoke from your first shot inevitably hid your target, fanning was particularly dangerous. Wyatt Earp blamed Levi's failure to hit Frank on "hurry." Judging from the excited way he talked and acted before the shooting began, it might well have been due to fury.

A great deal has been said about the speed with which frontier gunmen could draw their weapons. No doubt they were fast and skillful in comparison with ordinary gun-toters, partly through natural aptitude, partly because of constant practice. But their six-shooter was in fact a clumsy machine, and the ammunition they used was so defective that it frequently missed fire, as in the fight just described, or when Walker tried to shoot Nat Haywood (described earlier in this book). Sometimes two out of five cartridges proved defective.

The .45 caliber Buntline Special[2] carried by Wyatt Earp, Bat Masterson, Charlie Bassett, Bill Tilghman, and Neal Brown, was eighteen inches long. Even the popular Peacemaker—the .45 caliber frontier model single-action Colt revolver—was fourteen inches long and weighed three pounds loaded. How "fast" could anyone be in wielding such a hog-leg (as it was aptly called), particularly when such a "thumb-buster" was fired by pulling back and releasing the hammer with the most awkward of the fingers? No wonder more stress was laid upon coolness and accuracy than upon speed. Only a cool head *could* rely upon such a primitive contraption and such unreliable ammunition as it carried.

CHAPTER 20 · HORSETHIEVES

OF ALL the criminals who infested western Kansas in those early days none caused more exasperation or aroused more bitter feeling than horsethieves. All that country, it seemed, had here a horsethief, there a horsethief, everywhere a horsethief. In all the files of Dodge City newspapers there is scarcely an issue which did not have at least one—and generally three or four—stories of animals stolen, thieves arrested or pursued, rewards offered, and killings. When, in 1873, the depression set in and the railroad stopped building at the Colorado line, a multitude of railway builders found themselves without a job. And when, in 1874, there were no more buffalo in Kansas and as yet few farms and ranches, or cattle, stealing horses offered the most profitable and exciting way of life. A man who was not sufficiently educated to clerk in a store or skilled enough to be a cowboy or a gambler found stealing horses almost his only means to make a living. And the horse had the advantage of providing transportation for the thief. Moreover, since horses generally had to be turned out to graze, they could not always be closely guarded. During the seventies stealing horses developed into a regular crime wave.

First it was Indian ponies, then anybody's animal.

In Plains country a good horse was absolutely essential to a tolerable life. In that region of magnificent distances a man could walk himself to death and get nowhere, like a mud turtle on a world cruise. Such plainsmen abhorred walking, and a man afoot felt underprivileged and was, in all probability, a pauper. To sell one's saddle was the depth of desperation, and most men would walk a mile to saddle up and ride across the road.

A good horse was not only necessary to the business of a cowboy, a traveler, a hunter, or an officer, but the loss of it might very well result in serious exposure and even death from thirst, prairie fires, blizzards, heat prostration, or hostile Indians. A man afoot felt like an airman grounded.

Where good horses were so necessary and so desirable and where rough characters abounded, it sometimes happened that no questions were asked when a horse was offered for sale. The seller guaranteed no title, only offered possession, and the buyer purchased on those terms. Accordingly there was a universal hatred for horsethieves—even among horsethieves themselves, when their own animals were taken.

Often enough on the Plains the horsethief when caught was promptly hanged. In Ford County, however, officers made a mighty effort to deal with horsethieves by due process of law. But with mixed success.

In those days the laws of the State of Texas required every animal in any herd of cattle driven across the State line to be branded with the same brand. Of course, many of the animals had been branded before, and this extra brand, used only on the trail, was known as a "road brand." Horsethieves, like other shady characters in the West, seldom used their real names, and the monikers which they adopted or by which they were known were therefore called "road names." Horsethieves, more than any, found it convenient to have false names, and we may be sure that most of their names in the records were only road names.

Sometimes they operated singly and sometimes in great bands. Lieutenant Thomas B. Nichols, Sixth Cavalry, reported March 31, 1875, that on a march to intercept a party of Cheyenne Indians he "discovered the rendezvous of a large band of horsethieves, with corral and stables for sixty or eighty animals, ranch and signs of a sudden departure within a few days. This band appears to have lived here all winter and to have had in their possession considerable stock, chiefly shod horses and mules."

Let us briefly mention some of the exploits of these gentry.

In 1878, "a Government train of two wagons and eight mules was raided Tuesday night at their camp on Bluff creek, 37 miles south, and eight mules stolen. The train was en route to Camp Supply, and was in charge of soldiers. Sheriff Masterson and Lt. Guard, of Fort Dodge, with a couple of men, left Wednesday night in search of the stolen property and the capture of the thieves.

"Horse thieving is a little too bold and frequent to be longer endured without more stringent measures than a short term in the penitentiary. Some of these bold operators will some fine evening be taken in the most approved and summary style."

Again (a Fort Dodge item): "A daring horse thief attempted to persuade the post herder to deliver the herd of government mules over to him, but was not successful. He was pursued by Mike Sughrue, the corral boss, who sent a few bullets after them. A detachment of soldiers was sent out, under Sgt. Hamilton, but could not find the thief."

"Another exploit of a similar nature was made night before last. The door of Mr. Webber's stable was found to be forcibly opened and one of his horses taken out. Mr. Webber started in pursuit of the thief and found his animal among a herd of cattle and horses near the stock yards where the thief must have abandoned it for fear of pursuit."

In April, 1878, a horsethief was traced to Dodge City: "Last Wednesday Mr. M. A. Couch and three other gentlemen arrived in this city from Walnut creek, forty miles north of here, in search of four horses that had been stolen from them on the day previous. They immediately applied to the County Attorney for information and assistance, stating that they had tracked the horses to this city. Sheriff Masterson was sent for, and in company with Couch and party instituted search for the stock, which, luckily, they succeeded in recovering. Two of the horses were found in the river bottom southwest of the city and the other two were found in Mr. Bell's livery stable, where they had been placed the night before. The owners of the horses were very much pleased upon recovering their stock, and proposed starting immediately for home without making any search for the thief; but the Sheriff with an eye to giving his thiefship punishment for his wrongs, made search and discovered men whom he supposed to be guilty."

Sometimes a bold theft occurred in Dodge City itself. The *Times* carries this story:

"A bold robbery took place at 10 o'clock Tuesday morning at the residence of A. H. Webb, whose house is located on the hill north of the court house, and is the farthest house on the ridge. The thieves took two mares, two saddles, a Winchester rifle, clothing, etc., and safely evaded detection and pursuit. A description of the mares and thieves is given in another column of this page. This is the coolest robbery we have heard of for some time, and we hope the thieves will get their just desserts."[1]

In the same issue this item appeared: "Michael Riney's bay horse was missing from the picket pin, and is supposed to be stolen."

Again we have a week's haul reported in the same sheet:

Sheriff Masterson and officers captured in the city, Friday last, two horse thieves, who had stolen stock nine miles north of Great Bend. The prisoners had a preliminary examination before Justice Cook, and were held over in the sum of $800 each, but were subsequently taken to Great Bend, where they will no doubt be held for trial. A third person engaged in stealing with these two, managed to elude the vigilance of the officers, and escaped. The prisoners gave fictitious names before their trial, thus attempting to avoid identification.

On Sunday two more persons were arrested, charged with horse stealing, and having in their possession fourteen head of horses, supposed to be stolen, which they had secreted on the range south. The prisoners were taken before Justice Cook, on Monday, but the trial was postponed for ten days.

On Wednesday Sheriff Masterson received a dispatch from J. B. Matthews, at Fort Griffin, Texas, telling him to hold the two men arrested by him on Sunday. . . .

Horse stealing has taken a fresh start in the country, and since the wholesale conviction of thieves last winter that crime had not been on the rampage until within the past few months. The officers of Ford county are on the alert and watch with a vigilant eye every suspicious character lurking in our midst.

Under-Sheriff Masterson arrested a man this evening who had stolen a horse from Granada last week and sold him to a man near Offerle. The prisoner put up and was released. Policeman Joe Mason made six arrests this week. We are cheered to learn that our quondam friend ———— is in the dog house.

On Saturday last, Sheriff Christy and Deputy Sheriff Payne, procured the arrest of a man . . . living on a claim near Spearville, who is supposed to be the partner of the infamous Dutch Henry. He was first arrested in Wyoming Territory for stealing Government mules, but shot the two officers who had him in charge and made his escape. We think that great credit is due our officers, for the able manner in which they have worked up the case, and also to Sheriff Masterson of Ford County, for arresting the prisoner. He comes to trial on September 19.

Sheriff Bat Masterson Thursday night arrested one . . . charged with stealing a horse belonging to J. W. Duncan, living on Smoky river, at Hays crossing, on the 25th of April. The horse was not recovered. The prisoner has been placed in charge of a couple of officers and taken to Ellis county for examination. Horsethieves find hospitable reception at the hands of Sheriff Masterson. He is an excellent "catch" and is earning a State reputation.[2]

Not every man who suffered at the hands of horsethieves turned for help to the Sheriff[3] and his deputies. Not far from Dodge, on the trail to Camp Supply, Dirty Face Jones, the freighter, made camp on Bear Creek. It was his custom to lock his saddle horse up to his wagon every night with a log chain and padlock. Then he could turn his mules out safely, for the mules would not stray one hundred yards from the wagon. Jones gave it out that he was going to freight all that winter on the Camp Supply Road, that he was going to turn his mules footloose every night, and that if he couldn't find them there in the morning, he wasn't going to look for them. He was going to take his old *gun* out and when he found four men—whom he named publicly—he was going to kill them.

Dirty Face announced publicly that he was not going to hunt the mules at all. He was just going to "hunt them fellows and shoot them."

Sure enough, they stole his mules on Bear Creek. They had some new men in the gang and they had sent them out, and the new men had got Dirty Face's mules by mistake. The next night the leaders of the gang sent one of the new men to drive the mules back. Jones never had seen him before in his life, so let him come into camp and heard his story. He brought back all twelve mules and offered Dirty Face a buckskin money bag. Said he, "I brought you a hundred dollars. The boys give it to me to pay the damages."

Said that old-timer about the horsethieves: "When those fellows was hunting, they was hunting, and when they wasn't hunting they was doing something else. They would go down into the settlements of Kansas and make a raid and get a bunch of horses and mules and run them out along that route because they had water up there and there they could lose their pursuers." A party of thieves from Colorado would meet another with horses taken in Indian Territory, swap herds, ride home again, and sell the animals with impunity.

A favorite field of operations for horsethieves was the Indian Territory. The Indian reservations there were scantily settled, the military garrisons small, and the territory to be covered by U.S. marshals great. The Indians themselves were not well armed and few people had any regard for the rights of a redskin. Sometimes a camp would be softened up by selling them whisky, after which it was a simple matter to run off their ponies and head for parts north where the horses could be disposed of readily. A number of instances are recorded in which stolen Indian ponies were publicly sold on Front Street in Dodge City.

But stealing horses from Uncle Sam's wards on Federal lands had its dangers too. It brought the troops into the picture. Their exploits have been neglected and overshadowed by those of frontier Marshals and Sheriffs, but are nonetheless worthy of mention. After telegraph wire and iron rails crossed the Plains, troops could be readily alerted before the thieves had got clean away.

Often enough the troopers rode their horses for hundreds of miles and returned with nothing to show for their trouble. Sometimes they overtook their quarry, recovered the stock and captured the thieves.

On November 4, 1874, Second Lieutenant R. Hanna, Sixth Cavalry, in compliance with special orders left Fort Dodge at the head of a detail consisting of two noncommissioned officers, eight privates, and the post guide, Theodore German. The mounted party had four pack mules carrying rations. At Dodge City they entrained for Great Bend, Kansas, where the Santa Fe Railroad—and before it, the Santa Fe Trail—first touched the Arkansas River. They arrived at 10:00 P.M. and went into camp.

Meanwhile the Lieutenant made inquiries in the town looking for parties who could put him on the trail of three horsethieves who had been seen crossing the river below Great Bend with eighteen head of horses. The Lieutenant had orders to pursue and capture these men.

For five days Lieutenant Hanna and his men trailed the horsethieves, who resorted to all sorts of tricks to throw him off the trail. They would drive their herd of horses through a herd of cattle and so obliterate their trail. They crossed and recrossed the river, trying to confuse their pursuers as to the direction in which they intended to ride. Sometimes the troops were able to secure information from cowboys and settlers. In this the scout, Theodore German, was very helpful. Being dressed in civilian clothes, he would pretend that he was one of the horsethieves who had been left behind and was trying to catch up with his fellows, and so secured information that might have been withheld from men in uniform!

Every day the detail traveled from twenty-five to forty miles, following the common route of horsethieves coming from the Territory with Indian stock. This trail left the Arkansas River below Pawnee Rock. After following various creeks for camping purposes, the trail swung west, following the divide between Pawnee and Walnut Creeks until the settlements were left behind. On the ninth Hanna broke camp at 5:00 A.M. and within about five miles up Pawnee Creek he found the horsethieves' camp of the night before. They had not got up early enough in the morning to fool him. Standing on their camp ground, he could see them and their horses passing over a ridge south of the creek, moving in the general direction of Dodge City, then about thirty miles south.

It was clear the thieves had seen the troopers, for they were traveling fast and quickly passed out of sight behind a ridge. For six miles the troops pursued before they caught sight of their quarry again. The three thieves had their herd running at full speed.

The Battle of Guzzler's Gulch

The Lieutenant increased the gait to a gallop again and ran the thieves for ten miles before they stopped. By that time the troops were gaining on them so rapidly that they saw they would be overtaken and halted.

Lieutenant Hanna halted his men and rode up alone within two hundred yards of the horsethieves. He held up his hand and shouted, "Throw up your hands and surrender."

His only reply was three well-aimed shots, one of which killed his horse. The troopers returned the fire. The thieves ran about two hundred yards and took cover in a hole washed out by the water.

The Lieutenant dismounted the detail, leaving his horses in charge of one man, who took them to as low ground as could be found. One of the bullets from the thieves struck the man holding the horses in the hand, only taking the skin off between thumb and forefinger.

The dismounted detail advanced firing, but as the thieves kept the stolen stock with them and were good shots, armed with Sharps sporting rifles outranging the cavalry carbines, it was impossible to get the stolen animals without getting shot. Two hundred yards was as near as Lieutenant Hanna judged it safe to go. There he placed his men behind a low ridge which commanded the enemy position and began firing.

The thieves fought desperately and had apparently made up their minds to die fighting rather than to be taken.

The guide, Theodore German, was an excellent shot and a brave man. Lieutenant Hanna ordered his men to fire on the thieves and thus create a diversion from the guide, who habitually sat "at an aim" with rifle raised under cover. Whenever one of the thieves would jump up to shoot, the guide would cut loose. He was a much better shot than the troopers.

The guide also succeeded in shooting two of the saddle ponies, and wounded one of the thieves, who dropped the gun he was aiming, threw up his hands, and fell over backward.

Immediately afterward this man ran out of the hole, jumped on his pony and rode off about a mile. Then they saw him get off the horse, lie down for a minute, then mount and ride away.

German was sure he had hit the man in the chest.

Before the hour was out, a second thief was wounded, "judging from the howls of pain we could hear over in the hole." But the wounded man kept on shooting.

By this time the stolen ponies had drifted two hundred yards away on the opposite side of the hole, where they were grazing quietly. Lieutenant Hanna sent Sergeant Frank H. Mandeville,

Lance Corporal Francis D. Gaffney and Private William Latham
to circle the position, run off and secure the ponies. This took
time, which was improved by keeping up a hot fire on the two
remaining horsethieves.

When the mounted detail appeared near the stolen stock, the
thieves turned to fire at them. But in turning to fire at the three
troopers, the thieves exposed their backs to the main body of
troops, who took care to make them keep their heads down. The
Sergeant and his two men had to dismount and cut the hobbles
of the stolen ponies while under fire, but succeeded in running
off the ponies without a casualty.

The thieves still had one saddle horse in the hole where they
were, and while the troopers were rounding up the ponies they
tried to mount this horse and escape. The wounded man, too
badly hurt to stand, fell three times, unable to mount. Finally
the other put him on the horse, jumped up behind him and went
off at a gallop. The Lieutenant fired, trying to kill the horse,
but could not.

It was now two o'clock in the afternoon. The cavalry horses
had run nearly twenty miles, had had no water since six o'clock
in the morning, and it was twenty miles to water. Rather than
kill his horses the officer let the horsethieves go and headed south
to the Arkansas River. There they rested in camp for about five
hours, then traveled slowly downriver to within about three
miles of Dodge City. There they camped until eight o'clock
next day, having traveled fifty miles.

After breakfast the detachment rode the remaining eight
miles to Fort Dodge, bringing in twelve ponies and one mule.
Some of the ponies belonged to the Indians, some to the inter-
preter, Mr. Morrison. The total distance marched on this expedition was 208 miles. . . .

There are several stories in Dodge City papers indicating that
even certain officers of the law within Ford County's jurisdic-
tion were accused of yielding to temptation, and were arrested

and brought to trial on a charge of stealing horses or government mules.

It was hardly surprising that citizens organized to protect their livestock. Though the Dodge City papers make no mention of such an organization in the town, a correspondent in Dodge sent a letter (published in *The Commonwealth*, July 14, 1875) declaring: "The Arkansas valley is infested by a bold gang of horsethieves. A vigilance committee has been organized at Dodge City, and it would not be surprising if some of the telegraph poles were found ornamented some of these days."

Certain it is that the leading citizens of Offerle, near the eastern boundary of Ford County, met to form the Offerle Farmers' Protective Union because of the prevalence of horse stealing and other depredations. The enthusiasm manifested at the meeting showed its members were fully awake to their interests and that they would protect themselves at all hazards.

Here and there in western Kansas horsethieves were sometimes taken from jail and hanged by a mob. But the ringleaders of the mob were usually arrested and punished. About this time in Nebraska two men alleged to be cattle thieves were chained to a horizontal overhead pole so that their feet barely touched the ground. Hanging from the pole they were slowly burned to death. The Governor of Nebraska offered a reward of $10,000 for the apprehension of the villains who had perpetrated the barbarous outrage, and the Dodge City paper which reported it expressed violent indignation at that horrible crime. No wicked deed of this sort was ever committed in Ford County.

Indeed, there was a certain twisted gallantry in some of those knights of the saddle, a quality most apparent in the career of Dutch Henry. He was first heard from as a trooper in Custer's cavalry in the late sixties, but about the mid-seventies was accused of running off twenty government mules near Fort Smith, Arkansas, tried and sentenced to a term at hard labor. He escaped after only about three months and became the most notorious horsethief on the plains.

Henry Borne (the name is also spelled Born) was described as "a rather gentle-looking man . . . with black hair, eyes, black mustache, long face and Roman nose. His eyes are bright and penetrating and indicate quick intelligence." He dressed in a good suit of black and a white shirt. Henry might have passed for a professional man.

But his exploits soon made him a legend. He was quick with a revolver, easily controlled his confederates, and rode his fine sorrel horse as though the two formed one animal. He had the reputation of a skillful strategist, who usually evaded the law, but was ready to fight when cornered. Such was his success that it was said he had three hundred horsethieves working with him. Most remarkable of all his abilities was that of securing acquittal when haled into court.

In 1874 he was captured by the sheriff near Ellsworth, but was not taken until he had been wounded in the face. No record of this trial is extant.

In 1876 a Mr. Emmerson was looking for some missing horses near Dodge City when he met Dutch Henry. Perhaps not realizing that Henry was the horsethief, or else intending to warn him, Emmerson asked Henry, if he saw the animals, to hold them and send word.

A wire from Dodge brought out the Sheriff of Russell County, who held a revolver to the horsethief's head. Henry seized the hammer of the Sheriff's weapon, at the same time pulling his own gun. A bystander prevented Henry from firing. Then the Sheriff, after stabbing the bystander by mistake, finally wounded Henry and brought him down.

That night someone fired at Henry through the window of the jail, pierced the blankets of his bed but left him untouched. Henry wrote to Emmerson reporting that he had found Emmerson's animals, telling where to look for them. And there they were.

In Dodge City Henry was given a hearing, but never went to trial. But the settlers interfered, so that Henry grew revengeful.

Both in Kansas and Nebraska members of his gang were seized and held.

In December, 1878, Sheriff Bat Masterson learned that Dutch Henry was in Trinidad, Colorado. He wired officers there to arrest him, and caught the train to claim the prisoner. Bat had no requisition from the Governor's office, but as a witness before Judge Walker he so badgered and excited the legal gentleman, mentioning "unmentionable" matters, that Bat brought Henry back to Dodge on New Year's Day.

The charge was stealing those horses from Emmerson two years earlier.

Henry's plea was the statute of limitations. A jury of farmers, called to try the plea, gave a verdict refusing to sustain it. A special venire then empaneled was composed of citizens of Dodge. Henry offered a sob story of his earlier life, and swore that he had simply followed Emmerson's instructions and had never had any intention of stealing his horses. The citizens' jury, not being so prejudiced against horsethieves as the farmers, brought in a verdict of not guilty.

Henry left in a hurry, but on learning that no other charges impended, soon returned to Front Street. There he received something of an ovation.

However, in 1879 Deputy United States Marshal C. B. Jones of Kansas with Marshal Wilcox of Colorado ran the old fox to earth at the Commercial Hotel in Pueblo, caught him in bed asleep at midnight. Heavily ironed, Henry was brought before a judge in Denver and ordered back to Arkansas to fill his vacant cell.

CHAPTER 21 •
: BIBULOUS BABYLON

MEN of distinction while in Dodge City made their headquarters the Long Branch Saloon.

Charles Bassett, Ford County's first Sheriff, and A. J. Peacock opened the Long Branch in 1873. Later Chalkley M. "Chalk" Beeson bought it and William H. Harris became his partner.

This establishment endeavored to maintain a high-toned sporting atmosphere, serving only high-grade liquor, and its customers included the leading citizens—railroad men, cattle kings, buffalo hunters, and travelers who passed that way. The saloon took its name from the celebrated sporting resort on the Atlantic seaboard. Many of the men in Dodge came from New Jersey or other Eastern States.

There was no dancing in the Long Branch.

In 1876 there were nineteen places licensed to sell liquor in Dodge City, then a town of only twelve hundred inhabitants, and during the summer when the camp was full of transients and strangers, they all did a good business. But the rest of the year they had to depend for most of their business upon permanent residents. With one such place for, roughly, every sixty souls in the community, competition was keen.

Other well-known saloons on Front Street were Beatty and Kelley's Alhambra Saloon, Gambling-Hall and Restaurant, A. B. Webster's Alamo, Mueller and Straeter's Old House Saloon, the Opera House Saloon, the Junction Saloon, and on the south side of the tracks the Green Front.

George M. Hoover's establishment was remarkable in that it permitted no gambling—or dancing. Henry Sturm, like Hoover, conducted a wholesale and retail liquor store.

Of course, all the dance halls and most of the hotels contained bars, and no one could stay in Dodge City and be distant more than one hundred yards from some place of refreshment, open seven days a week, twenty-four hours a day. When a new saloon was opened or a new management took over, a magnificent free lunch was spread and the gang was expected to "get to the joint" in good shape.

In the earliest days on every American frontier the principal beverage was hard liquor, generally whisky, since the high proportion of alcohol in spirits made it more worth transporting with the limited facilities available. So in the beginning whisky was the principal beverage in Dodge and in the seventies mention is made in the local papers of the sale of three hundred empty whisky barrels in one year. As the population never exceeded three thousand persons, this would amount to an annual consumption of one-tenth of a barrel for every man, woman, and child. Of course, most of this liquor was drunk by the cowboys, freighters, soldiers, travelers, and hunters who visited Dodge.

But as railroad service improved and the town became more prosperous and less violent, carload after carload of beer rolled into Dodge every summer. As early as July, 1879, a facetious note appeared in the *Dodge City Times*:

"A young lady, Miss An Heuser, is stopping in the city at present. A great many gentlemen have called upon her and express themselves well pleased with her general appearance. The only criticism we have heard made is that the length of her neck is a little out of proportion to that of her body.

"The 'out of proportion' is to enable the fellows to embrace the neck. An Heuser is a delusion too many persons hug. It brings them to their beer."

Sturm and Hoover both advertised an extensive line of fine

wines. The officers at the fort, who in some measure set the social tone for Dodge City magnates, were great consumers of wine and champagne. It must not be supposed, therefore, that people in Dodge City limited themselves to three hundred barrels of whisky per year.

In the earliest days women of the town could frequent saloons at any time of the day or night, but in the eighties it had become the rule that they should not appear until after midnight. No such privilege for the demimonde existed in more orthodox communities. But in Dodge, where nearly every saloon contained a piano, the painted beauties came to sing and play, "and the sounds of sweet music, mingled with discordant strains from cracked voices, issued forth from those gilded palaces of sin and iniquity and were wafted away on the night air like the cyprian's beauty, never to return."[1] The bar did a thriving business during those early morning hours and there was also dancing. It was seldom that any disturbance occurred during these hours, though an occasional fight took place if one girl paid too much attention to another girl's favorite man. When that happened a battle royal commenced with everyone taking sides, until some recognized leader interfered to restore peace by calling for a round of drinks.

Among the gaudily dressed nymphs whose names are reported as frequenting these affairs are ladies distinguished by the fanciful monikers, "Little Dot," "Hop Fiend Nel," "Emporia Belle," "Scar-faced Lillie," and Miss "One Fin."[2]

In Dodge City the church social and the Firemen's Ball or a masquerade party staged by the Social Union Club enjoyed most favor. But in the nature of things the ladies of the evening —or rather of the early morning—were not invited to such affairs. They found their fun in the saloons and apparently had no lack of masculine company.

But in the beginning eastern Kansas had been settled by colonies of moral idealists sent out by the Abolitionists of New England to make Kansas free soil. Their long struggle with the

Border Ruffians of Missouri before, during, and after the Civil
War had only strengthened them in their pious convictions, and
now that that struggle was over, the New England conscience
moved steadily westward. It is doubtful whether the New
England conscience ever ran into a more immovable object
than old Dodge City.

But those idealists had given the State its motto on the Great
Seal of Kansas: "*Ad Astra Per Aspera.*" Dodge was hard—and
considerably lower than the stars.

The Murphy (Temperance) Movement gained strength daily.
A Dodge City paper as early as 1878 published an uneasy paragraph on this: "Slowly, secretly and noiselessly the Murphy
Movement is heading westward, taking towns by storm. It has
reached Larned," where three hundred persons signed the pledge
during one week. "Some of the most confirmed drinkers in
town are among the wearers of the blue."[3]

The State of Kansas passed a dry law in 1880 and it would
have gone hard with the men of Dodge City if they had ever
imagined that it could apply to them. There was a bleak moment
in March, 1885, when copies of the *Topeka Capital* containing
the official proclamation of the new prohibitory law arrived in
town. Three or four of the leading saloons actually closed their
doors on Saturday. On the Tuesday following, others announced that only "temperance drinks" could be purchased
over their bars. George M. Hoover offered cigars at wholesale;
his bartender, the only occupant of the house, was engaged in
scratching his chin.

But though George Hoover might close down, it was obvious
that Dodge could not long be other than *apparently* dry.

That same year Albert Griffin, a temperance lecturer, spoke
in Dodge and, according to Bat Masterson, stated that he intended returning with a State official, "to stay until every viper
engaged in the sale of liquor was crushed from existence."[4]

Bat declared in his letter to the paper: "This peroration was emphasized by a stamp of his foot, conveying the impression that it was intended as a threat."

Bat goes on to assert that Griffin advised his followers to rise up and drive the saloon men from the community by force.

However that may be, Griffin kept his promise to return to Dodge, bringing with him Colonel A. R. Jetmore of Topeka, representing the Attorney General of the State of Kansas. It was understood that these gentlemen were coming to institute proceedings against the saloon keepers of Dodge City. Some three hundred men met them at the depot, but having assembled merely out of curiosity, offered no insult to the strangers. They were promptly escorted by the Reverend W. G. Elliott and Dr. Galland to the Great Western Hotel, the temperance house, where they were quartered.

That afternoon excitement ran high on Front Street. The drys and the wets got to slugging each other in knock-down fights. These belligerents were "speedily calaboosed."

Such was the tension, however, that the public meeting planned for that evening was never held. At noon next day Griffin and Jetmore left on the train for Topeka without attempting any assault on the saloons. "They had seen enough with their own eyes and heard enough with their own ears to convince them that if prosecutions were commenced, hell would break loose and the devil would be to pay."[5]

The editor adds: "It ought to be evident to everybody familiar with the scenes in Dodge City last Monday, that the time is not ripe for an attempt to suppress the saloons in this place."

Then he concludes with some advice to the Attorney General's assistant:

"Lives and property of people who attend to their own business are safer in Dodge than in any other town in the state. Mr. Jetmore's residence in Topeka is opposite the capitol square, wherein robberies and murderous assaults frequently occur. It is dangerous for him to pass through that square after dark. Let him suppress the murderers and thieves of his own city before he attempts to regulate the morality of other localities. Let the state authorities prohibit crime at the capital of the state, and relegate to the local authorities the business of managing Dodge City."

Bat was furious at the invasion by the drys, assuming that they had come to enforce the law regardless and that they had been invited by his political enemies, who had defeated him in his campaign for Sheriff in 1879. Accordingly he lashed out, naming the supposed Dodge City "drys" in the most opprobrious terms and accusing them of nearly every crime in the book.

Bat then offered to deposit $100 with the bank in Dodge to be donated to any charitable institution in the State if he failed to prove that he could find a dozen respectable witnesses to support his violent allegations. He reminded them of the law of libel and invited them to sue him if his accusations were untrue. He also asserted that it had been said that the town had "long been a nest of outlaws, and that we elect our friends to office, and that most of the officers elected are more of a terror to the peaceable citizens than to their lawless masters."

Bat then launched into a spirited defense of the officials of the town:

"Now, let us see whom we have elected to office. The Hon. R. M. Wright is our mayor. Everybody in the state knows Bob Wright. His honesty and integrity have never been questioned at home or abroad. He is the largest tax-payer in the county, and is doing the largest merchandising business west of Topeka. He has represented us three or four times in the legislature. The president of our council is Ex-Mayor G. M. Hoover, and next to Bob Wright is the largest tax-payer in the county. He has been mayor twice, and served us once in the legislature, is now running a large flouring mill, and is president of the bank of Dodge City. Another of our council is Ex-Mayor James H. Kelley, who has served us as mayor four times, and next to G. M. Hoover is the largest tax-payer in the county. He has been identified with the town since its incipiencey, and everything he owns on earth is here. Another of our councilmen is Fred Gardner, who was twice mayor of Kinsley, and is now the railroad agent for the Santa Fe company at this place. He is a thorough gentleman and respected by all who know him. Mr. Henry Koch, the proprietor of one of the largest tonsorial institutions in the state, finishes the list of councilmen, and I defy any city in the state to make a better showing, or show a more representative body of men conducting the affairs of a city.

"William Tilghman is the city marshal. He is a member of the firm of Brown & Tilghman, also of the firm of Locke & Tilghman, and interested in one of the best stock ranches in the west, besides owning real estate in the city. This is our city government, that Mr. Griffin says is a terror to peaceable citizens. P. F. Sughrue is our sheriff and a better one cannot be found in the state. He has done more to suppress lawlessness in the unorganized portions of his bailiwick, when lawlessness existed there, than most any other man could possibly have done. B. F. Milton is our county attorney. He is a young man of sterling integrity, does not drink, smoke or swear, and is a gentleman whose character is above reproach. He has the happy faculty of knowing his own business, and cannot be bulldozed or intimidated by . . . any narrow-minded crank. . . . Let the good people of Kansas conclude for themselves whether Griffin or Jetmore have told the truth, after considering the showing I have made of the respective elements in this community."

After that Bat devoted a paragraph to advising Mr. Griffin that he "had better stay away" from Dodge.

The editor of the *Kansas Cowboy*, in which Bat's letter was published, quoted it in full, though not endorsing Bat's criticism of the citizens, adding, "However, the epistle would not be Bat's with any other treatment of the subject."

He points out that Griffin came of his own accord, not on invitation; that Jetmore instituted no prosecutions; and that the Attorney General, S. B. Bradford, who came himself a few days later, represented an administration conducted on common sense principles. "He realizes the fact that Dodge City has an individuality of its own, which is original and entirely different in character from that of any other locality in Kansas. Rules for the government of towns like Manhattan and Ottawa are not applicable to Dodge City. The town will work out its own salvation. It cannot be redeemed and purified by means of the lash in the hands of outside parties who are actuated by mercenary motives. One of the principal points of difference between Dodge City and other towns in the state is that hypocrisy does not exist here. Our wickedness is open to the glare of the sun. When we become civilized and pharisaical we will hide our deformities under the mantle of darkness and serve the devil in the livery of heaven. Mr. Bradford has won the respect of all parties in Dodge City and his visit here will be productive of good."

Strangely enough, in March, 1886, Bat Masterson joined the temperance forces, came to Dodge, and staged a general cleanup, closing saloons and ridding the town of gamblers.[6]

On March 19 the *Trinidad News* quotes a Dodge City correspondent thus: "The saloon men have all been arrested and are under bonds; nearly all of the saloons are closed. W. B. Masterson, a sporting man of considerable notoriety in the west, and the man who gave Griffin and Jetmore a ticket of leave from here last summer, has suddenly became a convert to prohibition, and to attest his sincerity has filed complaints against them. He bids fair to develop into a Sam Jones on the prohibition side. Mr. Masterson is a fearless fellow, and has buckled on his six-shooter and is making it as lively for the saloon men now as he did for Griffin and Jetmore last summer while they were in this city on their expedition against the saloon."

But it took more than Bat Masterson or the Temperance Movement to dry up Dodge. Even Carry Nation, if she had ever taken a whack at Dodge, might have blunted her hatchet!

Law enforcement in Dodge City was lax. Ordinances had been passed forbidding games of chance and houses of ill fame (1878);

closing liquor saloons on Sundays (1879); banning dance halls (1884); forbidding the sale of intoxicating liquor as a beverage (in 1887, years after Kansas went legally dry); forbidding the storage of liquor within the city (1889); and forbidding the sale of cigarettes, cigars, tobacco, opium or narcotics (1896). But Dodge City was still wide-open. For twenty years after State prohibition was instituted, liquor sellers in Dodge City were still in business, "the joints" (the word originated in Dodge City) paying a monthly fine instead of a tax. The last dramshop in Dodge was closed in 1903.

Most of the saloons in Dodge sold food. One day a citizen of the camp went into his favorite dramshop, took a seat, threw his feet on the table, and called for a glass of beer, a sandwich, and some Limburger cheese. These were promptly placed beside his feet.

But he called to the proprietor, complaining, "This cheese is no good; I can't smell it."

The proprietor shouted back, "Damn it, take your feet down, and give the cheese a chance!"

CHAPTER 22 ·
: THE BATTLE
IN THE PLAZA

In 1881 Dodge City was endeavoring to maintain law and order more strictly than before, particularly to rid itself of the criminals who continually drifted in, hoping to share in the prosperity of the booming town. Before the cattle drives could reach Dodge, Mayor Webster posted this notice:

All thieves, thugs, confidence men, and persons without visible means of support will take notice that the ordinance passed for their special benefit will be vigorously enforced after April 7, 1881.

Such people gave the town a bad name with the Texans and other visitors.

By this time, many of the old-time peace officers had left Dodge. Charlie Bassett and Mysterious Dave had gone by wagon toward Colorado a year before. Wyatt Earp was an officer at Tombstone, Arizona, where in March, 1881, Bat Masterson, while following his profession as a gambler in that town, served as Earp's deputy in one of the posses.

Gamblers and gunmen on the frontier were a restless lot, forever moving from one boom town or mining camp to another, as opportunity beckoned—yet just as frequently, turning up again in Dodge when the cattle season came on.

In Dodge, James Masterson carried on. He and A. J. Peacock were partners in a dance hall there. Their bartender was Al Updegraff, Peacock's brother-in-law. James Masterson was not content with the services of Updegraff, and urged his partner to join with him in firing Al. Peacock would not agree and insisted on keeping Al. The difference quickly grew into an open quarrel between Masterson and Updegraff, and hard words and insults flew back and forth.

The men of Dodge took sides in this quarrel, and though James Masterson had a number of loyal friends, he felt at some disadvantage and concluded that his life was in danger. At this time Bat Masterson was in New Mexico. There he received a telegram calling him to Dodge to settle the difficulty. Bat had lost one brother in Dodge. He did not hesitate, but boarded the next train with his pistol in its holster.

The train pulled into Dodge from the west at noon on Saturday, April 16. Bat suspected they might be waiting for him on the platform. He dropped off the train while it was still moving, and headed west down the street in search of his brother, Marshal James Masterson. As the train pulled on into the station it revealed Peacock and Updegraff walking across the street. Bat called to them, "Wait a minute, you two; I want to talk to you."

They both knew that voice, that familiar figure. They took his words for a challenge. Both ducked behind the near-by calaboose just south of the tracks and pulled their guns.

Bat was out in the open. But fortunately the railroad grade (which he himself had made) just there formed a slight embankment about three feet high. Bat dropped behind this and the steel rails which topped it. Then the shooting began. Bat's bullets sped south and east, knocking splinters from the corners of the calaboose. Peacock and Updegraff fired straight toward the stores on Front Street behind Bat.

Meanwhile, volunteers on both sides of the tracks joined in the battle. None of the three principals had more cartridges than he carried in his gun, and so the shooting did not last long, though long enough to cause a good many citizens to take cover, running out the back doors of the buildings as the slugs crashed in. One crashed into Dr. McCarty's drugstore, another through the front of the Long Branch Saloon.

There Chalk Beeson had a safe. Quickly he pulled the door open and got as much of himself as he could behind it. The fellows in G. M. Hoover's wholesale liquor store hit the floor as one bullet smashed a front window. A newspaper in the hands of a reader was shot through.

Some of Bat's friends, seeing him outnumbered, joined the fray. One of these took his stand at the corner of the street, laid the barrel of his rifle along the corner of the drugstore, and cut loose. Wright says, "No one seemed to know who did the shooting." There are those who believe that this man who came to Bat's aid in the unequal contest was a close friend and one-time fellow officer. Whoever it was, one of his shots passed completely through Al's lung and body.

In three or four minutes the fight was over. Updegraff had one cartridge left in his weapon, but had lost interest in the fight. At first his wound was believed to be mortal, but Al soon recovered.

The story goes that Mayor A. B. Webster, carrying a loaded .12 gauge Fox shotgun, stepped up to Bat and put him under arrest. Bat, now unarmed, offered no resistance.

The Police Court Docket recording his trial shows that Marshal Fred Singer made complaint charging, "that on the ———— day of April, 1881, in the City of Dodge City and County of Ford, State of Kansas, W. B. Masterson did then and there, unlawfully, feloniously, discharge a pistol upon the streets of said city."

Bat pleaded guilty and was fined eight dollars and costs; it is noted on the record, "Fine and costs paid."

As shown above, the month, April, and year, 1881, are on the record, but no day of the month is indicated. The entry falls in the Docket between one dated April 22 and another following dated April 25. But the *Ford County Globe* implies that Bat faced the Judge on the day of the fight. It adds, "A State warrant was issued later in the evening, for several parties connected with the affair, but they were allowed to leave town, with the understanding that they were not to return."

The *Ford County Globe* three days later comments: "Great indignation was manifested and is still felt by the citizens against the Masterson party, as the shooting was caused by a private quarrel, and the parties who were anxious to fight should have had at least a thought for the danger they were causing disinterested parties on the street and in business houses.

"Such was the nature of the affair that the officers thought best not to undertake the process of criminal prosecution, although many advised it. At any rate the citizens are thoroughly aroused and will not stand any more foolishness."

The day when Dodge shrugged off shooting scrapes on Front Street had passed. The people were highly indignant because of this fracas and the *Ford County Globe* declared that if such an occurrence happened again the men of Dodge City would not wait for the law to take its course.

The *Walnut City Blade* commented caustically—and somewhat unfairly: "It costs $8.00 to shoot a man through the lung in Dodge City—such was Bat Masterson's fine."[1]

They say the Mayor told Bat to leave town and not return.

Jim went off with his brother, dissolved his partnership with Peacock and resigned his office of City Marshal at Dodge. Bat settled in Trinidad, Colorado, and leased a gambling concession there.

Other communities sounded off about this affair. Al Updegraff published his account of the difficulty as follows:

The True Statement of the Shooting
at Dodge City.
Medicine Lodge *Index.*
Dodge City, Kan., April 21, 1881.

EDITOR GLOBE: There having been several statements published relative to the shooting that occurred here, in which I was wounded, and as my relatives and friends live in your city, I desire to make a brief statement of the affair for the purpose of correcting the erroneous statement heretofore published, that all concerned may know that I am not entirely to blame for it all. When I arrived here from Medicine Lodge I went into the employ of Peacock & Masterson, as bar-keeper. During the time I was so employed a friend of Masterson's robbed a woman of $80 by entering her room while she was absent. I advised her to have the party arrested, which she did, through the proper officers. Masterson thereupon came to me and insisted that I should make the woman withdraw the complaint, which I refused positively to do. He, Masterson, thereupon informed me that my services as bar-keeper was no longer needed, and I must quit. Mr. Peacock, the other member of the firm, thereupon insisted that I should stay, as I was right. Masterson having claimed to be a killer, then undertook the job of killing me, and attempted it on the following evening by coming into the saloon and cocking his revolver in my face. I got the best of him by a large majority, and notwithstanding his reputation as a killer, he hid out and was next morning arrested upon my complaint.[2] He or his friends then telegraphed an inflammatory dispatch to his brother, Bat Masterson, who arrived in due time, and met Mr. Peacock and myself midway between the two front streets and without any warning to us, commenced shooting at us. We of course returned the fire and soon drove Bat Masterson behind the railroad embankment where he lay down out of range of our fire. We were then fired at by parties from the saloon doors on the north Front street, from one of which I was shot through the right lung, now six days ago. I feel that I will soon be around again, and will not die as the party wished me to. The parties who participated in the affair against me were by the citizens bounced out of town, and I invite anyone who doubts this statement, to correspond with any respectable man in this place, who, I am satisfied will corroborate this statement.

Respectfully yours,
AL. UPDEGRAFF[3]

Bat and his brother published no statement of their case. The rumble of tenpins, the clink of glasses, the rattle of dice, and the squealing of fiddles began anew. Dodge was herself again.

One wonders how it happened that a man with Bat's reputation as a gun-fighter could empty his six-gun at Updegraff and Peacock without hitting anybody—unless perhaps, Bat was "distracted by the crossfire."[4] Also the way the three took cover before firing was not in the best tradition of Dodge City. The town was no longer what it had been.[5] But killings in Dodge were yet to come.

CHAPTER 23 :

: LUKE SHORT AND
: THE PEACE
COMMISSION

THE popular conception of a Western gun-fighter or gunman is that of a husky, rip-roaring athlete standing six feet or more in his socks, hard as nails, and able to outshoot, outwrestle or out-box any and all comers.

But as a matter of fact, few of the gun-toting gentry could measure up to any such standard. Many of the most celebrated were anything but athletes, and a surprising number suffered from some disease or physical or mental handicap or were less than man-size: Ben Thompson, five feet eight in his boots, fat and puffy; Doc Holliday, a consumptive who, according to Bat Masterson, "could not have whipped a fifteen year old boy"; the bucktoothed runt, Billy the Kid; Clay Allison with his crippled leg; Wild Bill with his female figure; Cockeyed Frank Loving; Wagner, killer of Ed Masterson, whose quarrelsome behavior was supposed to have been caused by a fall on his head from the saddle. Numbers of the gunmen were alcoholics; some, homicidal maniacs; and not a few were just kids in their teens when they killed their first man—mere juvenile delinquents.

It is clear that such men became pistol experts, not in spite of, but *because of*, their handicaps. Colt's "equalizer" was their only means of self-defense—and self-expression. Psychiatrists have a word for it.

There were, of course, gun-fighters who were sober, strong, intelligent, handsome men, like Bill Tilghman, Bat Masterson, and Wyatt Earp, who would rather "buffalo" a man than shoot him.

Some of the pistoleers were dandies and made it a point to be as fashionably or strikingly dressed as any modern gangster.

Luke Short was one of the dandies—one of the little fellows, standing nearly five feet six inches in his boots and weighing almost 140 pounds. A small package, but full of fight, with a round head that took a seven and one-eighth inch size hat. In the middle seventies he had worked as a cowboy on his father's ranch in West Texas, afterward trading with the Sioux Indians in Nebraska. Next he turned up in Leadville, Colorado. There for the first time he saw the game of faro dealt. Luke was fascinated.

One day in a gambling house a bad man with a killer's reputation took some liberty with one of Luke's bets and, when the latter politely requested the troublemaker to keep his hands off, the bad man grew angry and made rude remarks. The dealer well knew the bad man and was frightened half out of his wits. He expected to see Short riddled before anyone could raise a hand to prevent it. He did not know Luke Short. "Gentlemen," said the dealer in his suavest manner, "rather than have a quarrel I will make the amount of the bet good."

"You will not make anything good to me," said Short. "That's my bet, and I will not permit anyone to take it."

"You insignificant little shrimp," growled the bad man, at the same time reaching for his "canister." "I will shoot your hand off if you dare to put it on that bet."

Before the bully could get his pistol out, Luke—quicker than a flash—had jammed his own gun into the badman's face and fired it. Down he went. The ball passed through his cheek, but fortunately did not kill him.

Such things happened all the time in those days, so there was no arrest nor trial. But the incident gave Luke quite a standing in the camp. Owners of gambling houses hired him to stay around their places of business during rush hours to keep bad men from making off with their bank rolls. Luke had the knack of making friends and was soon popular with the quieter and better class of the sporting fraternity. He quickly learned to handle the pasteboards and was soon dealing faro on a percentage for the house. All dressed up in a tailor-made suit and a derby hat, he would never have been recognized in West Texas.

In Tombstone, where Luke dealt faro for Wyatt Earp in the Oriental, Luke had a run-in with Charlie Storms. Bat Masterson, a friend to both men, tried to prevent a quarrel. He held Storms, asking Luke not to shoot and afterward took Storms to his room, expecting him to go to bed. But Storms came back and pulled his pistol. This time Luke killed the man. The display of such courage, skill, and cool nerve earned for Luke the respect of the frontiersmen.

In 1883 Luke was in Dodge and well liked by the sports. He was popular with the cowboys too, since he himself was a Texan. But there were so many saloons and gambling places that even with a share in the Long Branch, the biggest and best-paying gambling house in Dodge, he was not satisfied. More especially as the new ordinance against gambling was not being enforced impartially.

Finally, Luke hit upon a sure-fire idea. He hired a very handsome young woman to play the piano in the Long Branch. Saloons stood thick along Front Street. The sound of the music carried through their thin plank walls and Luke made sure to have all windows and doors open when his dashing musician was playing, so as to reach as many ears as possible. On one side of the Long Branch stood the Alamo Saloon owned by A. B. Webster, the Mayor. In the other direction was G. M. Hoover's retail and wholesale liquor store. The fair pianist in the Long Branch made the crash of her piano resound in these rival establishments, quickly drained off their patrons, and Luke was in the money.

Now Webster was absolutely determined to run all the gamblers out of Dodge without delay. He had been elected Mayor on a "reform ticket" and was politically opposed to Short and his friends anyhow. So now he put the case up to the City Council. They passed Ordinance 83, which provided that no person was to have a dance hall in Dodge City or "any other place where lewd men and women congregate for the purpose of dancing." Also the ordinance provided that "no saloon keeper was to keep, maintain, or allow in his or her place of business any violin or piano or other musical instrument" and must "not permit them to be used to the annoyance or inconvenience of any person. Fine $10 to $100."

When the City Marshal informed Short that the music in his place must stop, Luke made no objection. "That suits me," he said. "I don't need music in my house in order to do business. And now I can save that expense."

What was Luke's chagrin and indignation to discover that evening that Webster had employed the pianist to work in the Alamo and that the cowboys had followed her there like a bunch of mules trailing a bell mare.

Now it was the basic principle of the frontier gambler never to let anyone run a bluff on him. The unfairness of the deal irked Luke. Promptly he hired several musicians from out of town. But once more the Mayor stepped in, sending two Deputy Marshals into the Long Branch to arrest Luke's musicians.

Luke was out at the time. When he heard the news, he went looking for an officer to give bail for his employees, but without success. All the time he could hear the music ringing from the Alamo.

Then suddenly he saw a special officer, L. C. Hartman, who had helped to make the arrests.

Hartman stood on the sidewalk a foot above the street. When he saw Luke coming, he pulled his gun and fired. Hartman missed. Luke fired in turn just as the officer started to run. When he jumped off the sidewalk into the dark street, he fell. Luke thought he had hit Hartman and without further ado hurried to the Long Branch, loaded his shotgun and stood off the town until morning. He refused to submit to arrest.

Next day they talked him into putting aside his weapons, suggesting that he go into court, plead guilty to disturbing the peace, pay his fine, and end the whole business. All Luke asked was a square deal. Accordingly he started to court with the officers, but found himself instead locked in the city jail.

The eastbound and westbound trains passed each other in Dodge at noon. Officers armed with shotguns marched Luke to the depot and told him to choose which train he would take. Resistance was useless. He caught the eastbound train for Kansas City.

Some of the fellows in Dodge threatened to kill Luke if he ever showed his face there again. But that was not the end of the story. Luke had invested everything he owned in the Long Branch Saloon. He felt he was surely entitled to recover the value of his property and wired Bat Masterson, then in Denver, to join him. Bat caught the next train and the two of them decided to go to Topeka and lay the whole matter before the Governor of Kansas. The Governor was annoyed at the goings-on in Dodge City, but explained that he could do nothing, since the local authorities there had informed him that they were amply able to keep the peace and wanted no interference. M. W. "Mike" Sutton, County Attorney, thought he could handle matters.

Bat and Luke assured the Governor that they thought they could reinstate themselves in Dodge, provided the State did not interfere. The Governor replied, "Go ahead, re-establish yourselves if you can."

Luke went west, rounding up friends on his way, while Bat hurried to Silverton, Colorado, to put it all up to Wyatt Earp. Wyatt, taking along four good gun-fighters—Texas Jack Vermillion, Dan Tipton, Johnny Millsap, and Johnny Green—

caught the train to Dodge. There on the platform stood Prairie Dog Dave wearing the badge of an officer.

Dave guessed at once what Wyatt was there for, and agreed that Luke had had a dirty deal. Finding Dave so sympathetic, Earp asked Dave to deputize his four companions as city peace officers, thus making it unnecessary for them to give up their arms. With these four worthies stationed at strategic points around the Plaza and several other friends dropping into the camp unobserved, Wyatt felt he had everything under control.

Even at that date Dodge was still a small town of little more than two thousand residents. The word that Wyatt was back quickly got around, and it was clear enough that the Mayor's supporters were none too anxious for a showdown fight. Hurriedly a telegram was sent to the Adjutant General of Kansas asking him to interfere. But the Governor was as good as his word, and no militia were forthcoming. Instead Colonel Thomas Moonlight, the Adjutant General, went to Dodge. When the Mayor's backers learned this, all the fight went out of them. It was not long until they and Wyatt got together.

"Wyatt went alone to the powwow, and, after letting the officials know that he had a correct idea of the controversy, concluded:

" 'Luke Short is at Kinsley. I'll wire him to come on. He'll stay in Dodge as long as he wants to, to continue business, or close out. If Ab Webster has a woman piano-player, Luke Short can have one. If Luke can't have one, no one else can. I have four friends in town with me. We're here to see that Luke gets an even break, and we can stay indefinitely. Does he get it?'

"Over Ab Webster's protests, the council agreed that Luke did. Short and Masterson came into Dodge on the next train."[1]

Says the *Globe*: "As soon as Bat Masterson alighted from the train on his late arrival into this city, Mike Sutton started for his cyclone building on Gospel Ridge where he remained until the truce was made.

"On the return of Luke Short and his friends it didn't take

Mike Sutton long to arrive at the conclusion that Kinsley was a much healthier locality and that town is now his abiding place. When Dodge City becomes too hot for Mike Sutton, hell itself would be considered a cool place—a desirable summer resort."

But Luke contended that the City Marshal's force was stacked against him, and that once his friends left Dodge, he would be run out again. So "The Dodge City Peace Commission" was set up—eight men appointed to choose new peace officers for the town.

W. H. Harris, Wyatt Earp, Luke Short, Bat Masterson, Billy Potillion, Charlie Bassett, Frank McLane, and Neal Brown made up the Peace Commission. Colonel Moonlight acted as chairman during its ten-day session at Dodge.

The Peace Commission had a group photograph taken. This is our best picture of that galaxy of Dodge City Marshals, gunfighters, and gamblers.

Of course, after this setback there was no pretense at enforcing the ordinances. The *Ford County Globe* reports: "Our city trouble is about over and things in general will be conducted as of old. All parties that were in on it have returned and no further effort will be made to drive them away. Gambling houses, we understand, are again to be opened, but with screened doors in front of their places of business.[2] A new dance house was opened Saturday night where all the warriors met and settled their past differences and everything was made lovely and serene. All opposing factions, both Saloonmen and gamblers met and agreed to stand by each other for the good of the trade. A not unlooked for result. The Mayor stood firm on his gambling proclamation, but as his most ardent supporters have gone over to his enemies, —he will have trouble in enforcing it. . . . Luke Short . . . we believe has come to stay."

Many a man will forgive another for doing him a favor. One in a hundred will forgive a man whom he himself has wronged. But not one in a thousand will forgive the man whom he has tried—and failed—to wrong. Luke Short, a friendly soul, soon realized that he could not be happy in Dodge. He sold out his interests and went to Texas. In Fort Worth he bought a large and elegant gambling house, the White Elephant. There he was obliged to kill another man in self-defense, yet in all his time in Dodge City Luke Short killed nobody.

But meanwhile the trouble in Dodge over music roused the indignant management of the Atchison, Topeka & Santa Fe Railroad to take action. They set out to tell Dodge where to head in. As we shall later see, within the year Dodge was to feel the force of their displeasure.

CHAPTER 24 ·
: BULLFIGHT

IN THE spring of 1884 Dodge City faced a prospect considerably less cheering than before. The depression which had set in the year before was making itself felt. True, it was not nearly so severe or prolonged as that earlier one of 1873-78 which had been such a spur to the westward movement. But in those earlier years with its bull teams, buffalo hides, and cattle drives, Dodge City had been too prosperous to feel the pinch. Now things seemed less favorable.

In the first place the severe winter just passed had taken heavy toll of range cattle and Dodge City papers quoted experienced cattlemen as predicting that the roundup would reveal losses of some thirty to sixty per cent. Moreover, much of the stock was in poor condition. Prairie fires in the fall and heavy spring rains had made the grass on the ground rot over large areas. Mountain lions and wolves were reported as playing havoc with young cattle. Far down in Texas, of course, the cattle were plentiful and fat, and even in the Panhandle there were many herds in fine condition which, could they have been brought to Dodge without losing weight on the drive, might have paid off well.

The *Fort Worth Livestock Journal* declared: "The well grounded suspicion of some of our leading drovers is that the drive this season will fall far short of what it was last year. No cattle worth speaking of have as yet been contracted. One reason for this is the fence cutting troubles and the uncertainty with cattlemen as to what the Legislature will do on the Herd Law

232

question. Northwestern stockmen have been here feeling the market but say they have more cattle now than they can handle if a Herd Law is enacted, and are therefore holding up. But the principal reason is given by a wealthy gentleman in the following words, 'Money is too scarce. We can't get hold of sums sufficient to enable us to invest as we want to. Then young cattle have been put back again to about last spring's prices which leave such a small margin that there is nothing really in buying at these prices. Cattle must come down.' "

No longer did the Dodge City papers content themselves with boasts and generalities. They began to report comparative statistics on business failures, increasing liabilities, and whistling to keep their courage up. The demand for cow ponies was falling, while the demand for draft animals mounted. Already in Ford County more than 3,000 acres were in cultivation, producing more than 75,000 bushels of wheat. Poultry, garden truck, and butter were beginning to be produced, and already in 1883 sheep were ranging the short grass, producing 38,000 pounds of wool in the County. Meanwhile the Kansas State Short Horn Breeders Association met in Topeka and predicted the days of the longhorn were numbered. The editor of the *Globe* published a rather pathetic story to the effect that all-wool blankets *might* be made out of longhorn hair!

All this had a discouraging effect on the usual robust confidence of the men of Dodge.

It seemed that everyone had a chip on his shoulder and wanted to fight. Jack Potter reports that when his outfit arrived at the line of the Cherokee Strip, they found the trail fenced and a sign nailed to a post bearing the word, CLOSED. The cattlemen coming round to Dodge by rail had had to appeal to the War Department, which sent troops down to cut the fence and open the trail.

But when the drive reached the Kansas line, they were stopped again by a quarantine. Hoof and mouth disease was rampant over the country and the Government was sending surgeons here and there to kill the cattle. The Texas cattlemen had to make special arrangements with the State of Kansas in order to cross the line.

Those who wished to take their cattle through to Ogallala found that a furrow had been plowed on either side of the trail from Dodge toward their destination. The trail so defined was from half a mile to six miles wide. Drivers were warned that a fine of $500 would be paid by anyone who crossed the furrows. Texas cattle, infected with tick fever, were deadly to Northern herds. And everywhere the nesters were belligerent.

But all these problems were temporary. There was much worse to be faced. Dodge City was losing prestige.

In fact the lusty young men who had come there to build and run the camp a dozen years before were now mature men, many of them married citizens with a stake in some business or trade. Bat was in and out of Dodge, always looking for greener pastures, trying his luck in Deadwood, Trinidad, Denver, Leadville, Tombstone, or Ogallala, yet always sure to turn up once more in Dodge. Wyatt Earp and his brothers, Doc Holliday, and other restless gun-fighters had left Dodge for wilder towns. The men of Dodge had been too successful in pacifying the gun-slingers. Their respectability was showing.

Newspapers over the country began to call attention to this change. It was natural enough that rival Kansas towns should call attention to this development. Thus the *Independent* published in McPherson, itself a Western town, declared:

"Dodge City is not the town it used to be. A few years ago at early candlelight nearly every saloon was turned into a public gambling or dance house. The 'girls' came out from almost every nook and corner and solicited custom with as much effrontery as the waiter girls do for their counters at a church festival. It was trying on a man's virtue in those days. The cowboys, with a revolver strapped upon each hip, swung these wicked beauties all night and made the sleeping hours hideous with their profanity and vulgarity. This has been stopped. No cowboy is allowed to carry weapons, few dance halls are allowed to run, and gambling is only carried on in private quarters. The saloons are yet running in defiance of law, but prosecutions are pending against all of them."[1]

Numbers of Eastern papers published such stories and, strange to tell, some of these were reprinted in Dodge City. Thus the *Kansas Cowboy* quoted:

"People in the East have formed the idea that Dodge is still the embodiment of all the wickedness in the Southwest, and that it is dangerous for a stranger to come into the town unless he has a strong bodyguard with him. The impression, however, is a false one. Dodge is a rough frontier town, and it is populated largely by rough people, but they are not at all vicious. They are open-hearted and generous. I would have less fear of molestation in this wild, western town than I would have on the side streets of Kansas City or Chicago late in the evening.

"Dodge is a typical frontier town. Cowboys and cattle dealers constitute the bulk of the population. Incidental to these are hosts of gamblers and saloonists. The yearly 'round-up' has not yet been completed. In May the cattlemen begin to drive in their cattle for the round-up, which lasts nearly a month. The drive this year probably numbered 450,000 cattle. Of these doubtless 100,000 will be shipped from here, the balance being driven on further. Dodge is a lively business town. The amount of freight received here over the railway is enormous, as this is the base of supplies for the immense country of which this is the centre."[2]

The editors in Dodge were hard put to it for stories of violence that spring. Almost the only story of the kind is of a pistol whipping—and *that* took place as far off as Cimarron. The editor of the *Democrat regrets* "the quiet and orderly condition of Dodge City on Christmas day." He goes on to remark that citizens can now indulge in argument without resorting to violence!

There was enough going on in Dodge to lend a good deal of color to such stories. In March a petition was circulated to abolish dance halls. And a hotel keeper sought an injunction in the District Court and damages in the sum of $1,500 because of the alleged nuisance caused by disorderly neighbors who, it was alleged in the complaint, "openly, notoriously, continually, unlawfully, persistently, and maliciously maintained a brothel or bawdy house in what was known as and commonly called a dance hall" and in which, it was alleged, "large numbers of lewd women . . . congregate and stay, and there, in said buildings on said lots dance, drink, get drunk, fight, stab, cut, shoot and so forth. . . ." There, it was complained, "the dancing is not so frequent but nonetheless, severe . . . loud and vulgar language is often used, curses . . . plainly and distinctly heard by the inmates of said hotel."

But the election of city officials showed no disposition on the part of the citizens to take issue on the question of a wide-open town. For the two-gun metropolis had not reformed. It was still as sporting and daring in spirit as ever before. A. B. Webster, formerly Mayor, proposed a plan to bring the reputation of Dodge City back, to make it once more a center of national interest.

Dodge had always been a sporting community, celebrating the Fourth of July with gusto. Webster proposed to stage a Mexican bull fight on the Glorious Fourth, and within two days sold the project to the businessmen and raised a budget of $10,000 for the festival.

This promised to provide the kind of publicity on which the town's reputation had previously thriven. But as it turned out, the publicity was more lurid than the backers of the bullfight had counted on.

The newspapers all over the country played up the story and hardly one but called to mind or exaggerated the now legendary sins of Dodge.

Meanwhile, Webster, the promoter, and his allies were busy finding matadors and bulls and an arena for the bout. The Dodge City Driving Park and Fair Association was organized with

H. B. (Ham) Bell as president; vice-president, D. M. Cockey; secretary, J. S. Welch; treasurer, A. J. Anthony; general manager, A. B. Webster.

Webster found in W. K. Moore, an attorney in Paso del Norte, the man to find the matadors. He hired the troupe and acted as their manager and press agent. This canny Scot endeavored to convince the public that the bullfight would not be cruel or brutal, giving out reassuring interviews to newsmen. The *Kansas Cowboy* quoted him as follows:

"Mr. Moore is a native of Scotland and has lived in Paso del Norte ten years. He is a professor in one of the Mexican colleges. He wishes to disabuse the prevailing opinion in the minds of the American people as to the nature of a bull fight. He says that fight is not the proper word; that athletic exhibition would be more suitable. There is nothing barbarous in the proceeding. The bulls are not tortured, the only weapons of offense used by the men being small darts. The excitement and interest in the 'sport' (as termed by the Mexicans) consist principally in witnessing the skill and dexterity of the men in evading the assaults of the bull. Mr. Moore says it is an error to classify it with pugilistic contests. The governor of Chihuahua is a bullfighter and can handle the lasso with as much skill as the most accomplished cowboy."[3]

Such publicity seemed to be needed, for the American Society for the Prevention of Cruelty to Animals which, four years earlier, had successfully stopped a bull-baiting exhibition in New York City, appealed to the Governor of Kansas by wire and by mail: "In the name of humanity I appeal to you to prevent the contemplated bull fight at Dodge City this day. Let not American soil be polluted by such atrocities."

In the letter it quoted the Laws of Kansas, 1879, Chapter 81, Section 264: "Every person who shall maliciously or cruelly maim, beat or torture any horse, ox, or other cattle, whether belonging to himself or another, shall on conviction be adjudged guilty of a misdemeanor, and fined not exceeding fifty dollars."

It was rumored that Governor Glick would stop the fight, but by the time the Governor received that letter the bullfight was over.

Even in Dodge City a minister stood in the pulpit and publicly prayed that the town might be spared this "stench in the nostrils of civilization." And some of the businessmen began to worry, fearing that all this criticism would damage the future of their fair city.

But all this criticism was wasted on Webster and his colleagues. It was claimed that he had received a telegram from the U.S. Attorney's office to the effect that bullfighting was against the law in the United States and that the Mayor made an answer that has become a classic in the West: "Hell! Dodge City ain't in the United States."

But most of the men of Dodge were heartily in favor of holding the fight. For a decade or more they had been rather proud of their sanguinary glory, and all the more so because they felt it was largely a thing of the past.

At the same time they expected to have a heap of fun. The fight gave everybody something to talk about, something to bet on, and to keep the spotlight on their town. They had a high old time over the bulls provided for the arena. D. W. "Doc" Barton, believed to be the first man to drive a herd of cattle from the Texas ranges to Dodge, was chosen to select the bulls.

There were plenty on the grazing grounds to choose from and Doc combed the herds to find the most ferocious, pugnacious, and active bulls. By the end of June he had corralled twelve at the arena.

The men of Dodge knew cattle and all agreed that Doc's bulls looked ugly enough. When anyone approached to inspect them it was "enough to bring them pawing and plunging against the corral fence till the boards bent like paper and the braces creaked with the strain."

One declared, "By nature a Texas bull is all the time as mad as he can get."

The *Ford County Globe* published a humorous story about the entries: "As some of them are liable to be numbered with the dead before our next issue, we deem it proper to give a short sketch of these noted animals, together with their pedigrees. These pedigrees are kindly furnished by the famous bull raiser and breeder, Brother Barton, of the great Arkansas River.

"Number 1 on the list was Ringtailed Snorter, the oldest and most noted of the twelve. He has been in twenty-seven different fights, and always came off victor. Pedigree: Calved February 29, 1883; sire, Long-Horns; dam, All Fire, first of Great Fire, who won big money in a freeze-out at Supply in 1882. . . ."[4]

Public sympathy was with the bulls. Of course it took nerve to face one of Doc Barton's demons. But after all, the Mexicans were aliens, the bulls fellow countrymen. Cattlemen felt that Ringtailed Snorter and his fellows were fighting for the honor of the cattle country and for Dodge. A good many bets were laid favoring the animals. After all, the prosperity of Dodge from the beginning had rested on the prowess and quality of horned cattle—oxen, buffalo, longhorns—and shorthorns.

As the week of the Fourth arrived expectation was high. The Sunday before, the bullfighters arrived and the newsmen did their stuff: "They are a fierce lot, and fear is an unknown sensation to them. They have followed this avocation from boyhood. They have had many narrow escapes from death and have been seriously wounded at times. They understand that the people want an exciting and dangerous fight, and they are ready to satisfy them. Some day, they all feel, they will come to their death in the bull pit, but they like the life and would not be satisfied to leave it. Yet they are as intelligent a party of men as any person would wish to meet. Their all-redeeming trait is that they cannot be forced to drink a drop of strong liquor."

That last claim of total abstinence has a hollow ring, as though intended to pacify critics of this sporting enterprise.

The five Mexicans were only part-time matadors. Their chief, Captain Gregorio Gallardo, was a tailor in Chihuahua. But the papers billed him as the most famous of all famous bullfighters in the history of Old Mexico. An astonishing number of local men could remember seeing him kill bulls at Paso del Norte a few years or months before. His two Toledo two-edged blades were three feet long. One the manager claimed was 150 years old and had belonged to Gallardo's great-grandfather, a famous Spanish bullfighter.

The picador, Evaristo A. Rivas, was an official inspector of public works in the state of Chihuahua; his son, Rodrigo, was an artist. The other two, Marco Moya and Juan Herrerra, were musicians from Huejuquilla and Aldama, respectively.

Visitors piled into Dodge, and the backers of the bullfights rubbed their hands. The Santa Fe brought carloads of visitors from parts east, and cowboys from all over the Southwest, booted and spurred, tanned under their big hats, with money in their pockets, strutted through the streets. The Plaza was jammed, the gambling games running full blast, the saloons doing a big business. Metropolitan newspapers had sent correspondents, and their stories did the occasion justice.

There were maybe five hundred cowboys in town. They all wore broad-brimmed, white felt hats, with leather hat bands and double-breasted flannel shirts. Some had on leggin's and spurs. They were nearly all well dressed, and a few stylishly and expensively attired. All seemed to have money, and they were very free with it. A man who had "bucked" the tiger unsuccessfully could generally get a stake from the first fellow herdsman he met. There was not a pistol to be seen, except in the belts of the Sheriff, the Marshal, and their deputies. Not a shot was fired all day. Not even a single, solitary firecracker was heard, nor a single cowboy coursing up and down the street as if he owned the town. One reporter complained, "All the profane language that your correspondent heard was in the hack while going to the bull fight, and that was enunciated by something that wore a Mother Hubbard dress."

Everywhere were cow ponies, wagons, and rigs tied along

the streets or picketed on open ground. Everybody was waiting for the big parade.

About two o'clock the promoter and manager of the affair, Webster, led off with Manager Moore toward the fair grounds. Behind them in a body went the town officials; then came the longhorn standard of the Cowboy Band and their music. After these, bullfighters in their blue tunics, red jackets, white stockings and black pumps paraded, seeming "the perfection of litheness and quickness, and were heartily applauded as their dark handsome faces looked on the crowd gathered along the streets."

The Association owned a tract of forty acres between the town and the Arkansas River where they had laid out a half-mile track and an amphitheater seating four thousand. Here in front of the grandstand an arena one hundred feet in diameter had been enclosed with an eight-foot plank fence. Inside the fence at regular intervals eight escapes or wooden screens provided cover for bullfighters if they should need it. To the west of the arena and connected with it by a chute was the corral holding the bulls. Alongside the chute there was a wider passage through which the bodies of the bulls could be dragged out.

The seats around the arena were packed to capacity. A third of those present were children and women. The seating of these last offered a problem, because the ladies of Dodge City fell into two well-defined groups. To avoid intermixture of the demimonde with the respectable ladies a deputy sheriff had been ordered to separate the sheep from the goats.

It may be regretted that we have no record of his proceedings, which might have been more amusing than the bullfight itself.

The band and the press were seated over the entrance gate and on either side leading citizens sat in their boxes. Opposite these were the cowboys and their companions. One writer reports that the ambition of every cowpuncher seemed to be to get a big fat girl and a high seat at the same time. While the crowd waited for their first bull, the time was filled with calling and kidding between the selections rendered by the Cowboy Band.

At half past two Mr. Chappell, a track horseman and rodeo rider, assisted by the bullfighter Juan Herrerra and a red cape, penned the bulls up behind the post. There they sawed off the tips of their horns and rasped the ends smooth.

It was 3:40 before the bugle sounded for the grand entry.

Then the bullfighters, now in costume, entered the ring. Gallardo in a scarlet tunic and knee breeches with a green sash; Rivas in a yellow tunic trimmed with red, yellow breeches and a white cap with horns. The other two matadors wore red and blue. These four marched in on foot. The picador, dressed like any cowboy, was in the saddle. Having circled the arena, bowed to the officials, they waited for the bugle.

Again the bugle sounded and a red, fierce-looking bull, apparently full of fight, rushed in. As he passed the entrance a decorated barb, or *banderilla*, was flung into his neck on either side. Enraged at this, he charged without delay.

Gallardo flung out his cape and began the play, leading the bull on to charge at him, luring him from his course with the cape, whirling to escape the horns as it passed. Several times Gallardo had to take cover behind one of the wooden escapes. The bull completely circled the ring, then stood in the center and defiantly pawed up the earth, hiding himself in clouds of dust. The other three matadors now closed in. But no matter how often and how fiercely the bull charged and wheeled he could not touch them, and every time he passed another dart was flung into his back until colored streamers flowed from horns to tail.

This bull gave the matadors and the crowd their money's worth. Here was a bull fight displaying all the skill and agility, all the deftness and tricks of the bullfighter's profession.

At the end of half an hour the bull was tired. Mr. Chappell was called on to rope him and drag him out.

The roping excited the cowhands, who longed to have a display of their own skills. They set up a cry, "Throw him." Chappell, willing to oblige, found the bull too strong for that and had to drag it back into the pen. There the bull charged him, scratched his horse, and broke away. At length he was dragged back into the pen.

Aroused by this exciting contest, the crowd expected another bull equally good, but the second bull wasn't having any. He had no heart for a fight, fled from the bullfighters and had to be let go. The third bull also had little fight in him. Nor had the fourth. But of all the bulls the fifth was the greatest coward. In his endeavor to escape he got jammed into one of the escapes and had to be whipped out by a cowboy in the front row above him. He fled to the pen amid the jeers and the catcalls of the audience.

The crowd began to wonder if they could ever get their money's worth. Someone demanded that they bring back the first bull. Others took up the cry. Earlier it had been announced that Gallardo would kill the last bull of the day with his sword. Now the crowd wanted to see the program carried out as advertised. So back the red bull came into the arena.

Manager Moore handed down the Toledo sword to Gallardo. It was his task to incite the bull to charge at him until it offered the right opening for the death thrust. The animal had to run upon the sword held from a position directly in front. The thrust could not be fumbled and must end in death before the bull reached his antagonist.

And now the crowd was quiet. The bull, now fiercer than ever, charged furiously. Gallardo gracefully swept it past. It wheeled and charged again, thrusting its horns into the red cape.

But each time the bull came closer, barely missing the man's unprotected side.

Then suddenly everyone leaped to his feet. The matador was down. Some hoped, some feared, everyone expected the bull to gore him; but luckily for Gallardo he fell near one of the escapes. He threw himself lengthwise between the horns and crawled to safety behind it. The bull nearly tore the escape down trying to get at him, then backed furiously away.

Gallardo, though bruised on his left thigh, stepped out to finish the fight. The crowd roared applause as he bowed and signaled the Cowboy Band to continue the music which should accompany the killing. Gallardo walked directly toward the bull until, when almost upon him, the sullen brute left his stance and charged.

But the bull did not offer Gallardo the opening he needed and again the cape swung into play. Once, twice. The fourth charge gave him his opening. The swift steel struck home, pierced through to the vital spot. The bull suddenly slowed, stumbled down and lay quiet.

The *Ford County Globe* reported: "Thus ended the first day's bull fight in Dodge City, and for all we know the first fight on American soil. The second day's fighting, with the exception of the killing of the last animal in the ring, was more interesting than the first. . . . The matadors showed to the people of America what bull fighting really was. No one could see it and go away saying that it was not a genuine bull fight. It was not that torturous or inhuman punishment inflicted upon wild animals as the term 'bull fighting' would seem to imply, save and except the single animal that was killed. The punishment, tortures or cruelty was even less than that inflicted upon animals in the branding pen."

The *Larned Optic* crowned the celebration with a news item which indicated that Dodge City still afforded plenty of opportunity for a good time: "Quite a number of our boys visited Dodge last week to see the bull fight. Some of them returned looking as though they had had a personal encounter with the animals."[5]

But this is not all the story of the bull fight at Dodge City. The bull stabbed on the second day was dragged out of the ring and onto the prairie where it was left awaiting disposal. What was the owner's surprise, when he came back, to find the animal gone. A few days later he discovered the bull among his other cattle, apparently none the worse for its experience. This true story—or legend—gave everybody in Dodge intense satisfaction. The honor of the cattle country had been vindicated.[6]

The bullfight had convinced most outsiders that Dodge was still wild and bucking. But for all their bravado, the citizens knew better.

The night after the bullfight, a very much disgusted reporter said to a citizen, "Where's all your dance houses and places for fun? I've been listening for music for the last half-hour and can't hear a demisemiquaver of a note. I though you had a lively town at night, if it *was* stiller than a mute school by day."

The citizen sighed and smiled, and said: "There isn't any music any more outside the church melodeon. I honestly think there ain't anything here that will make music bigger than a jew's-harp. This used to be a bully town for racket and noise. Every saloon had a piano and a bass viol and several fiddles, and some had concert organs and drums, and musicians' salaries have been as high as $2,000 a year, with board and drinks thrown in.

"But it ain't that way now any more." (Another sigh.) "There's nothing left but the stockmen's band."

"And how did all this come to be changed? Who was it that so unsympathetically stopped the mellifluous warbling and the mazy dance?"

"Oh, it's the Santa Fe Railroad. Everything that happens here is the Santa Fe. The Santa Fe giveth and the Santa Fe taketh away. I reckon they own half this town anyway. Their Boston management was down on so much noise. They said you couldn't go through on the train by day without thinking you were in Pandemonium, and at night you couldn't sleep. The Dodge City music was of the double-barbed kind and seemed to stick in their ears. So the railroad people asked to have it stopped.

"There was a big kick, but the Santa Fe men said, 'Gentlemen, we made this town and we can unmake it. If you'll stop your hellish din, we'll build a roundhouse here, and a reading room, and a hospital, and enlarge the pens, and put down more side tracks, and give you reasonable rates on freight. If you don't want to be reasonable, why, we'll take the pens further west, and we won't make any improvements, and then maybe some of you will be selling corner lots cheap.' The end of it was that the pianos and organs were sold at low prices for cash, and the musicians sought a more genial clime." (Sigh number three.) "I wouldn't stay if I didn't have to play the organ at church."[7]

CHAPTER 25 · **: MYSTERIOUS DAVE**

IN THE earliest years in Dodge the peace officers were hired killers who shot it out with gunmen. Then, as we have seen, following the example of Wyatt Earp and his deputies, officers buffaloed and arrested offenders and haled them into court to be fined or banished from Dodge City. And now in the camp's last years as a cowtown, having little occasion to shoot visitors, officers began to shoot each other. In the columns of the *Kansas Cowboy* for July 26, 1884, the following headlines and story appeared:

MORE BLOOD

ASSISTANT MARSHAL THOMAS NIXON SHOT AND KILLED BY DEPUTY SHERIFF DAVID MATHER

About 10 o'clock last Monday evening, as Assistant Marshal Thomas Nixon was approaching the opera house saloon from the north, he was confronted by Deputy Sheriff Mather, who fired four shots into the body of Nixon, the immediate provocation for which is unknown. One ball penetrated the heart of Nixon, causing instant death.

This killing is one of the most notorious in the annals of Dodge City. Both the principals were well known and the public interest in the affair has never faded.

Dave Mather, known from his inscrutable face and stealthy manner as "Mysterious Dave," was not a man with whom most people could readily make friends. When people met Dave on the street, they passed by without a word unless he spoke to them. Robert M. Wright in his book declares that "it was and is an undoubted fact that Dave had more dead men to his credit at that time than any other man in the West. Seven by actual count in one night, in one house, and all at one sitting."[1]

But Wright offers no proof to back his statement.

According to the newspaper, Mather had been a resident at Dodge City at intervals for several years. He had served both as an Assistant Marshal and Marshal of the city and "in similar capacities at other rough places and is known to have killed several men while in the performance of his duties." The editor adds that Dave was "a native of New England and a lineal descendant of Cotton Mather."

As is usual in such cases, various stories are told to account for the hard feelings between the men.

But according to the *Kansas Cowboy*: "A feud of several months' standing existed between the parties, growing out of the closing up of the dance hall in the opera house which was operated by Mather & Black. Mather suspected Nixon of being the cause of the breaking up of the dancing business."[2]

On the Friday preceding the killing, the *Kansas Cowboy* alleges, "Nixon was looking through the window of the opera house, in which a performance was being conducted, when he was observed by Mather, who was inside. Mather invited Nixon to come inside. Nixon declined and beat a retreat downstairs, followed by Mather, who applied to Nixon vile epithets. Nixon turned and fired a shot at Mather. The ball lodged in the side of the building and cut out a splinter which struck one of Mather's fingers, inflicting a slight wound. Nixon was arrested and tried for this shooting on Monday, but was acquitted."

That night Dave shot him.

P. F. "Pat" Sughrue was among the bravest officers in western Kansas. As Sheriff of Ford County, he repeatedly proved his courage.

On one occasion in Dodge he stepped between two well-known gunmen bent on killing each other, arrested both, and so prevented the duel.

Another time at Ashland, when a drunken cowboy—after shooting up the town, wounding a lady and smashing a small boy's nose—was seized and lynched by indignant citizens, Pat arrived, arrested every man in the mob, and jailed them all in Dodge.

In making another arrest, he met with armed resistance. An opponent fired in the Sheriff's face. Thereafter, Pat's cheek bore the powder mark—his blue badge of courage.

It was now his duty to arrest Dave.

The *Kansas Cowboy* reports that "Mather immediately surrendered himself without resistance to Sheriff Sughrue and was lodged in the county jail, where he has since been confined. Nixon's body was conveyed to the engine house, where it remained until after the holding of the coroner's inquest over his remains on the following day. The inquest was conducted by Professor W. H. Lybrand, justice of the peace. The verdict of the jury was that Nixon came to his death by pistol shots fired by Mather and that the act was premeditated."

The preliminary hearing was held at the courthouse in Dodge City at ten o'clock Wednesday morning before Justice Lybrand. Messrs. Whitelaw, County Attorney, and Gryden, City Attorney, appeared for the State; and Messrs. Sutton, Haun, and Swan for the defense. The prisoner is described as having "a calm demeanor" such that "a stranger would have been unable to have determined from any expression of countenance . . . who among them it was who was soon to meet the ordeal of life or death before a jury of his peers." At the opening of the court, the paper reports, the house "was nearly filled with spectators," but "there was no appearance of any excited feeling as is frequent in murder trials, and before court adjourned at twelve o'clock there was not a dozen spectators present."

For all that, many in Dodge City were shocked by the killing of Tom Nixon. A local paper reports: "Mr. Nixon was one of the oldest residents of Dodge City; in fact, he lived here before the town had an existence. He was a buffalo hunter and had at one time a large number of men under his employ. He was a genuine frontiersman, with a somewhat rough exterior, but under his vest beat a warm and sympathetic heart. In all business relations he was honest, prompt and reliable. All the old settlers had a warm side for poor Tom. As a token of respect to the memory of the deceased most of the business houses were closed on Tuesday afternoon, with crape attached to the doors. The funeral services were held at the residence of the family, and were conducted by Elder Collins. There was a large attendance of sympathizing friends. An invalid wife and several children survive the deceased. At the time of his death he was assistant marshal of this city and had been serving as such since the last municipal election. . . ."

J. T. Whitelaw, prosecuting attorney of Ford County, Kansas, filed his complaint accusing Dave Mather of the murder of Thomas Nixon. Mather's petition for a change of venue was granted by J. C. Strang, Judge of the Sixteenth Judicial District of the State of Kansas.

Soon after, a writ of habeas corpus was granted admitting the prisoner to bail, with bond fixed at $6,000. The bond was promptly signed by L. E. Deger, J. S. Welch, George S. Emerson, Saul A. Bullard, Fred Singer, Dave Mather, M. W. Sutton, J. H. Crawford, N. B. Klaine, S. Garland, and F. Martin. The *Kansas Cowboy* comments thus: "They are of the best, most solid and substantial men of Ford county, representing a capital of more than $100,000. David is therefore again at large among the people. He seems to have had no difficulty in getting a bond."

Meanwhile the *Kansas Cowboy* reports (August 2, 1884): "The young man who was shot by a stray bullet when Mather killed Nixon is still suffering severely from his wound. It is near the knee joint, and may give him a great deal of trouble yet. The hot weather has a tendency to aggravate his afflictions."

So much for contemporary accounts derived from newspapers and legal records. Now for the sworn testimony of the witnesses.

Dr. C. A. Milton (Sworn) Says:

I have practiced medicine in Ford County, Kansas two years and three months, I am a graduate of Rush Medical College Chicago, Feb. 1881, I graduated. I was called upon to examine the body of Thomas Nixon, deceased, I saw the body about ten or fifteen minutes after he was shot, he was dead then. I found seven wounds in the body and one ball lodged under the skin there must have been four shots at least. My examination was not thorough enough to enable me to tell about the course of the balls, I can tell the exits and entrances. I found that that one ball entered in front about 3½ inches to the right of the *medvin* and at the eighth rib, another entered the left side just below the ribs between the crest of the *Ilium* and the last rib, another about four or five inches below this point in front and directly over the crest of the Ilium, another entered the back about the second Lomber vertebra about one and one half inches to the right side. One ball made its exit on the right side the crest of the Ilium another at the left nipple, another over the pubic bone about two inches above.

I found a ball lodged under the skin of the body under the upper portion of the right arm.

Probably all of the wounds would have been fatal, three of them them at least—one was necessarily immediately fatal. The cause of the death of the deceased was gunshot wounds, those I have described.

I made the examination on the day following the death at about ten o'clock, It was on July 22nd.[3]

Testimony of Fred W. Boyd:

On the night of July 21st, 1884 at about 10 o'clock I was in the Opera House in Ford County, State of Kansas, Dodge City, I was there at the time of the shooting of Thos Nixon I did and did not see deceased at the time he was shot, I saw his back, I was about eight or ten feet away from him when he was shot, I was talking to a man when I heard the name "Tom" called, No other language was used except this word, I then look around at him he was standing leaning against the facing of the east door facing Walter Streators

I think deceased had his right hand up against the door and the left back across his body, he was looking in at a game in the room, a report of a revolver immediately followed, Tom Nixon then said "Oh! I'm shot" or "I'm killed", I think he said "I'm Killed". He turned before the revolver was fired there was nothing that I could see in either his right or his left hand, Nixon fell immediately after the first shot was fired, three successive shots followed his falling. Shots in quick succession, he had fallen before the last three shots were fired, I did not see Tom Nixon draw or attempt to draw any weapons, I did not see the party who did the firing at the time of the shooting or immediately after.

Cross Examination

I meant when I said I was in the Opera House that I was in Opera House Saloon.

I was standing south of the middle of the gaming table towards the door, I had stood there five or ten minutes not over ten perhaps not over five, Al Reudy was standing by me, we had just met as I heard the name Tom called, I had just came from the Oil House to that place where I was standing, I did not discover Tom Nixon till his name was called, I don't know how long he had been standing there, I do not know from what direction or where he came from to that place, when Nixon's name was first called he paid no attention, when his name was called the second time he turned around, his exact position as he leaned against the door is as I have described, when he turned he turned to the right, when he turned around he turned out of sight of the door from where I was standing, It was not over a breath from the time he turned around till I heard the first shot, I did not see his back at that time, I got a glimpse of his back as he turned around then he got out of my sight, the other three shots immediately followed, I did not see Nixon when he fell, I heard him fall, he fell immediately after the first shot, I did not see him after he was down, he used the words "I'm killed" just after the first shot, I moved some twenty feet north toward the restaurant door and staid there ten or fifteen minutes, I am positive that I saw Tom at the door before any shot was fired. I am positive that he stood at the door when I heard his name called twice.

s/s F. W. Boyd

3rd Witness, Andrew Faulkner (Sworn) Says:

At about ten o'clock on the night of July 21st I was in Dodge City, Ford County, Kansas at Nels Cary's Saloon sitting out at the east side of the saloon, I was at the head of the stairs at the time Nixon was killed, I did not see Tom Nixon till after the first shot was fired, I saw him a second or two after the first shot was fired, I saw him a second or two after the first shot, that is I saw a man whom I afterwards knew to be Tom Nixon. When I first saw him he was lying down at the east door of Nels Cary's Saloon, I saw only one man near him at that time, I took the man to be Dave Mather, the man that did the shooting was followed by two others, Three shots were fired after Nixon was down, after the shooting Dave Mather started and walked to the foot of the stairs and then came up the steps, I recognized him as he came up it was Dave Mather, He had a revolver in his right hand as he came up the stairs, I don't know of my own knowledge who fired the first shot I did not see it fired, Four shots were fired, I saw the flash of three of them, I walked right down stairs and saw the man who was shot, it was Tom Nixon.

Cross Examination:

The first I saw of the man I afterwards found to be Nixon was when he was lying near the door, This was after the first shot, His head was on the door step of the east door with his feet out towards the edge of the sidewalk, I saw the lower half of his body when I look down after the first shot, I was standing at the head of the stairs when the shooting commenced, I was standing against the bannisters looking into the window of the Opera House, I think the body of Nixon had not been moved before I first saw it, He was lying on his right side and back together with his feet to the east, a little north east

s/s Andy Faulkner

H. V. Cook (Sworn) says:

I was near the Opera House the night Tom Nixon was killed, I was at the S. E. corner of the sidewalk standing there, Tom Nixon was close to the east door when I first saw him, He was walking toward east door, I saw Dave Mather at that time, I saw Tom Nixon when the Defendant shot him, Defendant said to Nixon immediately preceding the shooting, "Oh! Tom", Nixon at that time was walking towards the east door of the saloon, He turned to the right when Mather called to him, nearly facing him, As he turned Mather shot, I did not see anything unusual about Nixon's hands after he fell, He made no demonstration at all towards Mather that I saw, He fired four shots at Nixon, Nixon was lying on the sidewalk while the last three shots were fired, He fell as soon as the first shot was fired, Mather advanced to fire the last three shots, He was about four or five feet away from the body when the last three shots were fired, Mather turned around and I think went up stairs, I saw a person running up stairs that I would take to be him, Nixon was coming from the south when I first saw him.

Cross Examination:

I stood on the east edge of the side walk near the Opera House at the time of the firing, I had come from Sturme's place, I stood there when the first shot was fired then I up this way north, I had got about twelve feet this way when the last shot was fired, I did not see any persons standing around there, Nixon was not leaning against the door facing as far as I could see, He was walking and turned, Nixon was lying struggling a little when received the last three shots, He fell partly against the door and then on the left side partly and partly on the back, His feet were north east, Nixon was about two feet from the door when he got the first shot, He fell with his head in the door, The last three shots were fired into him after he was down, I did not see Nixon just before he was shot lean up against the east door, I heard Mather say "O Tom", Mather was ten or twelve feet north from the door when he said this.

Re-direct:

I think he fell on his left side and back, It might have been the other way, on the right side, It is possible that he might have leaned against the door facing for a moment but he was walking when I noticed him, I did not hear Nixon speak after he was shot.

Re-Cross:

As I was coming up from down the street I saw him coming from the north, He might have been leaning against the door facing for an instant, I started on after the first shot and then stopped when I heard the others Nixon was shot He was facing the door just before he was shot, Mather was about twelve feet from him when he fired the first shot.

s/s H. V. Cook

Archie Franklin (Sworn) says:

At the time of the shooting of Tom Nixon by David Mather on the night of July 21st, 1884 I was standing leaning against one of the supports of the porch I had been there about ten minutes a young fellow by the name of Bud Gohins was with me, Tom Nixon was north from me standing or walking along when the first shot was fired, He was facing north when the first shot was fired at him, He was not making any demonstration toward the man who did the shooting before the first shot was fired, I could not understand what Nixon said I could not tell what the man that did the shooting said, both spoke but I did not understand either one, Mather fired four shots, Nixon did not fall after the first shot, He fell between the second and third shots, Mather advanced after the first shot, I could not say that he shot Nixon at all after he was down, I heard Mather tell Nixon just before he shot that he was going to kill him, That was before the first shot was fired. He then immediately commenced to fire, Nixon had no weapon of any kind in his hand at that time, He made no effort at all that I saw to get his gun.

Cross Examination:

I first saw Nixon that evening at the dance hall, I next saw him right down on the corner where the shooting was done, I went with Nixon from the dance hall to Wright & Co's. and then I sat down there, we sat fifteen or twenty minutes when Patton the man I was working for came along, We got some money from him and then went down to the corner the boss going into the barber shop to get shaved, I next saw Nixon at the corner, He was coming from the west going east at the time the shooting occurred, When I was on the corner Mr. Nixon came down and turned the corner, He got just a little way past the east door when he met Mather, Nixon came walking around the corner and got a little ways past the east door going north before I heard them exchange any words, Mather was at the foot of the of the stairs there, Tom advanced about two steps and Mather did the same and Mather did the same towards him and then began shooting, Mather told him just before he shot that he was going to kill him, I did not understand all that was said but I heard him say that he would kill him I will swear that he did not say "I will go you one" He said something just before this that I did not understand I will not swear that he did not say at any any time during the conversation, "I will go one", I did not understand all that was said, I kinder think that he said said you have lived long enough but I am not sure enough to swear to it, When Nixon turned around the corner Mather spoke first, I was not leaning against the lamp post, the post I was leaning against was near the center of the sidewalk going north and south, There was no man to the east of me on the edge of the sidewalk at the time of the shooting, I judge that Nixon was about four feet from the door at the time of the first shot.

Re-Direct:

I was watching Nixon and it is not possible that he could have leaned against the door and I not see him.

Re-cross:

Nixon fell close to the door

s/s ARCHIE FRANKLIN

W. B. Masterson (Sworn) says:

I was among the first to get to the body, I was probably about the first that took hold of him, He was lying on his right side and back with his head south west and his feet north east, His right hand was up and his left was by his left hip, This was about a minute after the last shot was fired, He had his revolver on, he was lying on it, It was in his scabbard, It looked as if it might have fallen partly out or been drawn partly out, I did not see any other weapon on him or in his hands.

Cross Examination:

It was a leather scabbard, one of those made for a short Colts pistol, Heavy leather, His pistol was on with the handle turned back, Nixon's legs from the knees down were drawn up towards the body, His head lay on the door sill

s/s W. B. MASTERSON

P. F. Sughrue:

I am the officer that arrested Dave Mather, He did the shooting with a Colts 45 calibre

Cross Ex.:

The revolver was a Colts 45, I did not see the pistol while it was being shot.

s/s P. F. SUGHRUE, *Sheriff*

The court then instructed the jury in the difference between premeditated murder and killing in self-defense.

The verdict was filed the thirty-first day of December, 1884, A. R. Bowman, Clerk, by H. C. Bingham, Deputy Clerk:

THE STATE OF KANSAS, EDWARDS COUNTY, SS
In the District Court, 16th Judicial District.

The State of Kansas	[VS.]	Dave Mather
Plaintiff		Defendant

VERDICT

We, the Jury impaneled and sworn in the above entitled case, do upon our oaths find the Defendant not guilty.

GEO. HILL, *Foreman.*

CHAPTER 26 ·
: FIRE AND ICE

IT SEEMED for a time that the killing of Tom Nixon had brought back the bloody years of old-time Dodge, and the energy shown in promoting the bullfight gave promise of continued prosperity. The recent depression of 1882-83 had passed and no town west of Wichita could show such growth. Boosters were bold to say that, even without the Texas cattle trade, Dodge City would thrive. Plans were even made to replace the ramshackle old rookeries and breakneck sidewalks on Front Street.

But, in fact, the days of the cowtown were numbered. One disaster after another beset her.

For thirteen years the ramshackle firetraps lining the streets had stood unscathed with no better protection than the rows of water-filled whisky barrels down the middle of Front Street.

Dodge City had many things to be proud of: the Dodge House, the Varieties, Kelley's kennel of hounds, the courthouse, school and churches, the Long Branch Saloon, the Cowboy Band. Of them all, however, none ranked higher than the Fire Company.

Its members were all leading citizens. Their well-furnished hall with its handsome Brussels carpet and its library of books and periodicals was the most attractive public gathering place in Dodge. Smoking was strictly prohibited there. The members formed an elite, and men moved heaven and earth to be invited to join.

The firemen of Dodge gave the best balls, the most agreeable parties, and excelled those of other towns in their drills and entertainments. When they turned out in their uniforms (most of which consisted of long-handled red-flannel union units), drawing their hose cart behind them, the spectacle was most impressive. No parade was complete without the Fire Company. The Dodge City Hose Team #3, consisting of fifteen men, made the record-breaking run in national competition at the annual firemen's tournament in Denver, thus winning the National Hose Cart Championship.

There had been a few small blazes as early as August, 1877. The new fire bell clanged and the firemen came rushing to the Engine House, pulled out the machine, and ran to the Lone Star Dance Hall.

"Poor Minnie Lee was sitting on a doorstep sobbing violently over the loss of her wardrobe." The fire had started in her upstairs room from an upset lamp. It was soon extinguished.

Up to 1885 there had never been a fire in Dodge involving loss to insurance companies. This was generally due to the fact that its (mostly one-story) business houses never closed their doors. Its saloons were frequented at all hours, and its streets by day or night were never empty of pedestrians. When fires did break out they were always discovered before they could spread.

But in January fire broke out in a grocery store on the north side of Front Street one Sunday afternoon. The flames spread to the Union Restaurant and the building where the *Kansas Cowboy* was printed. A thousand people gathered, and it was clear that everything in the block west of Bridge Street would go. But the people carried out everything possible from the lower floors. By heroic efforts the Iowa Hotel across the street was saved, though at one time its whole east side was blazing. The flames spread across the tracks and destroyed two warehouses; and spreading in the other direction down the street, a drygoods store, a hardware store, and a tin-shop went to kingdom come in a hurry with most of the stock. But when the flames reached the brick store just being erected by Jacob Collar, it stopped short. No less than eleven buildings went up in smoke.

On Friday, November 29, 1885, at ten-thirty in the evening fire broke out again—this time in an upstairs room between the Junction Saloon and the Opera House Saloon. By the time the flames burst through the roof it was clear that they were beyond control.

Fortunately during the two hours the conflagration continued there was not the slightest breeze to fan it. Hundreds of men did noble service in moving goods from the stores, tearing out awnings and parts of buildings and keeping exposed buildings in opposite blocks protected from the continual rain of sparks and embers which lighted up the scene. They hoped the fire would stop when it reached Bob Wright's brick building and corrugated iron warehouse in its rear. A force of men on the roof of the brick building fought heroically to stop the fire there.

But this time the brick wall was no barrier. The whole block east of Bridge Street on Front Street was consumed. The very business heart of Dodge was destroyed.

Goods rescued from the flames covered an acre. Around this ropes were stretched, and twenty-five men stood guard through the night. Says the *Globe*: "There are one hundred men whose services entitle them to a vote of thanks and a gold medal."

This conflagration was far more destructive than the one in January.

While the fire still raged Bob Wright contracted for a store on Bridge Street. The Long Branch Saloon erected a building for its business in front of the old stand on Front Street. The *Kansas Cowboy* comments: "If anybody thinks that Dodge is a dead town, let them come here now and get their illusion disspelled. . . . Not a single murmur has been heard to escape from the lips of any of the sufferers of the late fire. One hundred fifty thousand dollars went to glory, yet nobody cares a cuspidor about it."

But that was not the end.

Before December, 1885 was half out, another conflagration in the next block east swept away $50,000. Within an hour all the buildings were consumed.

Again in August of 1886 a fourth fire destroyed most of the Dodge House block (that nearest the railroad station). There was precious little left of Front Street then.

But by that time disasters had struck Dodge City which dimmed the fires.

By 1879 settlers, brought out by the railroads, had begun to swarm in and establish farms and ranches in western Kansas. With them came the windmill, the patent portable house, and multiplied roads. Barbed wire soon spread its network across the prairie. The first settlers on the bare prairie, having no fuel, had begged a Texan to hold his cattle on their lands so as to obtain cow chips for burning; but now, better established, they warned him off or fenced him out, fearing that the contagious Texas Fever, brought by Longhorns from southwest Texas, might infect their imported stock.

In Dodge City businessmen reacted quickly to this menace. A citizen's committee and the Santa Fe Railroad devised a scheme to carry on and bring Texas cattle to shipment as usual.[1] After all, they declared, it was only *Southern* Texas cattle which were barred from coming north of Parallel 34. They proposed to provide guides to lead all beef cattle by a devious trail to Dodge City. The committee announced that it would hold itself responsible for all damages done by cattle to growing crops along that trail, provided drovers followed it according to the instructions of the guide Dodge City would provide. This offer was made known to the cattlemen in Texas, but there was little response.

There were too many hazards. Already Ford County had under cultivation nearly 100,000 acres, more than 18,000 of them fenced. Moreover, the Dodge City trading territory was now well stocked with blooded cattle, so that even though no more Texas cattle came to Dodge, the town might still be a cattle market and shipping point. Winter wheat was beginning to be widely planted and there was a good market for horses and for wool. Even the rush of settlers, the passage of the Herd Law, and the near completion of the Santa Fe Railroad to Albuquerque in 1886 could not make the men of Dodge despair.

On New Year's Day, 1886, they celebrated as usual.

It was the custom for all the establishments on Front Street to keep open house for callers and to provide free the favorite drink in Dodge, "Tom and Jerry," to regular customers. There was much singing of "For He's a Jolly Good Fellow" and everybody "put on the dog" and made a day of it. Dr. Samuel J. Crumbine with three other "young bloods," as the cowboys dubbed them, had improvised an imitation tallyho from a two-seated spring wagon with a four-horse team. In this, dressed in Prince Alberts and top hats, they paraded through Dodge, dismounting at each friend's place to present their calling card especially printed for the occasion, six inches by ten inches, with one of their names on each corner and the State flower of Kansas, a large sunflower, emblazoned in the middle.

Before they had made all the proposed calls the air grew suddenly chill. A huge dark cloud swept down from the northwest and the first of the great blizzards of that dreadful winter swallowed the town.

The north wind howled by forty miles an hour and the air was full of snow, blotting out everything, so that a man walking from his house to his barn might lose his way and perish within a few yards of his own door. Unfortunately, the temperature did not fall to freezing and the wet snow soaked and penetrated clothing, clogged the nostrils, the ears and mouth, so that men caught out that balmy evening and unprepared with waterproofed clothing were soaked and chilled and perished from the cold.

C. M. Johnston, employed in the Santa Fe office at Dodge, had attended a dance that night and escorted his lady home early, as she had to catch a train. As he turned homeward the storm began. "The blizzard roared down like a flash. It almost swept me off my feet. I could only make progress by backing up against the houses, dodging from one to the other, but managed to reach home safely."

The storm raged until seven o'clock next day. In the morning people had to dig tunnels from their doors to get out, and when they looked across the prairie where so many claim shanties had been built, the houses resembled great white serpents, heads to the northwest, tailing out in the opposite direction.

By that time the snow had packed hard and frozen. A man could walk cross-country freely, right over the fences and gates.

The storm caught trains in the deep drifts where snow had filled cuts along the line. There were then no rotary snowplows, and for two weeks every available man was employed trying to clean out the snow. Engines hitched double-header bucked the drifts until they stalled. But the main work was done with shovels in the hands of some two hundred citizens. The division superintendent tried to keep an engine and coach moving to bring supplies to the front, but the ration train was stalled by another storm and a second load had to be carried out by mule-drawn wagons.

For the storm on New Year's Day was by no means the worst. On midnight of the sixth the sky was once more threatening, and by morning the wind was tearing down from the north forty-four miles an hour and the temperature had dropped to sixteen below. More snow fell and the storm continued without letup for eight hours.

During all this time the atmosphere was so highly charged with electricity that it was supposed an aurora borealis was overhead. So strong was the atmospheric electricity that telegraphic messages were sent to Fort Supply without any battery. Electrical conditions had prevented the signal office getting its telegraphic warning through in time.

There had been severe blizzards and high winds at low temperatures in 1873, '74, '75, and '76, and in 1882 the thermometer once dropped to twenty below. But nothing so severe and prolonged had ever been recorded in that country.

There was no mail; the town was snowbound; the drifts were the largest ever seen. In places the snow was ten feet deep. Sleighing was out of the question. Visitors remarked that Dodge was on its good behavior. However, this did not prevent a shark from passing a ten-dollar Confederate bill on one of the merchants.

The storm extended far south, east, and west of Dodge.

But that was not the end. Cold weather struck again on the twelfth, sixteenth, eighteenth, nineteenth, twenty-second, and twenty-third. There were twenty inches of snow, and the ice in the Arkansas River was a solid twelve inches thick. Almost every animal without shelter caught in this storm perished. Their bodies piled up against fences, filled ravines and ditches, irrigation ditches, and in places covered the river ice. Bill Tilghman lost several hundred head of hogs smothered by the snow in their pens, and cattle losses throughout the country ranged from twenty to one hundred per cent. Along some fences a man could walk for rods, stepping from one carcass to another and never touch ground. Nearly all the wild life perished, and jack rabbits around Dodge became almost extinct. When the snow melted, the earth was dotted with the carcasses of antelope, deer, coyotes, meadow larks, quail, and prairie chickens. Many horses were lost, and not a few settlers perished or suffered severe frostbite.

W. T. Roth, who lived twelve miles northwest of Dodge, was snowbound in town. Meanwhile, his wife and children tried to protect the cattle on his ranch. The wife and one of the daughters each lost an arm.

Three men, employed by the Eureka Irrigating Canal Company, came to Dodge to get groceries for their families, who were camped in tents five miles west of town. Finding the storm so severe, they put their horses in Ham Bell's livery stable and about three in the afternoon set off on foot. Robert Wade eventually found his way to a settler's home halfway to camp, but was speechless from the cold and could not give any account of himself or his comrades for an hour after.

When at last the two Hayter brothers were found clinging to a wire fence one was still alive, but soon died. Their widows and children, though in tents, managed to survive.

The snow was smothering and so dry that it went wherever air could go, sifting through shingles of new roofs to stack up on the bed beneath, or blowing through a keyhole to pile up on the floor as high as the keyhole itself.

Though there were no coyotes left to prey upon the carcasses of frozen cattle, other varmints soon went to work. With thousands of dead cattle lying about the prairies, men helped themselves to the hides. They used the old technique of the buffalo hunters, jerking off the hide with a two-horse team in double-quick time. Cattle owners published notices warning dealers to buy no hides bearing their brands without their written authority. But many an easy dollar was made by thieving skinners. It is an ill wind that blows nobody good.

But when, after that bitter winter, the snow had melted and the green grass covered the empty prairie where the bawling herds had ranged, cattlemen learned something of how Indians felt when their buffalo had been exterminated. It was no mere money loss, no mere loss of fine animals, no mere loss of prestige and credit. For any who had eyes to see, it meant the loss of the open range, the end of a lordly way of life.

CHAPTER 27 ·
· HOLY COWTOWN

EVERYTHING conspired to end the glory and prosperity of Dodge City.

It is too often forgotten that old-time Dodge had some pretensions as a cultural center. It was not merely that she dominated and supplied a vast area, not merely that her better establishments aspired to set a high tone, to serve only the best, but that the men of Dodge had been pioneers in bringing the good things of civilized living to the Plains.

Every institution that such a small, commercial, bustling city could maintain was established there.

Newspapers flourished. The first church was chartered in February, 1877, and by the end of the cattle trade Dodge had as many churches in proportion to her population as almost any Western town. And even while the Vigilantes were running wild in 1873, Dodge City had established a public school; and from then on the newspapers consistently gave as much space to school matters as to any other major interest of the town, printing school news and proudly giving the names and grades of all the pupils.

Dodge was always a center of sports. In the beginning bloody bare-knuckle prize fights were held there and brutal encounters of lapjacket. Cruel pranks were played when trained bears or the horses of tenderfeet were treated to a dash of hokeypokey.

But these rough sports soon gave way to gentler pastimes. Horse racing, baseball, and fishing flourished. Every sort of amusement available in those times had its fans, including square dancing. Dodge also welcomed the best singers, dancers, and actors who toured the West, and the circus soon became an annual treat.

Dodge long resounded with good music. A number of the young men in Dodge were enthusiastic musicians and the town was proud of its Cowboy Band, which also served the commercial purpose of attracting Texas cattlemen.

All this was most unusual in a Western prairie town. I well remember as a boy in frontier Oklahoma the horror and disgust which our local banker expressed when his son proposed to become a pianist. To the father—as to most men on the Plains at that time—a pianist meant simply a derelict who banged the ivories in some filthy honky-tonk. Rarely in Dodge City was a musician treated with such contempt as this item from the *Dodge City Times* describes:

" 'Paddy' is the name of a dashing young ranger who has been having a good time during the past week. Paddy got after a two hundred pound musician one evening just for fun, and it was amusing to see that musician run and yell for protection. But Paddy's fun had to subside. It could not last always. He informed us yesterday that the snakes in his boots were growing larger every day, and the delirium trememdums were upon him, therefore he had wisely concluded to change off to a cold water diet for a while."

Nor did Dodge forget the national holidays and traditional festivities of our culture. She celebrated the Fourth of July, Washington's Birthday, and New Year's Day in high style. The Union Church on Christmas Eve in 1879 was jammed to the doors for the town's first Christmas tree, and Lloyd Shinn—no mean writer—wrote a lyrical account of the occasion.

The buffalo hunters of Dodge had compelled the creation of one of the great mechancal inventions of the period—the Big 50 Sharps rifle, which destroyed the buffalo and settled the hash of the wild Indians. Dodge gunmen also helped to bring in the machine age by their frequent use of the first American machine to use interchangeable parts on a large scale—the Colt revolver.

As times changed, Dodge dreamed of a regular opera house, and when the roller skate came West, her citizens swarmed into the rink. The editor offered this gratuitous advice:

> Go to the rink young man,
> And skate with the girls, if you can.

The sole remaining dance hall was left standing empty, to be sold for a warehouse.

At the first cattlemen's convention in Dodge, no flowers or greenery being available to ornament the hall, it was decorated with a battery of bird cages from which canaries discoursed sweet music. The popularity of songbirds in Dodge long outlasted the cattle era; when Ham Bell became an automobile salesman, his agency was enlivened by feathered songsters.

In charity, Dodge City led western Kansas. Her gamblers would not permit anyone to surpass them in liberality. Her harlots aspired to appear benevolent, and her businessmen were always ready to do their share. Appropriately enough, Dodge attracted a philanthropist, Asa M. Soule, who promoted an irrigation canal, built a college, and contributed liberally to other civic projects.

In time the Beeson Museum was created, one of the most comprehensive and interesting collections devoted to municipal history in the whole United States, containing many a relic of frontier days, including the instruments and longhorn standard of the Cowboy Band, the grand piano and fine clock from the Long Branch, Ben Thompson's shotgun, photographs of earlyday worthies, along with branding irons, account books, documents, weapons, pictures, and trophies of every sort.

But now in 1886 comes Bat Masterson—of all people—to file complaints against saloon keepers and close their doors!

By this time, the men of Dodge, if sadder, were a little wiser. A. B. Webster, candidate for Mayor, declared: "Personal prejudices and factional feelings should be put aside and every man should press his shoulder to the wheel and work for the prosperity of the city. . . . The unprecedented prosperity which we have enjoyed has been forced upon us. Dodge City is not indebted to its citizens for that. There are many improvements to be made if we are to keep pace with our neighbors."

Dodge had tamed others. Herself she could hardly tame.

For after the saloons were closed, clubs and blind tigers took over, and their owners, having no licenses, were regularly fined —and tolerated. Some well-known names appear as defendants in the Police Court Docket. Likewise the inmates of brothels were hauled up periodically for fining; the names of a dozen women recur in the Docket for 1888.

But most of the sporting men and women soon left Dodge for greener pastures farther west. First stop was at Trail City on the Colorado line, a camp astride the new National Trail from Texas to Ogallala, Nebraska, and the Red Cloud Agency in South Dakota. For a brief time Trail City bade fair to rival Dodge. But the National Cattle Trail was never authorized by law, and cowmen began to ship their beef by rail. The bawling longhorns came no more, and Trail City faded to a ghost town.

Many substantial citizens of western Kansas, like Charles F. Colcord and Bill Tilghman, moved south when the Indian Nations were opened to white settlement, and played a great and honorable part in building Oklahoma.

A few remained in Dodge. There the fight for "progress" still went on, until (shades of Calamity Jane!) on March 5, 1888, a woman was actually fined five dollars and costs because she "did then and there, unlawfully, feloniously, appear on the streets of Dodge City dressed in male attire."!

In time Front Street was patrolled by the mumbling nondescript Ben Hodges, carrying an old revolver locked fast with rust.

And Bat Masterson, considering discretion the better part of valor, declined appointment as a United States Marshal in the West, went to New York City, and became a sports writer on the *Morning Telegraph*.

NOTES

Chapter I

1. See *The Trail Drivers of Texas*, compiled and edited by J. Marvin Hunter, published under the direction of George W. Saunders, Cokesbury Press, Nashville, Tennessee, 1925.
2. See *Fighting Indians of the West*, by Martin F. Schmitt and Dee Brown, New York: Charles Scribner's Sons, 1948, p. 173.

Chapter II

1. See Chapter XVII.
2. Quoted from *Boot Hill*, by Josephine McIntire, Boston: Chapman & Grimes, Inc., 1945.

Chapter III

1. *Kansas Cowboy*, August 9, 1884.
2. *Frontier Doctor*, by Dr. Samuel J. Crumbine, Philadelphia: Dorrance and Company, Inc., 1948, pp. 70-71.

Chapter IV

1. *The Story of the Santa Fe*, by Glenn Danford Bradley, Boston: R. G. Badger, 1920, p. 95.

Chapter V

1. Idaho, 1864; Wyoming, 1871; Montana, 1872; Nebraska, 1875; New Mexico, 1880; South Dakota, 1883; Colorado, 1897.
2. For the story of the Sharps rifle see *The Sharps Rifle*, by Winston O. Smith, New York: W. Morrow & Co., 1943.
3. August 18, 1877.
4. Fearing legislation to preserve the buffalo, the railroads conspired to keep secret the actual number of buffalo hides shipped over their lines. But Colonel Richard I. Dodge, Commandant at Fort Dodge, managed to get some authentic figures for the years 1872-74:

> *Hides*
> Total number of hides shipped on the Santa Fe Railroad, 459,453; other railroads, 918,906; total, 1,378,359

Pounds of Meat
  1872: None
  1873: Santa Fe, 1,617,600; other railroads, 3,235,200; total, 4,852,800
  1874: Santa Fe, 632,800; other railroads, 1,265,600; total, 1,898,400
       Grand total: Santa Fe Railroad, 2,250,400; other railroads, 4,500,-
                800
           Total: 6,791,200 pounds

Pounds of Bones (including water splashed over them to increase the weight)
  1872: Santa Fe, 1,135,300; other railroads, 2,270,600; total, 3,405,900
  1873: Santa Fe, 2,743,100; other railroads 5,486,200; total, 8,229,300
  1874: Santa Fe, 6,914,950; other railroads 13,829,900; total, 20,744,850
       Grand total: Santa Fe Railroad, 10,793,350; other railroads,
                21,586,700
           Total pounds of bones shipped by all railroads: 32,380,050

Each year Colonel Dodge estimated that the Santa Fe carried about 19,000 robes; the Union Pacific, 10,000, not counting perhaps 5,000 disposed of otherwise. The robe crop, including what comes from the Northern Plains, he believed to be in the neighborhood of 90,000 a year. Of the robes, skins, meat, and bones shipped over the Santa Fe much the greater quantity was shipped out of Dodge City.

Dodge believed that there was an Indian-dressed robe sent in for every five rawhides. In the years 1872, 1873, 1874 he finds a total of 1,215,000 buffalo killed by Indians; 3,158,730 killed by white people; a grand total of 4,373,730. This took no account of those killed by Mexicans and Canadians. Railroad figures compiled later by the Santa Fe are as follows: hides shipped out of Dodge City 1871-87, 5,860,000; value, $40,000,000.

These figures are taken from *The Hunting Grounds of the Great West* by Richard Irving Dodge, London: Chatto & Windus, 1877, p. 140.

Chapter VI

  1. *Oklahoma: Footloose and Fancy Free*, by Angie Debo, Norman: University of Oklahoma Press, 1949, p. 130.

Chapter VII

  1. The foregoing story is here reprinted by the permission of Mr. Heinie Schmidt of Dodge City from his column, "It's Worth Repeating," in the *High Plains Journal* of Dodge City, June 15, 1950, and of the Editor of the *Journal*.

Chapter VIII

  1. According to the *Ford County Globe*, February 17.
  2. For the Indian side see *The Fighting Cheyennes*, by George Bird Grinnell, New York: Charles Scribner's Sons, 1915: for the hunters', *The Life of "Billy" Dixon*, by Mrs. Olive K. Dixon, Dallas: P. L. Turner Co., 1914. I have myself described the fight in a book recently published: *Warpath and Council Fire*, New York: Random House, 1948.

3. Billy Dixon's biography lists the men who took part in the fight, but in some cases their full names are not given. Through the courtesy of Mr. Stuart N. Lake, I am able to complete four of these, as follows:

William "Dutch" Henry (This, of course, was not the celebrated horse-thief, "Dutch Henry" Borne; nor was it that Hendry Brown who once ran with Billy the Kid, and was lynched after the bank robbery at Medicine Lodge, in 1884.),

William "Billy" Keeler ("Old Man Keeler," as Dixon called him, was one of the craftiest and most courageous Indian fighters and buffalo hunters on the Plains.),

William Barclay "Bat" Masterson,

Thomas "Tom" Shepherd.

Also, Ike Shadler (Shaidler or Sheidler) was one of the brothers killed in the wagon.

4. *Dodge City Times*, December 1, 1877.

5. My information comes from interviews with Josiah Wright Mooar recorded by J. Evetts Haley. Mooar's story has never before appeared between the covers of a book. The gist of it was first published by James Winfred Hunt in one of a series of articles entitled "Buffalo Days" in *Holland's, the Magazine of the South*, March, 1933, pp. 8 ff. Retold here by permission of *Holland's* and Mrs. Victoria Hunt. See also "The Comanche Indians at the Adobe Walls Fight," by Rupert N. Richardson in *The Panhandle Plains Historical Review*, Vol. IV, 1931, pp. 24-38.

Chapter IX

1. *Clowning Through Life*, by Eddie Foy and Alvin F. Harlow, New York: E. P. Dutton & Co. Copyright, 1928, by E. P. Dutton & Co., Inc.

2. *Kansas Historical Collections*, Vol. 7, 1901-2, p. 415.

Chapter X

1. *The Longhorns*, by J. Frank Dobie, Boston: Little, Brown & Co., 1941, p. xvii.

Chapter XI

1. It is believed that "Bat" gained his nickname using his walking-stick to bat down offenders that season of 1876. S.V.

2. *Wyatt Earp, Frontier Marshal*, by Stuart N. Lake, Boston: Houghton Mifflin Co., 1931, pp. 172-73.

3. *The Ben Lilly Legend*, by J. Frank Dobie, Boston: Little, Brown & Co., 1950, p. 57. See also *I'll Die Before I'll Run*, by C. L. Sonnichsen, New York: Harper & Brothers, 1951, for the bloody feuds of Texas.

4. *Wyatt Earp, Frontier Marshal*, pp. 173-74.

5. *Ibid.*, pp. 179-84.

Chapter XII

1. William Barclay "Bat" Masterson had served briefly as a deputy under City Marshal Wyatt Earp in Dodge during the summer of 1876. At the end

of June, 1877, he was appointed Undersheriff of Ford County and served with Morgan Earp as deputy to Sheriff Charles E. Bassett until January, 1878, when Bat became Sheriff. Before this, as early as September 22, 1877, he was listed in the *Dodge City Times* as a City "Policeman," though still referred to in the same issue as "Under-Sheriff."

Bat was the first elected Sheriff of Ford County, Bassett having been appointed. In November of 1879, he was overwhelmingly defeated by George T. Hinkle and thereafter left Dodge for Leadville and Denver. He frequently returned to Dodge and served on the Dodge City Peace Commission in 1883. He was never City Marshal of Dodge. His brother, James Masterson, became City Marshal in November, 1879.

Bat Masterson's last "official" appearance in Dodge City was in 1886, when he returned to close the saloons.

2. *Clowning Through Life.*

Chapter XIII

1. *Dodge City, The Cowboy Capital, and the Great Southwest* by Robert M. Wright, Wichita: Wichita Eagle Press, 1913, pp. 303-5.

2. *Ibid.*, p. 299.

3. As Ed was shot in the abdomen from the right, and Wagner in the bowels from the left, some have thought it possible that Ed fired the second shot while the men stood facing each other. Once before, as we have seen, Ed had fired after being wounded. At any rate, they say, Ed was able to walk across the tracks and the Plaza—a distance of sixty yards—before he fell. Most accounts, however, give Bat full credit for avenging his brother and shooting Ed's assailants. S.V.

4. *Ford County Globe*, April 16, 1878.

5. *Ibid.*

6. Unhappily the Docket of the Police Judge of this date has disappeared from the official files of Dodge City.

7. This account of Edward J. Masterson's death closely follows in the main the contemporary newspaper accounts, with additions in part derived from interviews with old-timers recorded in George G. Thompson's *Bat Masterson; The Dodge City Years*, published in the Language and Literature Series, No. 1, F. B. Streeter, editor, General Series, No. 6; printed by the Kansas State Printing Plant, Topeka, 1943, and elsewhere as noted.

8. See his biography by Stuart Lake, pp. 200-201.

9. The Docket of the Police Judge for the time between July 4 and July 16 shows 11 trials, 1 dismissal; the defendants being accused as follows: 3 disorderly, 5 carrying a pistol; 1 carrying a butcher knife; 2 disturbing the peace. Arrests made: by Wyatt Earp, 3; by James Masterson, 4; by John Brown, 4.

10. *Dodge City Times*, February 1, 1879.

11. See *The Peacemaker and Its Rivals, an Account of the Single Action Colt*, by John E. Parsons, New York, 1950, page 91, for reproduction of Bat's letter, quoted by courtesy of Colt's Manufacturing Company.

Chapter XIV

1. "Famous Gunfighters of the Western Frontier, (Second Article) Wyatt Earp," by W. B. (Bat) Masterson, in *Human Life*, February, 1907, p. 9.

2. *Clowning Through Life.*
3. *Wyatt Earp, Frontier Marshal*, p. 206.
4. *Clowning Through Life*, pp. 112-13.
5. *Wyatt Earp, Frontier Marshal*, p. 206.
6. *Ibid.*, pp. 206-7.
7. *A Lone Star Cowboy*, by Charles A. Siringo, Santa Fe, New Mexico, 1919, pp. 101-2.
8. *Fighting Men of the West*, by Dane Coolidge, New York: E. P. Dutton & Co., Inc., 1932, pp. 81-82.
9. Ford County was created in 1867 and was organized by proclamation of Governor Osborn April 5, 1873.
In 1877 Clark County and all territory lying south of the Fourth Standard Parallel and west of the Counties of Hodgeman, Ford and Clark were attached to Ford—an area of approximately 9,500 square miles. This information is given in a table in the back of the statute book, but is not included in the statutes.
In 1881 the Sixteenth District was organized to include Ford County. To be attached until their organization were the following Counties: Clark, Meade, Seward, Stevens, Kansas, Stanton, Grant, Arapahoe, Foote, Sequoyah, Kearney, Hamilton, Greeley, and Buffalo. Foote and Buffalo Counties ceased to exist when all their territory was included in Lane and Gray Counties.
In 1885 the Counties of Finney, Scott, Wichita, Greeley, Hamilton, and Seward were detached.
The above information was taken from the Laws of Kansas, 1866-89, WPA records and the correspondence of Governor Osborn.
10. The same letter quoted above, dated 10/27/35.
11. There is no record in this docket of the arrest of Clay Allison by James Masterson or any other officer in October, 1878, or at any other time.
12. In a letter to Floyd Benjamin Streeter, dated at Wichita, September 17, 1935, quoted by permission.
13. *Wyatt Earp, Frontier Marshal*, p. 184.
14. *Clowning Through Life*, p. 105.

Chapter XVI

1. *Ibid.*, pp. 105-7.
2. *Wyatt Earp, Frontier Marshal*, p. 217.
3. Other accounts published later state that Kennedy headed west out of Dodge, but the newspaper account states quite definitely that he was seen to ride east on the Fort Dodge Road. S.V.

Chapter XVII

1. The October 3 issue tells the story.
2. See Dr. H. O. Simpson's article, "Early Day Gunmen Gave Color to Picturesque Setting of Dodge City," in the *Topeka Daily Capital*, December 9, 1934.
3. The account here given is from the story in the *Dodge City Times*, August 4, 1877, which includes the testimony of witnesses at the inquest, certain details supplied by M. W. Sutton, and the coroner's record.
4. *Dodge City, The Cowboy Capital*, p. 185

Chapter XVIII

1. *Wild Bill and His Era,* by William E. Connelley, New York: The Press of the Pioneers, 1933, pp. 182-83.
2. *Marshal of the Last Frontier,* by Zoe A. Tilghman, Glendale, California: The Arthur H. Clark Co., 1949, p. 108.
3. *Charles Goodnight, Cowman & Plainsman,* by J. Evetts Haley, Norman: University of Oklahoma Press, 1951, pp. 433-34.
4. *The Longhorns,* p. 273.

Chapter XIX

1. In his series on gun-fighters in *Human Life,* 1907.
2. Colt's Single Action Army or Frontier Revolver, manufactured in 1873, calibre .45, was first made in two patterns. Later a third with a shorter barrel was added to the series. Most of the peace officers during old Dodge City days carried one or the other of these models. Colt's catalogs list these as follows:
Cavalry Model, with 7½ inch barrel, weight 37 to 40 ounces, unloaded.
Artillery Model, with 5½ inch barrel, weight 38 ounces, unloaded.
Civilian Model, with 4 ¾ barrel, weight 36-7 ounces, unloaded.
This was the first revolver for center fire ammunition to be manufactured by Colt's. It was first issued to the U. S. Army in 1873. Since the smaller calibres were made simply by boring smaller holes in the same size barrels and cylinders, the smaller calibres sometimes actually weigh more than the big .45's, size for size. For example, the .32-20 weighs 6 ounces more than the .45. Different handles and different steels varied the weight of weapons of the same model somewhat; catalog weights vary. The Civilian model was later "made with a 4¼ inch barrel with a rod ejector attached, and also a 3 inch barrel without the ejector." See *The Peacemaker and Its Rivals* by John E. Parsons, New York, 1950, pp. 48, 96; and *The Evolution of the Colt from the Year 1836,* etc., etc.

Chapter XX

1. August 9, 1879.
2. September 13, 1879.
3. During the first twenty years of Dodge, Ford County Sheriffs were as follows: Charles E. Bassett, William Barclay "Bat" Masterson, George T. Hinkle, P. H. "Pat" Sughrue, Fred Singer, Hamilton Butler "Ham" Bell, and Chalkley M. Beeson. Bat Masterson was never Marshal of Dodge, though Wyatt Earp, when appointed Assistant City Marshal in 1876, for a time made Bat his deputy.

Chapter XXI

1. *Kansas Cowboy,* September 26, 1885.
2. In the *Kansas Cowboy* for September 26, 1885, the story, "Dodge City by Lamp Light," names the men and women of a dozen couples who held rendezvous in the saloons at these hours.
3. *Dodge City Times,* January 19, 1878.
4. *Kansas Cowboy,* August 29, 1885.
5. *Ibid.,* July 4, 1885.
6. *Ford County Globe,* March 16 and 23, 1886.

Chapter XXII

1. See *Ford County Globe*, April 19, 1881.
2. Updegraff's complaint does not appear in the Dodge City Police Court Docket for 1881.
3. *Ford County Globe*, May 10, 1881.
4. See "Frontier Etiquette" in the *Topeka Commonwealth*, May 28, 1881.
5. For the details of my account of Bat's gun-fight see copies of the *Ford County Globe*, April 19 and May 10, 1881, and George C. Thompson's *Bat Masterson; the Dodge City Years*, 1943. Thompson drew some of his information from interviews with Ham Bell and Thomas Masterson, Jr.

Chapter XXIII

1. *Wyatt Earp, Frontier Marshal*, pp. 360-61.
2. Before the age of fly screens this phrase meant simply doors through which passers-by could not see.

Chapter XXIV

1. *McPherson Independent*, July 9, 1884.
2. July 12, 1884.
3. *Ibid.*
4. *Ford County Globe*, July 1, 1884.
5. *Larned Optic*, July 11, 1884.
6. See "The Bull Fight at Dodge," by Kirke Mechem, *Kansas Historical Quarterly*, Kansas State Historical Society, Vol. II, No. 3, August, 1933, pp. 294-308. Newspapers giving accounts of this fight are as follows: *Kansas Cowboy*, July 12, 1884, which quotes the *New York Herald* and the *St. Louis Globe-Democrat*; *Dodge City Democrat*, July 5, 1884; *Ford County Globe*, July 8, 1884.
7. *Kansas Cowboy*, July 19, 1884.

Chapter XXV

1. *Dodge City, The Cowboy Capital*, p. 215.
2. *Kansas Cowboy*, July 26, 1884, p. 5.
3. For those who are interested in medical technicalities here follows the cross examination of Dr. Milton following his testimony:

Cross Examination:

I made the examination principally with a view to ascertain the cause of death. It was a matter easily determined as to the cause of death, I made no post mortem examination, examined wounds with fingers and probes, I cannot tell positively where any particular ball that went in came out, I do not know where the ball that went in near the spinal column came out, that ball either passed out of the body or lodged under the skin, I found there were four entrances and three exists and one ball under the skin, I know there were four balls that went into the body, three of which passed out and one was under the skin.

I can tell that the ball in front at the region of the eighth rib entered there from the fact that parts of the clothing were in the wound and from the appearance of the edges of the wound, I need no other fact except the clothing there to prove this. The skin around the wound had a bruised appearance and the hole was round, that wound as a place of entrance was larger than any of the others.

This wound was about three inches higher than on a direct line through to the wound on the back.

The wound in front over the crest of the Ilium is one which it is impossible for me to state positively with absolute certainty as to positive knowledge whether the ball entered there I could be more certain if I knew the distance the pistol was from the body at the time of firing. It is impossible to make absolutely certain observations from superficial examinations of this one wound, of some things I am certain as the wound in the breast, I made no wounds on the body except under the arm in cutting out the bullet.

I examined the wounds with my fingers and the probe, the examinations I made are what physicians term superficial examinations, I did not explore the cavity, I do not know of my own knowledge the distance the parties were apart at the time the balls were fired and received, if the pistol is near the body of the hit it is more difficult to tell the entrance and exits than when farther apart.

The reason for this is that a ball entering in close proximity may make a more ragged wound more like the exit of a ball, the place of exit may be smaller than the place of entrance; if the ball comes from quite a distance the entrance is smaller and the exit larger, my judgment is that from the character of the wounds in right breast the pistol could not have been more than three or four yards from the body.

Re-direct:

The wound in the left nipple was an exit as I am positive from these reasons. The hole had an irregular appearance more like a cut than a round hole. The wound in the cavity was about an inch below the wound in the skin and I found that a rib had been broken and the parts of the rib were pushed forward at an angle and a piece of the rib was detached and lying loose on top of the rib in front.

Re-cross:

It is possible for a ball to enter the body be deflected and come out on the same side of the body.

Re-re-direct:

It is possible that the ball which entered deceased's body at the crest of the Ilium might have been so deflected by the bones as to have come out at the left nipple, I am unable to answer as an expert as to the chances that such a thing is the case, I could not tell unless I knew more about the position of deceased's body.

Question: What are the chances that the ball so entering would have come out at the left nipple if the deceased were standing up, it is possible?

Answer: I will say that it is possible but not probable that the ball would come out at left nipple if the person shot were standing up, this is a bare possibility.

Question: As an expert, isn't there more intrinsic probability of the fact that the ball which entered from from behind in the back is the one which made its exit from the left nipple, the body being in an upright position at the time?

Answer: I think there is more probability that the ball entering in front was the one that came out at the left nipple than that the one from the back did so, because the wound on the back was on the right side of the spinal column and the wound on breast was on left.

Question: Suppose the body to have been in a reclining position, which is the more probable?

Answer: I think that the probability would still be in favor of the ball which entered at the front.

Question & Answer: If the body were lying on the left side the line from the wound in back to wound at left nipple is pretty direct and the bullet might have passed on that line.

Defense asks, Could the body have been placed in such a position that the wound in back and at left nipple could have been made by same ball?

Answer: Yes if the body were inclining forward towards left side.

Question: Could a man standing erect and struck in the back by a bullet have that bullet have its exit at the left nipple?

Answer: I think not.

Question: In your judgment as an expert, which bullet had its exit at the left nipple most probably?

Answer: I think it more probable that it was the ball that entered at the crest of the Ilium, I would like to add to that, that on more careful consideration I think the ball which entered on the right side in front was most probably the one that came out at left nipple.

s/s C. A. MILTON, M.D.

Chapter XXVI

1. See *Livestock Journal*, July 14, 1885.

BIBLIOGRAPHY

BRADLEY, GLENN DANFORD, *The Story of the Santa Fe*. Boston: R. G. Badger, 1920.

CONNELLEY, WILLIAM E., *Wild Bill and His Era*. New York: The Press of the Pioneers, 1933.

COOK, JOHN R., *The Border and the Buffalo*. Topeka, Kansas: Crane & Co., 1907.

COOLIDGE, DANE, *Fighting Men of the West*. New York: E. P. Dutton & Co., Inc., 1932.

CRAWFORD, SAMUEL J., *Kansas in the Sixties*. Chicago: A. C. McClurg & Co., 1911.

CRUMBINE, SAMUEL J., M.D., *Frontier Doctor*. Philadelphia: Dorrance & Co., Inc., 1948.

DEBO, ANGIE, *Oklahoma: Footloose and Fancy Free*. Norman: University of Oklahoma Press, 1949.

DIXON, OLIVE K., *The Life of "Billy" Dixon*. Dallas: P. L. Turner Co., 1914.

DOBIE, J. FRANK, *The Longhorns*. Boston: Little, Brown & Co., 1941.

DODGE, RICHARD IRVING, *The Hunting Grounds of the Great West*. London: Chatto & Windus, 1877.

EDWARDS, J. B., *Early Days in Abilene* (*Abilene Chronicle*, 1896), reprinted as a book, Abilene, Kansas, 1946.

FOY, EDDIE, and ALVIN F. HARLOW, *Clowning Through Life*. New York: E. P. Dutton & Co., Inc., 1928.

GRINNELL, GEORGE BIRD, *The Fighting Cheyennes*. New York: Charles Scribner's Sons, 1915.

HALEY, J. EVETTS, *Charles Goodnight, Cowman & Plainsman*. Norman: University of Oklahoma Press, 1951.

HAYES, JENNIE LORENE, *Kansas Cow Towns, 1865-1885, A Thesis Submitted to the Graduate Faculty in Partial Fulfillment of the Requirements for the Degree of Master of Arts*. Norman, Oklahoma, 1938.

HUNTER, J. MARVIN, Compiler and Editor, *The Trail Drivers of Texas*, Published under the Direction of George W. Saunders. Nashville: Cokesbury Press, 1925.

Kansas Historical Collections, Topeka.

LAKE, STUART N., *Wyatt Earp, Frontier Marshal*. Boston: Houghton Mifflin Co., 1931.

LOWTHER, CHARLES C., *Dodge City, Kansas*. Philadelphia: Dorrance & Co., Inc., 1940.

MCINTIRE, JOSEPHINE, *Boot Hill*. Boston: Chapman & Grimes, Inc., 1945.

PARSONS, JOHN E., *The Peacemaker and Its Rivals, an Account of the Single Action Colt*. New York: William Morrow and Company, 1950.

RAINE, WILLIAM McLEOD, *Famous Sheriffs & Western Outlaws*. Garden City: Doubleday, Doran & Co., 1929.

Guns of the Frontier. Boston: Houghton Mifflin Co., 1940.

SIRINGO, CHARLES A., *A Lone Star Cowboy, or Fifteen Years on the Hurricane Deck of a Spanish Pony*. Chicago: M. Umbenstock & Co., 1885.

SMITH, WINSTON O., *The Sharps Rifle*. New York: W. Morrow & Co., 1943.

STREETER, FLOYD BENJAMIN, *Prairie Trails & Cow Towns*. Boston: Chapman & Grimes, Inc., 1936.

The Kaw; the Heart of a Nation. New York: Farrar & Rinehart, 1941. (Rivers of America Series.)

"The National Trail," pp. 22-23 in *Some Southwestern Trails*, El Paso Texas: Carl Hertzog, 1948 (27 pages). (Reprinted from *The Shamrock*, October, 1946.)

THOMPSON, GEORGE G., *Bat Masterson; The Dodge City Years*, Language and Literature Series, No. 1, F. B. Streeter, editor, General Series, No. 6; printed by the Kansas State Printing Plant, Topeka, 1943.

TILGHMAN, ZOE A., *Marshal of the Last Frontier*. Glendale, California: The Arthur H. Clark Co., 1949.

VESTAL, STANLEY, *Warpath and Council Fire*. New York: Random House, 1948.

WARMAN, CY, *The Story of the Railroad*. New York and London: D. Appleton & Co., 1911.

WELLMAN, PAUL I., *The Trampling Herd*. New York: Carrick & Evans, Inc., 1939.

WIGGINS, OWEN D., *The History of Dodge City, Kansas, A Thesis Submitted in Partial Fulfillment of the Requirements for the Degree of Master of Arts, Colorado State College of Education*. Greeley, Colorado, August, 1938.

WRIGHT, ROBERT M., *Dodge City, The Cowboy Capital, and the Great Southwest*. Wichita: Wichita Eagle Press, 1913.

Periodicals:

HUNT, JAMES WINFRED, "Buffalo Days," *Holland's, the Magazine of the South*, March, 1933.

LAKE, STUART N., "Tales of the Kansas Cow Towns," *Saturday Evening Post*, Series, 1930.

MASTERSON, W. B. (BAT), "Famous Gunfighters of the Western Frontier, (Second Article) Wyatt Earp," *Human Life*, February, 1907, p. 9.

MECHEM, KIRKE, "The Bull Fight at Dodge," *The Kansas Historical Quarterly*, Volume II, No. 3, August, 1933, pp. 294-308.

RICHARDSON, RUPERT N., "The Comanche Indians at the Adobe Walls Fight," *The Panhandle Plains Historical Review*, Volume IV, 1931, pp. 24-38.

SCHMIDT, HEINIE, "It's Worth Repeating," *High Plains Journal*, Dodge City, June 15, 1950.

SIMPSON, H. O., M.D., "Early Day Gunmen Gave Color to Picturesque Setting of Dodge City," *Topeka Daily Capital*, December 9, 1934.

ACKNOWLEDGMENTS

I wish to express my deep appreciation for the unfailing help given me by Mr. Kirke Mechem and his efficient staff, the Kansas State Historical Society in Topeka; to Mr. J. Evetts Haley, for permitting me to use his voluminous interviews with old-time buffalo hunters; to Dr. Samuel J. Crumbine, for much information regarding his days in early Dodge City; to Mr. F. B. Streeter, Librarian of the Fort Hays Kansas State College, for his invaluable assistance in research; to Mrs. Zoe A. Tilghman, for much helpful information and permission to quote from her biography of William Matthews Tilghman; to Dr. Charles Evans, Secretary of the Oklahoma State Historical Society; to Dr. E. E. Dale, Curator of the Phillips Collection at the University of Oklahoma; to Mr. Heinie F. Schmidt, President of the Dodge City Historical Society; to Mr. C. M. States, of Dodge City; to the late Mr. Elmo Scott Watson, of Denver University, for the use of his files; to Mr. L. F. Sheffey, of the Plains Panhandle Historical Museum, Canyon, Texas; to the city clerk of Dodge City and the county clerk of Ford County, Kansas, for access to their records; to Mr. Stuart N. Lake for his generous aid.

Also for access to their records: the National Archives; the Library of Congress; and the State Historical Societies of Nebraska, Wyoming, and Montana.

I owe a great debt to my stepfather, James Robert Campbell, who lived in Newton and other towns in western Kansas in the seventies and eighties, and who, having been a research man for Hubert Howe Bancroft, had much to tell of old Dodge City.

Some of this he derived from Mr. O. B. Hildreth, father of my brother-in-law, who was an employee of the Santa Fe Railroad, active in promoting immigration into western Kansas, and frequently in Dodge City.

I am also indebted to Mr. Victor Hull for permitting me to make photostats of items in the Boot Hill Museum; to Miss Ina T. Aulls of the Denver Public Library; to Miss Letha Barde for access to the notebooks and correspondence of her father, Fred Barde; to Mr. H. Bailey Carroll and the Texas State Historical Association; to Mr. Bob Duncan; to Miss A. Blanche Edwards, of Abilene, Kansas; to Professor Paul Eldridge, University of Nevada; to the University of Texas Library; to Dr. Leroy R. Hafen and Agnes Wright Spring of the State Historical Society of Colorado; to Mrs. Charleen McClain, editor of *Holland's Magazine*; to Mrs. Harriet Horst of Newton; to the editors of the *High Plains Journal* published in Dodge City; to the librarian of the *Kansas City Star*; to Mrs. Leila Hudson (T. H.) Reeve; to the late Chris Madsen; to Professor Foster Harris; and to the Dodge City Chamber of Commerce.

I wish also to thank the following: Mr. J. L. Rader, Librarian at the University of Oklahoma; Mr. William McLeod Raine; Mrs. Olive K. Dixon; Mr. William G. Reed, Assistant Librarian of the Historical Society of New Mexico; Dr. Carl Coke Rister; Miss Mary Stith, University of Oklahoma Press; Mr. Paul I. Wellman; Dean A. B. Adams; Miss Lela Barnes; Mr. R. C. Barrett; Miss Louise Barry; Mr. R. F. Blackburn; Mr. Glenn P. Bradley; Miss Josephine Cobb; Miss Mary Elizabeth Cody; Mrs. Marion Dancer; Miss Elizabeth B. Drewry; Mr. Raymond P. Flynn; Mr. Dwight Franklin; Miss Llerena Friend; Mr. George Bird Grinnell; Mr. R. H. Justin; Mr. William E. Langdon; Miss Helen M. McFarland; Mr. Lyle Miller; Mr. Ward Perkins; Mr. John H. Seger; Mrs. F. B. Streeter; Mr. Ernest Dewey; Professor Winston O. Smith; Miss Harriet Smither; and to Margaret Roberts and Wylodean Saxon, my secretaries.

I wish also to thank the following: Mr. Stuart N. Lake for

kind permission to use passages from his *Wyatt Earp, Frontier Marshal;* E. P. Dutton and Company for permission to quote from *Clowning Through Life* by Eddie Foy and Alvin F. Harlow; Mrs. J. W. Hunt, for permission to quote from "Buffalo Days" by James Winfred Hunt, published in *Holland's, the Magazine of the South;* The Arthur H. Clark Company, for permission to quote from *Marshal of the Last Frontier* by Mrs. Zoe A. Tilghman; Dorrance and Company, Inc., for permission to quote from *Frontier Doctor* by Samuel J. Crumbine, M.D.; Little Brown and Company for permission to quote from *The Longhorns* by J. Frank Dobie; the University of Oklahoma Press for permission to quote from *Charles Goodnight, Cowman & Plainsman* by J. Evetts Haley; Mrs. Josephine McIntire for permission to quote from her *Boot Hill.*

Having been born in the Flint Hills of Kansas, having been raised in a prairie town about the size of Dodge City, and having afterward lived in Oklahoma Territory in its early days where Bill Tilghman and other former citizens of western Kansas were to be met with any day, I find it quite impossible to make due acknowledgment to all those many friends who have helped me to know and to understand since I first became interested in Dodge; but I am grateful to them all.

STANLEY VESTAL